Birdies, Bunkers and Bar Stools

Jottings from a Lifetime in Golf Writing

For Michael,
a worthy winner,

The Jubilee Trophy.
2016

Barry Ward

Birdies, Bunkers and Bar Stools

Jottings from a Lifetime in Golf Writing

First Printing: 2013

ISBN 978-1-291-41915-3

www.posh-golf-travel.com

Front cover original illustration by Mickey Durling.

Typesetting and design kenandglen.com

Dedication

For Shirley, who started it all in Bermuda,
and for Christine, who encourages my addiction.

Contents

Golfing memories are made of this...

For a man who once forgot his wife's birthday and, soon afterwards, our wedding anniversary, attempting to recall 50-plus years of playing and writing about golf has been an exercise comparable to extricating a ball from the Road Hole bunker armed only with a putter. Frustrating doesn't begin to sum it up.

At this remove the only certainty is that my career high points have out-numbered the lows and while the latter have perforce been personal (the yips, anyone? or the shanks?) the highs have been mainly professional, the consequence of watching great events, meeting memorable players and visiting sumptuous golf resorts around the world in search of colourful copy for various magazines and newspapers.

It's been a heck of a life but in truth it hasn't been all milk and honey. There's been a price to pay for the good life: recurring dengue fever, missed flights and interminable waits at strange airports for some less than salubrious aircraft, questionable hotels, second rate courses, to say nothing of lost luggage, obstreperous immigration officials, arrogant speed cops on the make....

Also on the debit side have been some hairy situations: a night flight to Bangkok where our 747 was a feather in the firmament; the turbulence was so frightening that my fellow passengers were either screaming or chanting prayers. I requested a farewell glass of champers but it never arrived.....Driving on flooded, single track roads through a storm in the Atlas Mountains of Morocco was fun, too.

Then there was being lost and out of fuel in a Casablanca shanty town that made Soweto look like Mayfair; and being unable to find water with my car radiator imitating a volcano during a pitch-black, midnight drive across central Spain with neither a spot of light nor a drop of water to be found. I relieved the situation simply by doing what came naturally: No, I didn't have a bucket....

On a lesser scale have been flights caught by the skin of the teeth after being stuck in peak hour traffic in Dublin, Lisbon, Bangkok and Madrid (don't even *think* about driving in any of these places). On each occasion I literally abandoned my rental car in front of the departure terminal and ran for it, dragging my golf clubs behind me. Couldn't do that these days......

1

Sheer blissful addiction aside, watching great events, playing great courses and recording unforgettable experiences in my travels around the globe has left me with memories to savour. I am indeed a lucky old golfer. Envious chums have frequently suggested alternative employment and though I have often threatened to find a proper job I've never quite got around to it. How it all began still leaves me bemused...

The moment of truth is an integral component of golf and my first such took place in 1956 in Bermuda, where I was introduced to the game by a pretty lady golfer. I became irrevocably hooked, a dyed-in-the-wool addict. The lady became my partner, on the course and off.

One thing led to another as the gods continued to smile upon me and another moment of truth came in 1961 when I arrived at Royal Birkdale to cover my first Open Championship. Gale force winds off the Irish Sea had demolished the small tented village and incessant rain left players and galleries soaked to the skin. But I was in seventh heaven. I couldn't believe my good fortune....

Since those happy days my life has encompassed visiting countless golf-mad locations hither and thither, watching great tournaments and playing in excess of 2,000 courses in 46 countries in pursuit of enlightening copy about golf tourism and the clubs and resorts that sustain what is now a huge industry. It's a far cry from those sun-kissed days in Bermuda when I began my improbable journey with what now appears an equally improbable routine.

I was a sports writer for the *Royal Gazette,* a daily paper published in the wee hours which meant we reporters worked at night. This played havoc with my social life but it left my days free for golf: thus I played 18 holes every morning.

But not at weekends, though: then, fit as a flea on a butcher's dog, I would play 54 holes every Saturday. It wasn't quite dawn to dusk but it was pretty close, with a stop only for lunch and a reviver. You'll gather I was committed

My first great thrill in the game came the day I bettered the 100 mark. I had shot 104 in the morning, then 98 in the early afternoon and finished at sunset with a 94. I never looked back. By then a member of Belmont Manor Golf Club, whose par 69 course overlooked Hamilton Harbour, I was initially given a handicap of 24. But within a year I was playing off 12. More significantly, my great passion brought about a major change in my life. It proved to be the second step in my journey.....

The Bermuda Tourist Board had just launched the Goodwill Tournament, an international pro-am that attracted teams from all over the world. The Sports Editor needed a golf writer to cover it and as I was the only staff reporter who played the game I was elected. And as they say in the classics, the rest is history.

A favour for a visiting Australian journalist proved to be my next stepping stone, a sports writing job in London. Writing for the Sydney *Daily Telegraph* group, my brief was to cover any sport in Europe which involved visiting Australians or which would be of interest Down Under. Thus, only a few days after taking up the post I was covering tennis at Wimbledon before dashing to Lancashire where I found myself at Royal Birkdale and rubbing shoulders with the great players of the day. I thought all my birthdays had come at once. It was an eye-opening experience for a tyro golfer, and two of those legendary players gave me an insight into the realms of the game at the highest level; they were scenes that have stayed with me to this day.

The first involved Australia's Kel Nagle, the defending champion. I was soaked and frozen but I tracked him, enthralled, as he crafted what was arguably one of the greatest rounds seen in the Open. When few in the field could better 80 in conditions that were close to unplayable, Kel returned a 75. In gale force winds, on many tees blasting across the line of flight, he seemed to have the ball on a string, shaping it this way and that and at no time that I recall hitting it more than 20 feet off the ground. It was pure golfing magic.

The other memorable example, one since marked by a plaque that is still *in situ*, came courtesy of the legendary Arnold Palmer. I was close enough to touch him when he produced the moment and the shot of the tournament. Also nearby was Henry Cotton, who described it as "the bravest shot I've ever seen."

It came on the 15th, now the 16th, in the final round. Arnie was on the rampage, in the hunt for his first Open title, and level with Dai Rees at the top of the leader board when his tee shot on the demanding par four faded on the wind and came to rest in deep rough. Disaster beckoned. Not only was his ball in wet, clinging rough it was almost touching a thumb-thick sapling.

With the green still some 160 yards away, through a cross wind and up-hill to boot, most players in the field doubtless would have opted for a sideways pitch out to safety, hoping perhaps for a bogey at worst. Not Arnie. He took his six iron and, his huge hands a blur, he gave it everything he had, removing the sapling and a doormat-sized patch of rough in the process. The ball finished maybe 20 feet from the flag and a safe two putt par left the great man in the lead. Up ahead, Rees dropped a stroke on the 17th; Arnie held fast to win by one.

My notes and the printed report of this momentous championship have long been lost but those two events have been indelibly etched upon my memory. The one involving Arnie, indeed, became significant in the sense that his charismatic style and his spectator appeal rejuvenated the Open. So much so that the classical Birkdale links required modification to better accommodate the huge galleries he attracted.

Spectator movement had created problems, both of crowd vision and mobility. So it was deemed apposite to modernise the links, a project undertaken by F.W. Hawtree, father of Martin and then head of the architectural family which has long been associated with the club.

His solution: to re-site several tees, allowing easier movement for the huge galleries who, formerly given freedom of the fairways, were now guided along prescribed routes by a system of constructed pathways and fencing. He also created a new hole, the short 12th, to replace the par three 17th, which had been one of the major bottlenecks, and shortened the opening hole for similar reasons.

To off-set this, new tee positions lengthened several holes by between 20 and 60 yards and the par five replacement for the old 17th meant that the finish was now one of the longest and toughest in the world, with three of the final four holes in excess of 500 yards.

The results were seamless and successful: the course retained its challenge without blemish and within a decade several major events, and the vast galleries they now attracted, endorsed the Hawtree formula as the correct solution. Indeed, many players regard Birkdale as their favourite Open venue, holding it in similar affection to Muirfield, at once fair, cerebral and technically challenging.

Most current American professionals have acknowledged their debt to Palmer, the first great international player of the modern age. We British are also in his debt and for similar reasons: through his magnetism and dramatic playing persona he transformed the Open Championship into one of the great sporting events; he made the world sit up and take notice.

Arnie's victory at Birkdale in 1961 and at Troon in 1962, and his subsequent Open appearances, brought a vast increase in the number of spectators and a subsequent rise in ticket revenues and prize money. And, having won, he was smitten: he came to love the event and the challenge of links golf and persuaded his fellow US pros that playing in the world's oldest event on our great links was a necessary part of their golfing education, an invaluable addition to their playing CV. Until that time few of their leading players came to the Open more than once, mainly because of the time factor in travelling and qualifying and the minimal rewards. But Arnie built the Open into his playing schedule and his rivals began to follow him over.

A side effect, one still in evidence today, is the constantly escalating prize money prompted by hugely increased revenues from world-wide television that his presence initiated back in the 1960s. So, to my ever-lasting good fortune, my introduction to the Open coincided with Arnie's arrival on the British golfing scene and the transformation, the re-birth if you will, of its principal event.

How lucky can you be?

Mind you, the infrastructure was rather less sophisticated in those days. There was no Media Centre as we know it now: we had a draughty Press tent large enough for perhaps a dozen wooden tables and chairs sufficient for maybe 20 or so reporters: the in-coming scores were hand-written in chalk on a blackboard and after typing their reports my colleagues had to queue for use of a phone in the clubhouse or the local pub. I would type my copy on the standard Cable & Wireless yellow forms and find the nearest post office capable of transmitting it to Sydney.

These days the Media Centre opens the week before for final qualifying at nearby courses and then for 20 hours each day from the Sunday of the week of the championship. Now it accommodates close to 500 writers from all corners of the world whose copy is transmitted by lap top via the central IT system, and whose desks have telephones upon request; the leader board brings current hole-by-hole scores of every player in the field; there is continuous closed circuit television coverage of play, vital for those whose deadlines are a barrier to walking the course; there are interview rooms where the leading players arrive after each round; there are all manner of research facilities and an information desk managed by the Press Officer; there is a major media restaurant offering day-long catering; there are convenient parking facilities and virtually every form of assistance a writer might require. It is truly mind-boggling, ultra professional and indicative of the management and planning which makes the Open such a major event and a joy to experience. Birkdale '61 was never like this!

The Open has long been an annual personal highlight but each year has also brought others and my time with *Golf Monthly* combined extensive travel with playing great courses around the world. The trips came via regular invitations from national and regional tourist boards in the USA, Ireland (regularly!) Tunisia and France, among others, and I've written books on golf in Scotland and Morocco, so frequent have been my visits there.

My wanderings began long before this, though. Back in 1973 I was in Sydney and editor of *Golf Australia* when I was invited to the opening of the Pacific Harbour resort in Fiji. It had a very fetching course by Trent Jones Sr. but it was also memorable for another reason: while there I succumbed to dengue fever which had me bed-bound for most of the stay and 20 pounds lighter when I returned to Sydney. Worse, it recurred at the same time each year for six years. The joys of travel, eh?

I'd moved there in consequence of the dreadful winter of 1962-63 when London was frozen solid for months and my Bermudian wife was desperate for some sunshine. Having established myself with the Sydney *Daily Telegraph* a move Down Under seemed apposite. Let's just say that in professional terms it was enlightening...

A protracted newspaper strike forced me into magazine publishing , hence my post with *Golf Australia*, but at least I extended my golf writing CV, via several Australian Open and Amateur championships, the Eisenhower Cup at Royal Melbourne and the Espirito Santo ladies event at the nearby Victoria Club. In playing terms my golf reached its peak during my time in Australia. My handicap dropped to single figures (very briefly as low as five) and on three occasions I scored in the 60s. Those were the days!

The low points came in Australia, too, when the shanks and the yips came in quick succession. I had an enviable short game and was a demon putter — hence my low handicap — but suddenly my game went sour on me. I was forced to stop playing, so bad were the shanks/sockets (playing a three wood I once hit the ball between my legs!).

But the break did the trick for me. Venturing out again after several weeks I was faced at the first hole with a 50 yard pitch over green-side bunkers, precisely the shot that had started my problems in the first place... Concentrating on tempo and and maintaining my height the result was better than I dared hope. I holed it for a birdie and everything was fine thereafter, proving that confidence holds the major key in golf. The yips required a modicum of self-duplicity but confidence was a major factor here, too.

My once smooth stroke had disappeared: It became a nervous twitch when faced with short putts, even tap-ins. So I had resorted to putting back-handed, but with a standard right hand grip, when faced with anything around four feet or less. The results, while better, were inconsistent because my cavity-backed putter wasn't designed for cack-handed operations! So I tracked down a two-faced, centre-shafted model that could be used either way (I still have it somewhere....) and learned to putt proficiently with a right-handed grip but a left handed stance. It worked and after about a month I reverted and rediscovered my old stroke. So normal service was resumed. I'd beaten the yips! It's a solution I commend to the stricken.

It was a solution born of necessity: I was playing in some hot company in those Sydney days. I was a member of the Long Reef and Moore Park clubs and it was at the latter that I enjoyed some of my happiest days in golf. I was one of a group of single figure players who teamed up each week in club events and ran cut-throat, private competitions in conjunction, even in the monthly medals.

In true Aussie style we'd bet on anything and everything we did on-course: eagles, birdies, most pars, fewest putts, longest drive; nearest the flag on the short holes (but it had to be within the length of the flag stick), sandys (down in two from a bunker), plus of course the overall scores. It would take an hour afterwards, amid much raucous laughter and joshing, to settle the bets. Huge fun, and it brought a razor sharp competitive edge to our play that saw consistent improvement all-round. One of us would invariably win the medal or the event of the day in singles competitions. I frequently recall those happy days and think about the good guys. I hope they're still around and knocking in the putts....

My golf these days is, shall we say, rather more prosaic! Health set-backs followed in rapid succession: a tumour in my inner ear, which affects my balance, and tendon problems in both hands that eventually brought the amputation of my right ring finger. This meant that I could neither over-lap nor inter-lock my grip. I couldn't play for almost two years and when I resumed I had to switch to the baseball grip and adapt my plane as well as adopting more user-friendly clubs. So my handicap now is comparable to my collar size and rapidly approaching that of my inside leg measurement!   But at 80 years of age I still play three times each week; these days simply for the joy of it, for the exercise and the fun to be had with a bunch of like-minded old grey beards, the club seniors. Though still working and writing, I have reduced my travels somewhat but I accept some invitations to "come and see our new resort course."

Recently I was in Scotland and, the icing on the cake, I carded an ace, my fifth, on the 16th hole at Irvine (Bogside) to prove that there's life in the old dog yet! Shortly I shall be off to Marrakech, which I view as the capital of North African golf, and then to the Cote d'Azur, one of my favourite destinations. I hope to see Bermuda again soon, back where it all began in 1956.

Having reached the age of semi-retirement travel has lost its allure of bygone days and I have put the brakes on, so to speak. The odd jaunt aside, I have dropped anchor at home in Rutland. Which of late has encouraged the thought that perhaps I should collate my outstanding memories of great events, of other times and other places, and record them for my nearest and dearest and anyone who cares about this wonderful game of ours.

Only then did I come to realise the difficulties I faced because my early material, pounded out on a typewriter for newspapers, had long since gone into oblivion, my files lost for all time after countless domestic moves. Only material produced for magazines in the age of computers and word processors has survived, and indeed not all of that.

What follows is a small selection of the latter, plus a piece or three dug from the memory bank or plucked from old printed publications that have somehow become fixtures in my golf library. They were written for various publications, chiefly *Golf Monthly* and, in recent times, my web site (www.posh-golf-travel.

com) but also for *Golf Links* magazine, the original *Golf News,* plus a number of trade and consumer publications and newspapers, *The Times* among the latter.

So my golfing love affair goes on; after 57 years my improbable journey continues. Plainly, the gods are still smiling upon me and my dear grannie was right when she said it was better to be born lucky than rich...

It's all been great fun. I hope you find as much pleasure in the reading I have in the recollection.

PROLOGUE

Golf: A Game for the Ages, A Game for Life....

Unknowing non-believers tend to ridicule golf as a male-only game for elderly snobs wearing outlandish sweaters and plus fours. If only they knew how wrong they are and, more importantly, what they're missing.

Golf is a game for the ages and all ages. Its history dates to 1457 but it is as modern as today with its high tech equipment and a place in the pantheon of televised sport, attracting millions of fans. It may claim to be the world's largest participant sport with more than 100 million players world-wide, most of them ordinary club members who appreciate what the game brings to their lives: camaraderie, unending challenge, common interest, exercise and a subsequent feeling of well-being, and the occasional sense of achievement when things go to plan.

Golf can be maddening, supremely satisfying, frustrating and uplifting, all in the process of 18 holes. As such, it can be a great test of character, concentration, patience and fortitude. A keen sense of humour helps, too. It may be the greatest game ever invented.

As a sage once wrote with more than a hint of truth: "Tis a devilish game played with instruments ill-suited for the purpose." Mark Twain described it as "a good walk spoiled," but he was only half correct. For 'tis indeed a good walk and that's one of the reasons why it is so popular with those past the first flush of youth.

Unlike most outdoor games or sports, where active participation declines as mobility and stamina decrease, golf can be played by people well into their 90s to whom a five mile walk that the average round of 18 holes entails brings a sense of good health and fitness that few non-golfers will recognise. This is no exaggeration, as I know from personal experience.

Because of ill-health some time ago I was unable to play for almost two years and when I resumed I could barely last the course, with a consequent decline in form. It took a good three months to become what I termed "golf fit" again, to the point where I could stay the pace with my colleagues.

9

It had been the only gap in a golfing life that has stretched over more than 57 years, in fact the game has been more than a pastime to me: it has been central theme of my daily life. Yes, I know: some people have all the luck!

It's been a tough life. My escalating handicap suggests I'm suffering from golf fatigue which I suspect is terminal. Once in low single figures, my handicap now roughly equates to my collar size and is rapidly approaching that of my inside leg measurement.

But, like most of my senior club colleagues in Rutland, when not travelling I still play three times each week, winter and summer, in all weathers. Because of this, we golfers are keenly aware of the seasons and the changing face of Mother Nature. There can be no more up-lifting sight than the landscape donning its mantle of Spring and nothing lovelier than thousands of trees changing their colours in the Autumn.

More than this, golfers frequently connect with all forms of wildlife. At my club, for instance, we have deer, badgers, hares, stoats, rabbits and a myriad form of bird life from ducks, moor hens and swans on the lakes to kestrels, kites and even ospreys gliding overhead.

A golf course is never a dull place! All this and a fascinating game, too. The non-believers truly don't know that they're missing.

When golf is a game of the soul

We were playing the Castlerock links on the Antrim coast and were nearing the end of our round when it happened. I'd teed up on the 18th and was taking a practice swing when I became aware that my playing partner was sitting down and holding his head, as though ill. When I asked what was wrong his reply spoke volumes.

"I just don't want this to end," was his plaintive response. No further explanation was necessary. I knew precisely what he meant.

It was a day made in Heaven. There was barely a cloud in the sky and a light breeze had the flags fluttering just enough to make things interesting. Short sleeves and sun visors were on duty and the grand old links, almost deserted, was in its usual impeccable order with the greens glinting in a late afternoon sun. It would be an insensitive soul who didn't appreciate his good fortune. But there was more to it than that, I was to discover.

Touring the region on behalf of *Golf Monthly,* I hadn't known my chum until we were introduced in the pro shop. It transpired that he was a US golf tour operator researching the region and, having landed only hours before, had made Castlerock his first port of call. He was chatting to the pro when I walked in and it wasn't long before our host suggested we pair up and play the course. My new-found friend hadn't been to Ireland before in fact, remarkably, he had never played sea-side golf or even seen a links.

"Then you've a treat in store, although believe me links golf is not always like this," I told him, as we stood on the first tee. It was to prove an understatement, and a memorable day for me, too. We both had handicaps of eight and, playing for the post-round drinks, had a nip and tuck battle with several birdies and barely a bogey between us. It was one of those days a golfer dreams about.

Hence his reaction on the final tee. He was a happy and enlightened man: he had discovered the soul of golf.

It's an elusive quality but is most readily discovered on a links because this is where it all began, centuries ago. You could find it easily enough, if you're lucky and have a sense of the history of the game, sufficient to recognise the work of the first great architects: Morris, Braid, Ross, Colt and Mackenzie, et al. Their creations are memorials to genius; their life spans were but fleeting moments in time, a blink, but their legacy will, with luck and global warming permitting, last into eternity.

A lonely links hemmed by a deserted beach with a restless sea stretching to an endless horizon, all this brings a palpable sense of history and time. Play such a place late of a summer's day when a lowering sun is pouring shadows into the nooks and crannies of the landscape and you'll be privy to an ethereal experience usually known in a cathedral at sunset, perhaps, or at the funeral of an old friend......

To some folk this is the very essence of the game, its soul and its heartbeat; the day at Castlerock aside, I've known it at various times over the years, at great links such as Portmarnock Old, Prestwick Old and Western Gailes and have been moved beyond measure each time.

A man could do no better than to hand in his final card on such a day, I thought, but a conversation with an old friend on just such an occasion went like this.....

"This is what it's all about, isn't it? You wouldn't be dead for a million dollars, eh?"

"You're right. Not even for two million..."

There have been other discoveries, other places, other times. One came at my present club in Rutland.

On the 17th tee of the Valley course at Greetham is a bench seat placed, just so, to allow views of the rolling Rutland countryside. On the seat is inscribed a legend in memoriam to a former member which states simply: "To know the true character of a man, first play golf with him."

The inscription ends with the late member's name and the citation "He was a gentleman and a golfer."

I hadn't known him but I owe him a debt of gratitude: his aphorism came to my rescue at a most difficult time in my life, after a long spell in the doldrums because of illness. He helped remind me of my memories of our wonderful game and made me re-think my attitudes, to golf and to life. He made me recognise that to be playing at all was a blessing.

Instead of being frustrated and angry at my lack of form and fitness I counted my blessings and began to enjoy the simple pleasures of the game; the challenge, the exposure to nature, the camaraderie, the exercise. It reinforced a long-held recognition, overlooked in the times of tribulation, that golf is good for the inner man and his soul.

Favourite courses? I've got a few......

As a golf writer I am frequently asked to name my favourite golf course. It's a question that's impossible to answer. Heck, after a lifetime travelling the world writing about golf I'd be stretched to name my favourite 50!

I've played some 2,000 or so courses in 46 countries over the years but most of them only once, often in the process of a fleeting visit. Only a handful, usually on resorts where I've stayed for two or three days or have returned after some years, have I played several times. I've seen a few courses that were, shall we say, less than good but most were beguiling, some unforgettable....

Here's a wish list of the latter that I'd give my trusty putter to play once more, before the Great Course Marshall taps me on the shoulder to say "Time's up, old boy." Some of them would be among my favourite 50. Most will be new to you but you'd love all of them.

I've opted for three from each country and they come in no particular order. If you have a few months to spare or are about to retire you could do worse than spend time travelling to play a few of them. I promise you won't be disappointed.

I start in the United Kingdom, because that's where I live and have played most of my golf.

England
The Alwoodley GC (Leeds); Silloth GC (Cumbria); Seacroft GC (Lincs).

Scotland
Machrihanish GC (Mull of Kintyre); Boat of Garten GC (Aviemore); Royal Dornoch (Highlands).

Ireland
The European GC (Co. Wicklow); Castlerock GC (Co. Londonderry); County Sligo GC, Rosses Point, (Co. Sligo).

Wales
St David's GC (Harlech); Caernavonshire GC (Conwy); Tenby GC (Pembrokeshire).

Africa
Amelkis GC, Marrakech, Morocco; Erinvale GC, Cape Town, South Africa; The Cascades GC, Soma Bay, Hurghada, Egypt;

Australia
The New South Wales GC, La Perouse, Sydney; Hope Island GC, Gold Coast, Queensland; Kingston Heath GC, Cheltenham, Victoria;

Continental Europe
Le Chateau course, Terre Blanche Resort, Provence (France); Praia D'el

Ray GC, Obidos, Lisbon (Portugal); Casa Velha do Palheiro, Madeira (Portugal);

The Caribbean

Teeth of The Dog GC, Caso de Campo, Dominican Republic; The Mid Ocean Club, Bermuda;
Sandy Lane GC, The Resort, St James, Barbados.

The United States

The Number 2 Course at Pinehurst, NC; The Ocean Course, Kiawah Island, Charleston, SC;
Falls Course, Magnolia Grove GC, Mobile, Alabama

That's 27 courses to die for, and I haven't included some of the great and famous courses I know and love. I could compile five similar lists without great difficulty. So when I'm asked to name my favourite course you'll understand why I scratch my head...

My favourite golf holiday venue? That's a tough one, too...

Asking a chap in our line of business to name his favourite golf holiday destination is rather like asking him if he's stopped beating his wife. The question invariably prompts a pregnant pause while he ruminates. If he doesn't hesitate you'll know he's probably telling the truth...

"I'd have to plump for Hawaii," our golf writer might respond, "or Pinehurst, or maybe Kiawah Island, or perhaps Cape Town." There'll be a slight break here for effect, while the questioner turns green with envy.

Then: "No, on second thoughts," he would add, "it has to be Ireland."

Such a statement tends to result in elevating eyebrows but it's the one I would make. In golfing terms, Ireland is the bee's knees, the cat's whiskers. The Emerald Isle has in excess of 420 courses, almost a quarter of them being links out of the top drawer and, as they'll tell any visiting golfer, all of them are ranked in Ireland's Top Ten! Irish golfers, lucky devils, have a grand sense of humour, too.

Throw in the welcoming populace and cracking accommodation at every turn; add the scenery and the Guinness and you'll have painted a picture of golfing holidays at their finest. And that's personal experience speaking. I've been there countless times over the years, usually to run the rule over a new course and to check out the 19th, and never once have I been disappointed. It's always a pleasure to arrive and too soon to depart.

I've written elsewhere that you could throw a dart at a map of Ireland and confidently take a golfing holiday wherever it sticks. If you don't have access to a set of darts, or are cack-handed, you could just as easily consult the all-knowing web site of Tourism Ireland, the national tourist authority, and spend several hours marvelling at the prospects.

A bonus for green-minded British readers: there's no need to fly. Take your car and your choice of club bandits to one of several mainland ferry ports and you'll have fun getting there, too.

Make it a week-long visit and if you're entering the country through Dublin hold your hour, as they say there, and investigate. The barmen are a dangerous lot of scallywags and the golf is as good as it gets. No argument; with more than fifty courses within the city limits Dublin is the world's greatest golfing capital.

But go prepared for all-night conversations, with a thirst you can hang your hat on and in good singing voice. The golf is a lovely bonus.......

INSIDE THE ROPES AT THE MAJOR VENUES

Smiling Seve gets serious to win at St Andrews

Hard on the heels of his third round Jack Nicklaus was musing upon how he might win the 113th Open Championship. Having opened with rounds of 76-72-68 he agreed that if he maintained the sequence a 64 would be most useful. So too, he joked, would a violent storm lasting the rest of the day.

"Anything can happen," said the great man. "The opera ain't over 'til the fat lady sings."

He wasn't to know, nor was anyone, that the fat lady was already rehearsing–in Spanish.

One of the great mysteries of golf in 1984 centred upon Seve Ballesteros, his lack of form and the paucity of his appearances, both in Europe and America. Doubtless the latter was the consequence of the former. Seve is not one to linger while fickle form changes partners. He'd rather be in Spain, quietly practising and enjoying his creature comforts.

So although it was agreed that one can never tell with such genius his arrival at St Andrews for the 113th Open Championship went relatively unremarked. Spanish golf writers being somewhat thin on the ground, the occupants of the vast press marquee were, depending upon their nationality and allegiance, ruminating upon the likely fortunes of Nicklaus, Watson, Langer, Norman and Faldo.

The last we'd heard of Seve's form was that he was still searching for that elusive feel, the great intangible that separates the genius from the mere superstar. It's not difficult to tell when he's lost it: a dark and sullen scowl replaces that beaming smile; strong men avoid him; ladies turn their heads; golf writers find others to extol.

It should have been obvious, then, that he wasn't at St Andrews for a stroll in the sunshine that baked the old town from dawn to dusk, just as it had most of the summer. Seve was smiling, even cracking jokes with the press. Something, obviously, had happened.

That something, it transpired, was a practice session with Vincente Fernandez and Jamie Gonzalez. They'd put their collective finger on the great man's problem: "They said my weight was going left to right instead of right to left." He executed a parabola, a half swing, sitting down. "You know what I mean?" In essence, it seems he was swinging around the ball, rather than through it.

Upon such tips are empires built. The next day Seve went out and started to slay them. Never more than two strokes behind the leader at any stage, he completed the championship with only five bogey holes—three of those coming at the 17th—and 17 birdies. His final round was comprised of 16 fours, a two at the 8th and his killing three at the 18th.

All the clues were there: we simply didn't spot them. He was smiling like a beacon and cracking jokes after his opening round of 69. We should have known that when Seve cracks jokes he's serious.

The fact is, though, that we were distracted, first by Bill Longmuir then, for three rounds, by a young Australian with an unlikely name: Ian Baker-Finch, known to his mates as Sparrow.

Longmuir, an expatriate Scot, repeated the giant-killing act he first displayed at Royal Lytham in 1979 to post a first round 67, five under, and a share of the lead with his chum Greg Norman and America's Peter Jacobsen. They were hotly pursued by young Baker-Finch whose 68 included an eagle two at the 7th, where he holed a wedge from 75 yards for a dream start to his first Open Championship. It was a dream that was to end in nightmare.

To add to the distractions, Jack Nicklaus came in with a 76 and Nick Faldo with a 69. Then Seve sauntered in with a 69 that included four birdies and a five at the 17th and, ominously, said he was driving well and putting even better.

"If I play two more rounds as well I will be in contention on the last day," he predicted. "The greens are so big it's very difficult to put the ball close, so most important to be a good putter."

Seve may not have been aware of it but he had precisely defined Tom Watson's game. With the possible exception of Ballesteros there's no finer putter in the world but in the early stages of the championship Tom left himself too many long ones, basically because his driving was below par and he couldn't get into the proper position for his shot to the green.

Charging the hole is not recommended practice at St Andrews and though he lipped a few times Tom was philosophical about his opening 71. He had that look about him and hopes were realised the following day when he returned with a 68, a round spoiled only by a six at the Road Hole where he was buried in the face of the bunker.

Seve, meanwhile, had also returned 68 and was now lying joint second with Nick Faldo, who had matched his two scores to be seven under, along with Lee Trevino.

Young Baker-Finch, though, was top of the pecking order, following his opening 68 with a robust 66 whose sole blemish on the card was a three putt bogey at the 4th. He wasn't overjoyed four holes later with "a terrible six iron at the 8th." He was 50 feet from the flag but the putt was never going to miss for two.

All the portents were good for the 23 year old who'd turned professional only three years before. He'd played a couple of practice rounds with Peter Thomson and Kel Nagle, who had unlocked a few Old Course secrets for him, and with an elegant swing always under tight control, allied to a seemingly nerveless putting touch, he thoroughly deserved his place on the leader board.

He held it, too, with a third round 71 though the Old Lady nibbled at the edges of his card on the homeward run in which he three putted the 10 and 11th and dropped the 14th and 17th.

Pulses quickened with the news that he had been joined in the lead on 11 under by Watson who returned with a 66 and the news that he hadn't played better all season.

"My touch was very good today. I put the ball where I had to, my distance was good and I misplayed only two clubs all day," said the defending champion.

Seve had dropped his third stroke in succession at the Road Hole, but that was his only error and it was off-set by three birdies for a 70 and nine under. He was still smiling and prophetic. "I make three fives at the 17th," he said. "That's par. I make four tomorrow. If not I play Monday!" No, he said, there was not much pressure. "I feel comfortable. Nothing to lose tomorrow."

His score was matched by Bernhard Langer, who returned a second successive 68, and a five stroke gap had opened up between the leading four and their closest challengers. For the finale, Watson was paired with Baker-Finch; Seve with Bernhard.

"I tell my caddie we have to beat Langer. He's a good player. We beat him, we beat the others."

This was the Seve of old at last; oozing confidence, swinging like an angel, putting like a magician.

The final pairings were to have a decisive influence on the outcome. They probably favoured Seve, though some would argue in 'the reverse and certainly Watson made light of the Spaniard's advantage of playing in front, of setting the target which, in the event, proved to be unreachable.

And in an Open Championship where the near miraculous became commonplace, where golf was replaced by pure magic, Ian Baker-Finch finally returned from the land of make believe to the one of total reality. In 14 holes he plunged from the heights to the depths as the Old Lady, not one to relish forced attentions, extracted her toll for the favours she'd bestowed over the previous three rounds. In nine holes the young Australian went from 11 under to six under, from the top of the leader board to the bottom.

Five holes later he had almost disappeared from view when a horrendous seven at the 14th put him a mere two under. He knew not an ounce of luck from the moment his second shot to the first hole spun back six feet from the front of the green into the burn. Then, trying to reclaim lost ground, his tempo quickening with every hole, he learned the cruellest lesson of all: that the Old Course must be coaxed if it is to be conquered, that patience is the ultimate virtue.

Seve knew the Old Lady's secrets, though. He tempered his Latin flair in a manner that had the canny Scots galleries nodding approval, taking irons off the tee, at most a three wood; plotting his course with conservative, slide rule accuracy, avoiding the bunkers and the myriad pitfalls, all the while spurred on by the brilliance of Langer who played the finest golf of the tournament, tee to green, but who couldn't have bought a putt in a summer sale.

Seve ran in seven straight fours, the birdie at the 5th putting him ten under, before an exquisite five iron to six feet brought him a two at the 8th. A four at the 9th had him out in 34, at which point he was one ahead of Watson and three in front of Langer.

Seve knew his worst moments immediately after the turn. The tide seemed to have turned, but he still had one ace to play, one promise to keep. He drove the 10th green, but three putted when he might have pulled further ahead. Then he under-clubbed at the short 11th and took three to hole out.

Watson by this time had birdied the 10th and was back in front; then he parred the 11th to hold his one stroke lead. Seve missed a four footer at the 12th and there were those who thought the writing was on the wall. But Watson hooked into the consommé off the 12th tee and took five. Back to level. He birdied the next; one ahead. Seve birdied the 14th. Level again. Then he parred the 15th and 16th and the moment of truth had arrived.

"I knew I needed two fours to have a chance," Seve said later. That was equivalent to one under. A tall order, but history shows that he went one better.

The day before he'd promised the media he would finally get a four at the 17th. He kept that promise, hitting a six iron approach 200 yards to pin high and almost holing the putt. He locked the door at the 18th with "the most important putt I've ever had" but by then it was all over. Watson had fallen foul of the Road Hole, and though he paced out his second shot to the 18th the eagle two he required to tie was never on.

We'd seen four days of magic. When the wand was waved for the final time the stocks had been exhausted.

Seve Ballesteros has described the 17th on the Old Course at St Andrews as "probably the most difficult par four in the world." The statistics of the 113th Open Championship endorse his view. Over the four rounds only 11 birdies were recorded there–a solitary one on the final day–and only 147 pars were scored. There were 254 bogeys and over the championship the average score was 4.79.

Few players disagreed with Seve's appraisal. "It's the most difficult par four in the world," said Ben Crenshaw, "because it's a par five." Jack Nicklaus holds slightly differing views: "It's a par four and a half," he says. There's another view: "I can't play that hole," said Greg Norman." I really can't."

It was apparent from the outset that, as usual, the Road Hole would hold the key to the championship. At 461 yards it is close to the maximum distance for a par four and its configuration extends the length. It appears to be a dog-leg, left to right, but in fact it's virtually straight although the ideal tee shot must be aimed over the Old Course Hotel grounds to a hidden fairway. Anything slightly right is in danger of going either out of bounds or onto the paved road, which is in play but well below the level of the green.....

So the line for the percentage tee shot is left of centre which invariably means playing the next one from the rough, a line which makes the steep faced Road bunker a magnet. From the left it is virtually impossible to hold the green via the aerial route, even if the player has the courage to go for it, and most opted to play long and left, chipping back to the flag from beyond the bunker which guards the left middle of the green, the flag position for the fourth round.

The second shot was seldom less than a long iron for most of the week–some even hit woods, although on three occasions Ballesteros hit the six iron from an almost identical position in the left rough. Only once, though, did he find the green and make four, and that came when it mattered most, in the final round. Then his six iron from 200 yards was always short but, coming out of rough with top spin, it ran on, trundling its way up and on to the green, leaving him a 35 footer. He played for two putts and the first almost made it, leaving him a tap-in.

Watson, coming up behind, had played into the perfect position, uncharacteristically fading his tee shot which, indeed, he thought had gone out of bounds. Arriving at the ball he knew he was 210 yards from the flag, with a carry of 190 yards. He was undecided about the club to use, he said, but finally opted for the two iron, the one which had won for him on the final hole at Royal Birkdale the year before. His ball took one bounce and flashed on to the road to within two feet of the wall. The rest is part of golfing history.

Jose Maria Faces His Moment of Truth

The moment of truth is an integral part of golf. Tournaments and careers frequently turn on a split second of inspiration or misadventure. Golfing history is littered with examples, none more so than that of the United States Masters, the Major that each April announces the season's opening in the technicoloured landscape of the Augusta National Golf Club.

Australia's Greg Norman has featured in many such moments over the years and his latest came in the third round of the 1999 Masters when he stood on the tee of the par three 12th, the nemesis for countless dreams, the focal point of the stretch justifiably known as Amen Corner.

At five under par he was leading the field and in the form that devours golf courses. But knowing Augusta and Greg's propensity for drama we should have guessed it couldn't last.

In the swirling wind that makes club selection a lottery at what is arguably the toughest par three in world golf, his seven iron flew the water, carried the green and soared over the rear bunker before it vanished into the rough that covers the hillside beyond. Now disaster beckoned. His run was about to reach a grinding halt.

First, though, a search, joined by Lee Jansen, his playing partner, their caddies, the marshals and assorted officials. No joy. The hunt became feverish, then frantic. Still no luck.

As events were to prove, he had been fortunate not to find his ball. Later discovered buried in several inches of pine needles, it was unplayable. Sure enough, he could have taken a penalty drop but so steep was the terrain, so intimidating the rough, that even he could have taken six, or seven.....

His five minutes expired, a disconsolate Greg trudged back to the tee to play a second ball. It floated onto the green and settled like a butterfly 30 feet left of the flag. Two putts and a double bogey five seemed likely, a seminal moment appeared imminent. It was. The putt tram-lined into the hole for a four and the amiable Aussie was still in the hunt.

"Ah!," said the wise ones. "The moment of truth. Norman will win here at last. It is written in the stars." But they had misread the stars. They made no allowance for a lion-hearted Spaniard overlooked by all but those closest to him.

Norman was still in the hunt by mid-round on the final day, when the cream had risen to the top and the event had become the usual cavalry charge with champions of various nationality and vintage leading the way. Few, though, would last the pace as they turned for home, brought undone by unfamiliar conditions.

It is a truism that the Masters doesn't really begin until the final nine holes on Sunday: with few exceptions, each year sees a dog fight down the home stretch with the event being decided on the final green. The 1999 Masters was to break that mould, but for totally unpredictable reasons.

Since its inception in 1934 tradition has dictated that rough was superfluous at Augusta National, for three principal reasons: several of the undulating fairways have an up-slope in the landing area, so a drive deficient in length and height of flight would check, leaving a difficult second shot, often to a green out of sight.

And although the fairways are generous, it has always been a placement course, perhaps the ultimate in target golf, demanding that the tee shot be pin-point accurate to find the correct position for the approach to the green given the flag position of the day.

The latter holds the key. The Augusta greens, convoluted in their configuration and an amalgam of slopes and mounds, are never less than hard and marble-slick. The legendary Sam Snead once described them as "like trying to hole a putt down a marble staircase." They may be the most intimidating greens in world golf: they're certainly the quickest, not least to those facing a downhill putt breaking two ways!

Plainly, then, the primary objective on each hole is an up-hill putt, which places a premium on the approach shot line and thus great emphasis on precision from the tee. In a nut shell, Augusta National was deemed tough enough without rough.

But that was before the advancement in golf equipment technology coincided with the arrival of a young virtuoso named Tiger Woods. Suddenly the ball was flying distances previously only the stuff of dreams. Tiger is prodigious but many others consistently clear 300 yards with the driver.

The consequence: some of Augusta's longest holes had been reduced to a drive and a medium iron — in 1997 Tiger frequently used the wedge en route to winning with a record score of 18 under par! Obviously something had to be done. A little tightening up was required.

So three or four holes were lengthened by moving back the tee; the 11th green was raised to toughen up the approach; fairways were narrowed by clumps of newly-planted trees and, most important of all as it transpired, the fairways were reduced in width by carpets of rough on either side. It was nothing excessive, you understand; just above an inch deep.

But it was enough, as events were to prove, to bring the field back to earth with a bump. Now the big hitters running out of fairway would be in danger of their next shot catching a top spin flier that such rough generates, instead of the back spin that brings the desired control. The consequence: even short iron shots hitting the greens were jumping forward with the top spin, running off the green or into the wrong position. It reaffirmed Augusta's insistence upon precision over length.

Worse, because of inclement pre-tournament weather the greens were harder than ever before and the organising committee, fooled by a gentle weather forecast, had chosen the most searching flag positions on the final day. When the predicted breeze matured into a full-blooded blow that attacked from all angles, Ian Woosnam, the former champion, declared them the toughest fourth round conditions he'd experienced in many years of playing at Augusta.

So when the leaders turned into the more demanding home stretch at the tail-end of the field the cavalry charge lost its impetus. Woosie, for instance, was close to the lead at four under par after four birdies in the first eight holes. Then the wheels fell off. Similarly Lee Westwood, another British hope with seven wins around the world last year, was five under and joint leader at the turn. Then he dropped three strokes in two holes and another at the 12th.

Playing behind came Steve Pate, whose second round 65 had vaulted him from the basement to the penthouse. He was now joint leader on five under and, Houdini-like, holing everything in sight. Alongside were another former champion, Jose Maria Olazabal, Greg Norman and Davis Love, with Bob Estes at four under and Nick Price three under. Several others, among them the much-fancied David Duval, were only one adrift. At that point any of eight or nine players could have won. But significantly Tiger Woods wasn't among them. He was never close.

Olazabal, whose immaculate short game and putting had been a feature throughout, made a big move at the 10th where he holed a 20 footer to go six under and take the lead. Thereafter, he was never out of it.

Norman joined him with a 30 foot birdie at the dangerous 11th and the pair, playing together, walked onto the 12th tee, once more the stage for great drama. The real moment of truth was at hand.

Norman this time left his tee shot clinging to the bank on the front edge of this slimly proportioned, acutely angled green. He was about 40 yards from the hole, now placed rear right, with Ollie in the back bunker, 25 yards from the cup. But Norman left his chip shot ten feet short and this time Lady Luck was smiling on another. He was to take two more, a bogey.

With the dexterity that is his forte, Olazabal conjured a running bunker shot that checked only when it neared the hole. A tap-in par. The smiling Spaniard remained six under, his lead once more secure.

Davis Love took a stab at it in his moment of truth that brought the shot of the tournament. Playing ahead of the leaders and lying second at five under with three holes to go, Love over-shot the green on the 181 yard, par three 16th, the ball stopping on the rear apron some 20 yards beyond the hole.

Now this green bears a strong affinity with a switchback, a marble roller coaster that falls steeply towards the lake that also guards the approaches. A ball landing on the top edge can break two ways as it gathers speed and charges the water. It's an evil configuration. In his first winning year, Bernhard Langer once putted at a 90 degree right angle, away from the hole, to make a birdie!

The flag was in its traditional fourth round spot, the rear left corner, at the bottom of the slope and about 15 yards from the water. So Love, facing an impossible task simply to make par, floated a soft pitch well left, maybe 15 yards wide of the flag and ten feet beyond it.

The ball checked, halted and then trickled at snail pace, back and down. Halfway there it was going to be close. Another yard and it was not going to miss. The ball caught the right lip and toppled in as the gallery erupted and Love leaped. The scoreboards said he was six under with all still to play for, still time for the Spaniard to crack.

Olazabal heard the roar but remained impassive. By now he and Norman were on the green at the par five 13th. The Aussie had arrowed a three iron to 25 feet and eagled it to go seven under; Ollie answered with a birdie from 20 feet. They were again joint leaders.

Greg dropped one at the next where his approach out of the rough jumped through the green. Ollie's two putt par was rock solid. Once more he was the lone leader and looking every inch the champion. Up head Pate birdied the 15th out of a bunker, holing another 25 footer, to equal Norman on six under, with Love on five and Estes four.

The par five 15th proved a turning point. Norman was bunkered and dropped one; Ollie sensibly laid up, pitched to 15 feet and got his par. Still seven under. Three holes to go and history beckoned, the climax of a poignant story.

Unable to walk for 18 months, his career seemingly ended by a foot injury that defied surgery, Olazabal was in despair until a German osteopath diagnosed the problem as emanating from the lower back. Months of manipulation and therapy got him back on his feet, hours of wading through the surf near his Spanish home strengthened both his legs and his resolve. To win the Masters again had been only a dream. Now, a year later, it was about to become reality.

It was fitting, perhaps, that Ollie was paired with Greg that day. When the Spaniard was in the depths of despair the Aussie was one who telephoned, offering sympathy and encouragement. When Norman similarly was *hors de combat* for seven months after shoulder surgery, Ollie was the first to call with words of hope and mutual affection. Now here they were, mano el mano, head to head, with the world watching.

Ollie virtually wrapped it up at the short 16th: Norman's tee shot was 10 feet long but straight, Olazabal's four feet away, on the high side with a wicked break. Norman missed the first putt but parred to stay five under.

With what may have been the finest putt of the week, Ollie simply let the weight of the putter head set the ball in motion and it curved into the centre of the hole for a birdie. Eight under. Now only disaster could prevent him taking his second green jacket and the $720,000 first prize.

He scrambled a touch up the 17th but held on. Two ahead with one hole remaining, he tip-toed up the 18th, and two putts later the Maestro was back, the Master once more.

He and Norman embraced on the green as the galleries rose in acclamation. Tears were close but Ollie, just as he had all week, proved his mettle. You couldn't imagine him crying in front of all those people. But he did later, at his Press conference. It was quite a moment. There had been many such that week....

The US Open: the highlights of Pinehurst No. 2, hole by hole

Why the USGA procrastinated in staging the US Open at Pinehurst is one of the great mysteries of golf. Virtually every other event of note has been held on its illustrious No. 2 Course: the Ryder Cup, the PGA Championship, the US Amateur, the World Open, the Tour Championship.

The Donald Ross masterpiece, opened in 1907 and rebuilt in 1935, has a permanent ranking among America's finest courses: it's invariably in the leading ten but in the eyes of many it is higher even than that.

"Pinehurst No. 2 in my mind cannot be out of anybody's top five golf courses in the world," says Raymond Floyd. "I have to put it in my top three. It is very, very special."

There'll be no hair-tearing or muted cussin', or at least not enough to write home about; no club slamming or scowls and caddies rolling their eyes skywards. Sure, there'll be some glazed looks along the way, and eyebrow raising will be a popular exercise.

Grins will be profuse, too, and high fives. Pinehurst has that effect on most folks and those who tee it up in the US Open Championship next month will be no exception. Because they'll be playing the fabled No. 2, one of the world's exceptional sporting creations. They're in for a rare treat.

For there will also be a paucity of architectural gimmicks, such as hidden hazards and penal collars of rough around the greens. Here such things are anathema. This course doesn't need fripperies. Every fairway bunker is in view from the tee and from the prescribed position everything is visible for the second shot. It's as fair a course as was ever laid out.

You'll gather this is not your typical US Open venue, most of which tend to give the players an attack of the vapours. At Pinehurst the golf is of surgical purity. The design, a living memorial to Donald Ross, demands supreme course management, limitless imagination, the touch of a brain surgeon, the short game of a conjurer and the nerves of a lion tamer.

It will help, too, if you've got a couple of major championships under your belt, or have won a swag of Tour events. An unknown bolter won't win here, in fact you could count the potential winners on the fingers of one hand. OK, maybe two hands...

Consider this: the rough will be four inches of clinging Bermuda grass; the fringe rough will be an inch and a half, just deep enough to stifle a recovery shot or, worse, encourage a top spin flier.

At this level, where the leading players talk of reducing the parameters of their bad shots, they'll consider the tree-lined fairways quite accommodating at between 24 and 30 yards wide. They won't be walking in single file, to be sure, but there's another factor: most of the greens are elevated a touch and angled, just-so; all are judiciously bunkered, several with off-set cross bunkers maybe 20 yards short of the front edge.

Many fairways bend a tad, too, so from several tees the target area for the ideal position is no more than 15 yards wide. This will not incommode most in the field but, like Chinese water torture, its effect is cumulative. Come the final day and nerves will be shredded, knuckles paled.

Thus, all the appropriate questions are asked on the tee box and there's more to come at the business end of most holes. Here the character of the design is most evident: here is where the real action will take place; here is where the US Open will be won and lost.

The greens average about 6,000 square feet which is not over-generous but, as we shall see, only half of that is cuppable area, offering a fair position for the flag stick. The reason: they are not only angled and elevated, they are also crowned, inverted saucers that will accept only the most precise and authoritative approach shots.

Find the middle of the green and there'll be the chance of a 30 footer and a two putt par. Be more than a touch askew–short, long or wide–and the ball will scamper off the green. To compound this problem the down-slopes are, like the greens, Penn G2 bent grass, shaven and as slick as can be. The ball will run a fair distance, 40 or 50 feet in some cases, before it meets the Bermuda grass fringe and brakes.

Then comes the major problem: getting it back up-slope in such a manner that it will stop within holeable range. And being askew by not much at all means the scenario is likely to be repeated. The short game, in all its infinite variety, will be at a premium.

"In the June heat the greens will be firm and running between 10 and 11.5 on the stimp meter," said course supervisor Paul Jett. "Any quicker and the cuppable areas will reduce in size even further. There has never been an Open course that will respond like this one."

A minority of the field will have played it before: the 1991 Tournament Players' Championship was held here but that was a limited field and the event was staged in November, when the Bermuda grass was dormant and conditions and weather quite at odds to that expected when the Open is played in June.

The players loved it, by all accounts, but the characteristics will be a mystery to most. Those who have played a windy British links in the Open Championship will soon get the message. Early in the piece the flag positions should be towards the front centre which will encourage the bump and run approach. Thereafter it's anybody's guess and the Devil will be calling in some debts.

On the distaff side of the Magic Circle, if golf's Tooth Fairy could wave her wand a few knowing players would happily settle for an aggregate of five or six below par. If that doesn't win it will go awfully close.

Take a look at the card and you'll get my drift. It reads 7,175 yards, par-70, with only two par fives, one of 610 yards. There's a clutch of strong par fours, two in excess of 485 yards, two one shotters of 200 yards or more, and three teasing short par fours, counterpoints in the symphony and each a potential danger zone. It all equates to a course of consummate challenge, of both technique and character, one that will refresh the image of this great championship.

In terms of balance and tempo the course comprises four distinct passages, beginning "pianissimo" and ending, as it should, with a crescendo. The four opening holes are down-wind and the players must take advantage of this, to gather credits for the examination ahead.

Two shortish par fours and the first par five, of 566 yards, are obvious birdie opportunities although any shot marginally off-line will nullify the chance. The route then turns into the wind for three holes and this is where Ross sharpened his knife: pars here will pick up strokes on most of the field.

The 5th is 482 yards but a par four, regarded as the toughest hole on the course, one where both fairway and green tilt right to left, away from safety. Then comes a one shotter of 222 yards: birdies here will be gilt-edged.

The 7th is 398 yards, a sharp left-to-right dog-leg with a cluster of six bunkers guarding the elbow. Some long hitters could gamble here, flying the bunkers to leave a flick wedge, but that's not a percentage shot. Most will play short, just as they will on several holes where precision takes precedence over power—Paul Jett reckoned few will use the driver on more than six or seven tees.

One of them is the 8th, another long two shotter, relatively trouble free apart from a dramatic down-slope on the left of the green. The 9th, at 179 yards, may appear innocuous but it flatters to deceive: the side-on green is fiercely defended and the slope at the rear is the route to perdition.

The 10th is 610 yards and although it has the largest green on the course at 7,500 square feet the betting is that even those who are capable will not attempt to get up in two. Guarding bunkers demand an approach from the right side of the fairway but even from the perfect spot the green configuration predicates a lay-up as the best option for the obligatory birdie.

Patience holds the key over the next four holes, too: they're all two shotters, of disparate character and tempo. Play smart and hope a putt or two falls is sound advice, particularly for those in contention and showing red on the leader boards. Because the moment of truth is nigh. It's make or break time.

Donald Ross believed that the long irons prove a player's ability and few are the holes at Pinehurst No.2 where they can be overlooked, either on the tee or for the second shot. In these days of inordinate length this applies even more than when he revamped the lay-out in 1935. No one will over-power this course, no matter how far they hit it. Ross would be mightily pleased.

The 15th offers a good example of his philosophy. At 202 yards to the smallest green on the course, one that is crowned, this is the hole that will offer a glorious anti-climax in the final round. Birdies here will come with golden plumage; par will be an imperative for anyone with realistic ambitions of becoming champion.

The 16th is a long two shotter of 489 yards but it probably plays 470 because it's down hill and slightly down-wind. It bends left a touch and there are bunkers 290 yards out, as the ground rises. There's oodles of space over the crest, though. Tiger and his ilk will be taking the driver here; the risk is negligible.

The approach shot is the vital one, to a green ringed by bunkers, so the shorter the iron, the higher the flight, the better the chance of a birdie. This tee shot could prove decisive in a crunch.

The breeze will be a factor in the championship but unless the weather turns freakish the maximum velocity will be about 15 mph, a mere zephyr by British links standards. But when it's across the flight it will be sufficient to nudge a ball off-target and that's the danger at the 17th, a slightly down hill 195 yarder.

This hole runs at right angles to the 18th fairway, in fact the green is near the final tee, opposite a clearing in the trees. So the right to left breeze coming down the 18th is unchecked. It's effect on all but a faded tee shot could be terminal. There are bunkers and trees to the left and bunkers right and centre, the latter the deepest on the course and just beyond a swale. There's a bunker rear right, close to the likely pin position on the final day. This could be another critical shot in round four.

The drivers will be out on the 18th tee; it's a rising fairway into the breeze and anyone in with a shout will want to be hitting no more than a medium iron into the green, to ensure a putt and a safe par or better. The elevated green runs away to the rear and from the right edge, the latter with a steep-faced bunker only a few feet away. Guess where the flag will be on Sunday?

There are more bunkers left and front right, the latter one of those Ross cross bunkers. It's some distance from the front edge, in fact there's a substantial apron thereabouts for anyone who tweaks his tee shot and is forced to play the percentages.

Considering the likely pin position on the final day it's a realistic target en route to saving par, although for those who cream the tee shot the head wind will help the approach hold the green, providing it's on-line.

So the home hole offers a birdie opportunity that in a high scoring championship could mean make or break. It's a fitting finale to what promises to be a glittering event on a peerless course.

The Open at Royal Lytham, where the dramatic is the norm

Royal Lytham staged its first Open Championship in 1926 and though only eight championships have been held there the great Lancashire links has been the venue for a chapter of events beyond the mere dramatic.

Whatever the outcome next month golfing historians are guaranteed at least one further fact to add to their collection of Lytham memorabilia, one record will either be broken or extended into the next century.

It is this: no American professional has won the championship there, although one has tied. Other than the 1926 championship, when the USA dominated the event won by Bobby Jones with "the shot that echoed around the world," it's only a mild exaggeration to say they've barely had a look in.

The 1963 championship saw America's Phil Rodgers lose a play-off to New Zealand's Bob Charles, with Jack Nicklaus a stroke behind, and Nicklaus went one better when he was second in 1979, three adrift of Seve Ballesteros.

But that, the odd brilliant round aside, is the extent of the US challenge at Royal Lytham, post 1926. Considering their success at the other venues it's an oddity that borders on enigma. Current form suggests no change.

Lytham must be a favoured venue for golf historians and other collectors of statistical memorabilia: the Open always throws up something noteworthy for them, a bone to chew on.

In 1926, Lytham's Open début, it was the victory by Bobby Jones, the first amateur to win since Harold Hilton at Muirfield in 1892, plus the fact that the next three places were also filled by Americans, a record unmatched until the Turnberry Open of 1977.

It was 1952 before the championship came to Lytham again and this one was notable on two points: it brought Bobby Locke's hat-trick of wins and it signalled the emergence of another great Commonwealth player, Australia's Peter Thomson, who was second.

Thereafter, Thomson was seldom out of the top six. He became the only player in modern history to win the Open three times in succession, a feat he completed at Hoylake in 1956, and scored his fourth win in 1958 — at Royal Lytham, the first Open to be televised.

A fact of astonishing proportions is that in 1957 Thomson was runner-up to Locke, as he was at Lytham in 1952. So between 1954 and 1958 he came close to being Open Champion five times in succession. He was also joint runner-up to Ben Hogan at Carnoustie in 1953, although with three others he was four adrift of the American. So Thomson was first or joint second each year between 1952 and 1958!

His victory in 1958 came via a play-off with David Thomas. It was only the fifth such in the history of the championship but it was replicated at Lytham in 1963, the first time an Open venue had seen successive ties. En passant: That year, Thomson covered the opening half of the first round in 29 strokes, then a record, en route to 66.

Bob Charles' win five years later was notable for other reasons, too: in becoming the first left-hander to take the Open, he set a record for the least number of putts in a round. He took only 26 in the third round, never used more than 31 in any round and literally putted Rodgers off the course to win the play-off by 140 to 148, single putting 11 holes in his morning round. And that on greens far from their best because of a harsh winter and a late spring!

Which leads to yet two more historical facts associated with Royal Lytham: it was the last time an Open tie was decided by a 36 hole play-off. From then onwards it became 18 holes until the present four hole system was adopted.

As in 1926 and 1952, the 1963 Lytham Open saw a major talent take centre stage in Britain for the first time. After falling at the 36 hole barrier in his initial championship at Troon the year before, Jack Nicklaus placed third, a stroke behind Charles and Rodgers.

What if....? Two fours would have done the trick for Nicklaus but he dropped a stroke at the 71st hole, when he over-clubbed his approach and ran through the green, and then drove into a bunker off the final tee. But another legend was in the making.

The Open next came to Lytham in 1969. It proved to be a milestone, in more ways than one: it brought the first televised golf broadcast in colour, and Tony Jacklin became the first home-grown champion for 18 years, beginning a resurgence in British golf that would bring unimagined rewards and set a pattern which continues to this day.

Charles led after 36 holes with rounds of 66-69, three ahead of Jacklin's 68-70, and one ahead of Christy O'Connor Sr., who came home in 32 with only 10 putts for a second round of 65, a course record.

Then the wind freshened and Charles faded as Jacklin surged to a two stroke lead with a 70. Out in 33 in the fourth round, he was beyond reach of the field, despite dropping three strokes in the later stages for a 72 and a two stroke victory.

A measure of Jacklin's performance is that this was one of the strongest fields in Open history with a large US contingent headed by Nicklaus and a galaxy of international stars. An indication: behind him were four Open champions in Charles, Thomson, de Vicenzo and Nicklaus, in that order, the latter five strokes away.

On a lighter note, 1969 was also the year in which the Bollinger champagne tent made its first and now regular appearance at the Open venue. At £3.50 a bottle doubtless Tony Jacklin celebrated in the appropriate style! What price these days, eh?

Another great Commonwealth champion also had reason for celebrating at Royal Lytham in 1974, the year the larger US-sized ball became obligatory for the first time in the Open.

Gary Player, never out of the lead and the only one to better par over four rounds, won by four strokes from Peter Oosterhuis, to complete his hat-trick of Open victories over three decades. It was a feat to equal that of Harry Vardon and J.H.Taylor at the turn of the century.

The championship returned to Lytham in short order, relatively speaking, only five years later, and it heralded the start of another golden era, that of Seve Ballesteros.

At 22, the dashing Spaniard became the third youngest winner in history, returning an aggregate 283. He was the only player to better par, pushing Nicklaus and Ben Crenshaw into second place by three strokes.

The scoreboard would show that the victory was largely due to a record-equalling second round of 65, which drew him within two strokes of Hale Irwin, the leader after 36 holes with a pair of 68s. But as always the scoreboard doesn't tell the half of it.

For much of the championship there was at least a two club wind and Seve, playing into it coming home, carded four threes in the last five holes, all par fours, for an inward 32.

The 65 inspired him to greater things, of that there's no doubt, but there was much more to it, as anyone who was there will testify. Seve knew that much of the rough had been flattened by the huge crowds — in excess of 134,000, then a record —- and so he took his driver and let it ride as only he knows how.

At the 13th in the final round, for instance, he carried a bunker some 290 yards out on the fly, found the rough off the 14th and 15th tees, was in a car park at the next and missed the final two fairways for good measure.

But with a short game that set new standards he played those final six holes in one under, for a final round of 70. Green-side bunkers? Like Gary Player in his heyday, Seve aimed for them. Throughout the championship he hit 15 in all and failed only once to get up and down. The historical statisticians were going bonkers!

Nine years later, in 1988, he did it again, pipping Nick Price at the post as he bettered his 1979 Lytham aggregate of 283 by ten strokes with rounds of 67-71-70-65. Price recorded cards of 70-67-69-69-275 but was beaten by two. There was a small consolation: it was the second lowest aggregate by a runner-up!

Truly, Royal Lytham, birthplace of champions, has seen many wondrous happenings! The sequence is certain to continue. What price a left-handed American professional winning the 1996 event?

The course guide: Links courses generally are somewhat lacking in visual appeal and Royal Lytham's may be the most unprepossessing of any, set as it is amidst suburban housing with no view of the Irish Sea or the coast line.

But it lacks for nothing in challenge, as you'd expect of an Open venue, and when the prevailing nor-west winds are on duty it can make strong men cringe. Uniquely for a major course, Lytham opens with a par three, with two others to follow on the outward loop, which for championship purposes is the shorter, 3,302 yards to 3,555, par 35 as against par 36.

That seven of the opening holes are invariably down-wind — the 4th reverses direction, the short 5th is at right angles — tends to unbalance the course somewhat, particularly in extreme conditions, although the railway line and OOB beckons to the right of the 2nd, 3rd and 8th. Then 33 or better is often followed by 43 or worse and 39 can represent good scoring on a remorseless loop requiring constant adjustment for subtle changes of direction and with a cruel finishing stretch.

Not that the first nine is a piece of cake: scores have to be earned and oft-times the tail wind is so fierce that it becomes an additional hazard. I recall Tom Watson in 1979 hitting a 9-iron second to the par five 6th and going through by 30 yards. "No control," he said. "Impossible to stop it."

That apart, precision is paramount at Lytham: as at the Old Course, there's a correct side of the fairway for every tee shot. Miss it by not much at all and the knolls and swales — to say nothing of the myriad, steep-faced bunkers — will do their worst.

The green approaches have been tightened in recent years, the bunkering imposing greater demands upon accuracy and shot-making skills. It is possible to run the ball in down-wind, but only from the prescribed position. The alternative to a lay-up is the aerial route but with a tail wind that means jumping into the lap of the gods.

Unless the tide turns mid-round the wind that ballooned the sails going out, as it were, will bend the mast backwards coming home. Hereabouts it roars in off the Irish Sea with lumps in it.

The return journey begins with a fine short two shotter that often flatters to deceive and a long par five whose fairway bunkers would hide a tank battalion. The 12th is the final par three but one of 198 yards with OOB only a whisker away to the right, and the 13th reverses direction, allowing a modicum of respite, if a hole with 16 bunkers can be said to offer respite.

Then the really serious business begins, a succession of long, rock hard par fours that make the ultimate demands: accuracy, judgement, courage, physical and mental strength, and shot-making skills of the highest order.

The 15th is a blind tee shot that must tackle the rising, curving fairway and anything less than perfection will leave a blind second, too, over dunes, cross bunkers and evil rough.

"God, it's a hard hole, " said Jack Nicklaus in 1974, when the average score there was more than a stroke over par.

The 16th brings another blind drive and an elevated green surrounded by bunkers, of which there are 15 in all, some in line astern down each side of the fairway, the remainder in clusters on two sides of the green. At 468 yards into a strong wind there are few tougher par fours anywhere.

The 17th will always be Bobby Jones' hole. It's another brute. It has 18 bunkers en toto, a crescent of them down the left becoming cross bunkers at the elbow, where the fairway bends left.

Catch one and you'll need divine guidance, or the talent to match Bobby Jones. Because only from the right half is the green visible through a gap in the sand dunes. From even the ideal spot it's a character-building second shot, over the cross bunkers to a green ringed by sand. As history proves, the championship can be won or lost here.

The home hole at Open time is, quite simply, the ultimate test of courage and technique for those who aspire to hold the claret jug. It measures only 386 yards from where the tigers prowl but the perfect drive has to thread its way between and over angled bunkers left and right of the fairway, with deep trouble beyond on both sides.

Six more bunkers sandwich the green, which is the largest on the course, with two more some way short squeezing the entrance. The tee shot is the key. In Jacklin's year his final drive flew the bunkers and split the fairway, prompting an unforgettable response by television commentator Henry Longhurst: "What a corker!," he said. Three shots later Jacklin was the champion.

The Magic of The Open at St Andrews

Arnold Palmer, who won it twice, said of it in his heyday: "There's golf, there's tournament golf and then there's the Open."

The late Gerald Micklem, the doyen of the amateur game in Britain, went further: "There's the Open and then there's the Open at St Andrews." You'll get the picture.

Well, July will see the staging of the 124th Open Championship and the 25th to be held at St Andrews and already the usual 1,600 aspiring entrants are licking their lips, some in anticipation, others in trepidation.

Those collective facial twitches are nothing to do with the prize money of £1.25 million, once more a record. Most of those 1,600 hopefuls won't get a bean and anyway they'd play for the glory, given only half the chance.

Which is rather more than they'll have considering that the regional and final qualifying rounds they face will reduce the number to a fraction of the 156 who will tee up at St Andrews on July 20. For of that 156 about 95 are exempt from qualifying for reasons of status or current world ranking.

So those 1,600 dreamers, most of whom are even now doubtless practising from dawn to dusk, are shooting for little more than 60 places on that first tee. Not good odds for their £75 entrance fee but the cost is irrelevant in the scheme of things. For many, the disappointment will be doubly acute if they fall at the last fence, in the two days of final qualifying over the four courses within half an hour of St Andrews.

So near and yet so far. That's where the hard luck stories will abound, of the one missed putt, the fluffed chip, the inexplicably silly mistake that cost entry to the greatest golf show on earth, the oldest major event in that sport at the world's most ancient golfing venue.

The tournament dates from 1860 but even that pales into insignificance in comparison with the history of the course. There's a written reference to the game being played there in 1457, when church elders tried to ban it, and the Noble Gentlemen of Leith, the forerunners of the Royal and Ancient, drew up the rules of golf for their first official competition back in 1754.

The championship was staged at Prestwick from 1860 to 1873, when it moved to St Andrews to be won by Tom Kidd with a 36-hole aggregate of 91-88-179. Kidd's first prize was £15. This year the champion will collect £125,000, plus several millions of pounds in commercial spin-off.

Every professional completing 72 holes will get a minimum of £5,000 and of those who don't make the 36-hole cut, the one in 156th place will get £650.

It's all a far cry from even 1955 when Peter Thomson's second win brought him the first £1,000 cheque from a total purse of £3,750.

Each year since the total prize money has risen inexorably–this year it is up £150,000 on 1994 — all financed by television fees and the vast and steadily increasing attendance: 35,000 in 1964 to 92,000 in 1974 and 193,000 in 1984. Gates of 200,000 plus have become the norm since the previous Open at St Andrews in 1990 when 208,000 paid to see the event.

Another record is assured this year because just as the Old Course always attracts the largest entry so it pulls the biggest gates, plus untold millions of a world-wide television audience. Players come from the four corners of the globe, from every part of Asia and Australasia, from every country in Europe, from Africa — Nick Price, the defending champion, hails from Zimbabwe — and from the Americas, South and North. Of the last, there's not a player ranked in the world's top 100 who can resist the championship that they readily agree is the greatest in the world.

They've been flocking here smce the charismatic Arnold Palmer made his debut in the Centenary Open of 1960 and helped usher in the age of televised golf. Arnold, second to Kel Nagle of Australia that year, fell in love with St Andrews and the Open and won the two ensuing championships.

To Arnold, and those who have followed his well-trodden trail, British links offer the ultimate test in golf. All have had to learn how to play in wind on crumpled, fast-running fairways and hard, bouncy greens. They had to adapt technique, learn shots they didn't play at home, accept unusual bounces and, to them, eccentric course design. In other words, golf as it was first played. The real thing. They loved it.

"Playing in the Open over a links completes a golfer's education," said Tom Watson, the five time champion. "This is true golf, as it was meant to be played."

Not everyone necessarily agreed, particularly apropos St Andrews. The great Bobby Jones tore up his card in frustration the first time he played the Old Course but came to love it and, indeed, won the 1927 Open there.

It's a test of character and imagination at any time. Flat and gnarled, almost bare of foliage, there's virtually nothing to aim at, little perspective. There are, though, lots of wicked, hidden bunkers — "just big enough for an angry man and his niblick" — guarding huge, silky greens, seven of them vast double greens.

The greens hold the first key. They're so large that 50-yard putts are not uncommon for lesser players and simply to change the flag positions can alter the whole character of the course. This affects the line of approach shots, which in turn affects the line off the tee at this level. Throw into the equation a brisk sea breeze and the problems are compounded.

Weather is the second key. As with most British links the wind off St Andrews Bay can switch direction with the change of tide. It's the original out-and-back links but in more than one Open the wind has been against up to the turn and, just as the players were anticipating relief, it reversed with the tide!

When it's really angry, when golf becomes a question of survival, breaking 75 is an achievement on the Old Course. Four days of suchweather will challenge man's character, destroy his resolve, his tempo and his technique.

But oft times it's fine: Scotland's east coast enjoys some of Britain's most agreeable weather and although still days are rare they are not infrequent. Then, flags limp, the Old Lady dozing in the sun is at her most vulnerable and the young bucks are quick to take advantage, before the mood changes

Hence the course record 62 by Curtis Strange in the Dunhill Cup, the 63 by Paul Broadhurst in the 1990 Open, and Nick Faldo 's remarkable scoring in the same championship.

Quite simply, the man ran amok. He started 67-65 for an Open record-equalling 132 for 36 holes, then carded a record 54-hole total of 199 en route to 67- 71 for a St Andrews Open record of 270, 18 under par and a five-stroke victory. Shouldn't be allowed!

The young lions will be hoping for similar weather come July, so that they can strut their stuff, shoot the lights out again. The old stagers, though, will relish a brisk sea wind, to keep things in perspective.

St Andrews 1995 will be nostalgic as well as historic. A new exemption clause allowing past champions to play until their 65th birthday facilitates the final appearance of Arnold Palmer, back to where it all began for him in 1960.

Back, too, for his final appearance, will be Jack Nicklaus, who made his debut at Royal Troon in 1962 — he missed the cut! — and first appeared at St Andrews two years later. Jack has always said he'd like his final Open to be at St Andrews, where he won in 1970 and 1978.

Just imagine: Palmer and Nicklaus paired together and coming up the vast, crowded canyon of the 18th for the last time....The applause will be deafening; there won't be a dry eye in the place as two more golfing giants offer the Old Lady their final salute and pass graciously into history.

Royal Birkdale is a Hawtree family affair

Some people, 'tis rumoured, would go to any lengths to become members of a royal golf club, particularly one which regularly hosts the Open Championship. The subsequent prestige is an irresistible lure, the club tie a mark of exalted status, a signal that its wearer has "arrived."

To some members of The Royal Birkdale, though, such sentiments must have seemed somewhat dubious between the autumn of 1992 and the winter of 1996. Then their great links was reduced to a shadow of its former pre-eminence, with temporary greens a permanent scenario and excavating bull-dozers a constant backdrop to their restricted golfing activities.

No one complained, though: stiff upper lip and all that was the order of the day, alleviated somewhat as other clubs threw down the welcome mat in Birkdale's time of trial.

If it was the worst of times it is has brought the best of times. It was far from a blessing in disguise, but from near-disaster has emerged a triumph of agronomy and innovation. The great links, for years one of the world's finest, has been polished beyond mere lustre.

The on-course problems that surfaced in the course of the 1991 Open finally were faced, and paid for. The recalcitrant greens were torn up, the problem identified and alleviated.

Now the golfing world is about to view the fruits of all the heartache and subsequent endeavour. It will be a revelation arguably without precedent in the Open Championship. It also completes another memorable chapter in the history of a unique family, the Hawtrees.

The root of the problem was just that, at root level in the sub-soil. Excavation disclosed a dense black substance impervious to every treatment, totally lacking in oxygen and too high in humus to allow any form of root growth. A lump the size of a small tea pot weighed about ten pounds. It might have been putty.

Its origins were a mystery; its effect was to repel the finer, deeper-rooted grasses, the bents and the fescues, to the benefit of the secondary more shallow-rooted grasses, poa annua, or meadow grass. The consequence was thatch, for an Open venue the equivalent of the poisoned chalice.

So each green was torn up, its foundations rebuilt, its root zone renewed, its turf replaced. The cost: £267,000 en toto, plus almost as much again for incidentals and architectural improvements that were viewed as a vital adjunct to such a major project.

Enter Martin Hawtree, the third generation of his family to contribute to the architectural history of the Birkdale links. It's a tale worth repeating.

The club, founded in 1889, moved to the present site at the turn of the century and leased the land from a prominent family. Some time in the mid-20s the land was acquired by the Southport Corporation and when the club's lease expired it was feared that the new owners might assume control and convert the site into a municipal course.

The fears proved unfounded, in fact quite the reverse happened. The corporation, seemingly more far-sighted that its successors, could see Birkdale becoming a major championship venue with obvious benefits to the town's economy.

With this objective, a new lease was granted, one of 99 years, on the proviso that within seven years the course be brought up to championship standard, complete with a suitably impressive clubhouse.

And so in 1932 the architectural duo of F.G. Hawtree and J.H. Taylor was contracted to meet the obligations of the lease. Their plan was to amend the route of play, to run the holes in the valleys between the sand hills, rather than over them, in the style that makes the links such a joy to see and play. The result, still largely in evidence, was a course at once tough but fair, one with minimal blind shots common to many eminent links, and with generally flat but deviating fairways. The new design brought a cerebral links, one which rewarded accuracy and imagination, as the roll call of its Open champions proves.

In time the club's honours board of major events exceeded all expectations until, in 1961, came the catalyst for further change.

His name was Arnold Palmer, a swashbuckling golfer with a penchant for setting championships ablaze with the sheer force of his personality and golfing bravado, seemingly playing on the knife-edge of disaster, but often triumphant, always enthralling.

Crowds flocked to watch him and at Royal Birkdale — the club had been so elevated in 1951 — the multitude was such that spectator movement created problems, both of vision and mobility. So after the 1961 Open it was deemed apposite to modernise the links once again. And once again a Hawtree was among the leading characters, this time F.W., son of F.G. and father of Martin.

His solution was to re-site several tees, allowing easier movement for the huge galleries who, formerly given freedom of the fairways, were now guided along prescribed routes by a system of constructed pathways and fencing. He also created a new hole, the short 12th, to replace the par three 17th, which had been one of the major bottlenecks, and shortened the opening hole for similar reasons.

To off-set this, the new tee positions lengthened several holes by between 20 and 60 yards and the replacement for the old 17th meant that the finish was now one of the longest and toughest in the world, with three of the final four holes in excess of 500 yards.

The results were seamless and successful: the course retained its natural beauty without blemish and within a decade several major events, and the vast galleries they now attracted, endorsed the Hawtree formula as the correct solution.

Now one of the favourite Open venues for the world's great players, all went swimmingly until 1991, the year of poor Ian Baker Finch, when eyebrows went skywards at the sight, and the response, of the once-famed Birkdale greens. Patchy, soft, discoloured and inconsistent, they had rebuffed every remedy tried by Tom O'Brien, the club's master greenkeeper.

Once more desperate times called for desperate measures. A cast of experts was assembled, from the Sports Turf Research Institute, the Royal & Ancient and even from the United States Golf Association.

The members concurred with their findings: the problem identified, agreement was reached to solve it. Martin Hawtree suggested that as the greens were to be excavated it would be a sound notion to modify their design, raising some to aid drainage, giving more contour and variation to others and to meld them more harmoniously into the dunes.

And so it came to pass, and in the process other potential improvements emerged: for instance, the tee of the short 7th has been moved 50 yards left so that the shot is now down the line of the green; the 17th tee has also been shifted 50 yards left, bringing a tighter driving line to a hole much improved by a green which now has an angled shelf running diagonally from front left to back right, where a new pot bunker awaits. As the 71st hole it could prove decisive in July.

The new 15th green is another beauty, in fact there's not one that doesn't catch the eye and many will catch the breath. And because they have reverted to true links style — hard and quick — they will offer greater challenge, both in approach and with the putter. Many bunkers are now much more in play and it has been estimated that the course will now play up to three shots harder overall.

At 7,018 yards, par-70, and with only two par fives, the stage is set for a searching Open Championship. A record round is in prospect, but not, we would suggest, a record aggregate. The Hawtree mystique should see to that.

A debutant's guide to St Andrews.

If you are a golfer making your maiden pilgrimage to St Andrews the tingle factor will come into play as you cross the Forth bridge that links Edinburgh with The Kingdom of Fife, wherein lies the Home of Golf. You scan the countryside for a golf course and the prickling mounts when the first comes into view. Now you know how Columbus felt when he spotted America.

It's about an hour's drive from the bridge to St Andrews but that only serves to heighten the exquisite agony of anticipation. By the time you reach the old grey town the hairs on the back of your neck are rising as ecstasy assumes total control of your senses.

The trio of awe-struck hackers with you are already reaching for their spikes. Quick as you can, you park the car and walk the few yards to the broad expanse of green visible at the end of the street. You turn the corner and stop in your tracks.

There it is. You're looking at the stage on which six centuries of golfing history have been played out. There's the Valley of Sin gnawing at that vast green, the Swilcan Bridge straddling the burn near the first green, the fluttering flag at the Road Hole just visible in the distance. Dappled evening sunlight pours shadows into the undulations that dimple the expanse of fairways and greens. You contemplate the fact that Old Tom Morris and Young Tom won their great championships here; so did Vardon, Braid and Taylor; Bobby Jones and Bobby Locke; Nicklaus, Player, Watson, Faldo and Ballesteros.

The ambience is awe-inspiring, ethereal. It is almost a spiritual experience, akin to standing in the vastness of a great cathedral. You wonder how on earth you'll ever get the ball off the first tee, let alone over the burn and onto the green. When your turn comes you hope, as with death, to face it with dignified courage.

St Andrews affects all first-timers this way; for many it never loses its romance. The old place has been involved in more love affairs that all the great hotels of Paris and London combined. It occupies a very special place in sporting history, one that will draw you back again and again.

The game is everywhere here, where it all began back in the 15th Century. Golf features in the names of shops, restaurants, bars, hotels and streets. And not including a nine hole course that's ideal for beginners, there are now five 18 hole courses with a swathe of others nearby, some equally venerable and romantic: Crail, Elie, Leven and Scotscraig spring to mind.

You'll want to play them, no doubt, but your priority is St Andrews, Golf's Mecca, the cradle of the game and the fount of much of its history. Be assured you'll have your hands full, but don't rush things, eh? There's always tomorrow. You must savour the time as well as the place.

You'll probably be surprised to learn that the Old Course is one of five, two of them fairly recent in origin. They are the Strathtyrum and the Balgove. There's also a modern practice centre, a new public clubhouse, a museum of golf and various innovations to cater for the vast number of visitors drawn to the town each week.

The 21st Century arrived early at St Andrews but the changes haven't been allowed to over-ride the historic ambience that permeates the town and its surroundings. The tingle factor remains unchanged for first timers, and for some veteran visitors too, upon reflection.. It will be doubly noticeable this year, when the Millennium Open takes place there in July.

In order of technical challenge here's a pen picture of the courses to be found at the modern St Andrews. For beginners and youngsters there is the Balgove, a nine holer with a par of 31. Then comes the Strathtyrum, another Donald Steel design built in 1993, an 18 holes of 5,200 yards, par-69. This is a holiday course with built-in undulations for variety and perspective. It's a fair challenge but not overly taxing.

The Eden, opened in 1914 to a design by Harry Colt, has been up-graded in severity of challenge, again by Donald Steel. Now it's quite a severe test, a course of considerable prestige, with small greens guarded by deflecting hummocks, some devilish bunkering and several areas out of bounds. The emphasis here is on accurate iron play. It measures 6,112 yards to a par of 70.

The Jubilee course, opened in 1897 to a design by Old Tom Morris, was up-graded some years ago to meet the need for a second championship course. It's a whisker over 6,800 yards with a par of 72 and a mark of its quality is that it has been the venue for the Scottish Strokeplay Championships, among other notable events.

You're in serious golfing country now. From the back tees it is long, a sound test with a tough six hole finish. For the less ambitious, there's an option known as the Bronze course, which uses variable forward tees. Great fun.

The New course is in fact the second most senior at St Andrews, built in 1895 when the game experienced its first boom and an increasing volume of visitors predicated the demand for a second course. Designed by Old Tom Morris, then the head green keeper and professional, it is considered the nicest and fairest of them all. Indeed, many locals prefer it to the Old.

Unchanged from the original, it is an out-and-back links in the old style, with a slight diversion for variety. Like the Old Course, it has some undulating fairways, lots of magnetic gorse and it makes all the demands known in golf, particularly over a tough five hole finish.

The size of the greens is, as it should be, governed by the length of shot required to reach them. Some are quite large and there's one double but they're all full of interest and in good order, as are all the courses at the Home of Golf.

There may be little to write about the Old Course that you may not have seen on television or first hand. Visitors and locals alike meet and chat along the footpath that runs in front of the Royal & Ancient clubhouse and the famous monument. They'll be there when you nervously tee off; some will be waiting when you play your final approach, over the Valley of Sin at the 18th, and they'll be peeking over your shoulder as you weigh up the down-hill, side-hill putt that's sure to follow. But whatever the quality of your shots they'll be sympathetic or appreciative.

They'll be golfers, too, you see. Virtually everyone is who lives at St Andrews, which is also home to one of the world's oldest universities. You'll be aware of the students as you wander around the narrow streets. Don't contemplate driving once in situ, incidentally: the walking is easy, the town is compact, and parking is limited. Strolling is part of the local tradition, particularly on Sundays when many people walk the course or cross it to reach the beach that rims St Andrews Bay, or the wonderful old putting green that edges the first fairway.

The Old Course is on common land, hence its accessibility to the public. It is a municipal course, managed by a trust (not the Royal & Ancient, as many presume) which is responsible for all the golf facilities in town. They set the fees, decide how the revenue should be spent and supervise the continuous programme of up-keep and expansion that has taken the town's golfing facilities to a peerless level in recent years.

You should be aware that actually getting onto the Old Course is not easy, unless you are a lone player, in which case you can "make-up", that is complete a foursome, simply by approaching the starter early in the day. You'll find his office near the first tee of the Old Course, in front of the R&A clubhouse.

For others in pairs or groups, all is dependant upon the daily ballot, held the day previously, that's necessary to filter the hundreds of daily applications to play the world's most famous links. Your best bet is to choose a hotel or a holiday company which will make the tee reservation on your behalf. You will, though, need to make your plans well in advance: eight weeks' notice is required for this purpose.

There are dozens of hotels, large and small, in town, many overlooking the Old Course. There are restaurants galore, an equal number of bars and the shopping is a delight.

Those playing the Old Course should make a bee-line for the new Links Clubhouse where there are locker rooms, secure storage for golf clubs, a pro shop and, on the upper floor, a handsome restaurant and bar giving all-day service. This will be a popular spot come The Open: the terrace overlooks the opening and closing holes of the Old Course.

Doubtless a few more love affairs will be launched in July as another chapter in golfing history is etched upon the parchment of time as the great players gather for the most venerable championship in golf on the world's oldest and most revered links. .

'Twas ever thus at St Andrews, the town that is a timeless monument to golfing traditions and a magnet to lovers of the royal and ancient game the world over.

A guide to Lytham St Annes, an Open town...

First class golf is only one of the attractions of Lytham St Anne's. To visit this quintessentially English resort on the Lancashire coast is to experience the best of domestic tourism. It wants for nothing in terms of facilities, services and ambience. Solid, peaceful and unchanging, it is easy to imagine life here in a pre-war era, when families and golfers would arrive by train for their annual holidays by the seaside.

Largely Victorian in origins, its architecture is a delight to behold. Handsome, pristine villas line the broad pavements, interspersed with venerable hotels that have pumped the economic lifeblood into the community for a century or more. Tradition and quality are evident at every turn, and they go hand in hand with good value at Lytham St Anne's.

In fact they are twin towns, with separate identities, although you'd be hard pressed to find the join. The locals say Lytham is the resort and St Anne's is where they live but like a good marriage the union becomes stronger with each passing decade.

As its name implies, the Royal Lytham & St Anne's Golf Club has bridged the imaginary divide since 1886, making a major contribution to the community's prosperity as the frequent stage for the Open Championship, first played here in 1926. Every seven years or so a torrent of wealth cascades into the town as the golfing world beats a path to its door but the spin-off is perpetual as visiting golfers make the pilgrimage, to play the great links and the three nearby courses whose names have become synonymous with the Open.

Fairhaven, St Anne's Old Links and Lytham Green Drive have all been venues for final qualifying and although the latter is no longer suitable (it's deemed too short for modern championship play) it remains a major attraction, not least for its superb presentation and facilities.

Unlike its links land neighbours, the Green Drive course is a tapestry of emerald, as lush as could be imagined and heavily wooded in parts. Trees influence play on most holes and they also protect the course from the wind that is a major factor on the adjoining links.

It's a fine club course, easy walking and tight but fair, with rough that will cost half a shot. At 6,194 yards to par 70, it has some short and tempting two shotters but the big hitters should think twice before chancing their arm. Sound course management is an imperative here.

You'll not find a prettier course in a long day's drive and when you see those greens you'll want to roll them up and take them home! There's a cracking clubhouse too and you'll be made most welcome, in true Lancashire fashion.

The club was founded in 1913, which was 12 years after St Anne's Old Links first saw play. This grand old course was laid out by Alex Herd, hard by the sand dunes that overlook the Irish Sea at the north end of town. So the wind is a major factor here in fact it holds the key on most days.

With the exception of three one shotters, all the holes run roughly north to south or the reverse and the prevailing wind is a westerly, or variations thereof, and invariably on the sharp side of brisk. To exacerbate those problems and unusually for a links, this one has four ponds that influence play on six holes. This compounds the interest in high summer when the fairways produce some fiery bounces. It offers pure links golf, traditional, demanding, exhilarating, the very essence of the game.

The course has been used for final qualifying for the Open since 1926 and a further measure of its quality is the number of national events it has hosted, the English Amateur, the British Ladies' and the World Seniors' Championship among them. Plainly, this is one not to be missed. It's a class act.

Those sentiments also apply to Fairhaven, although it differs in style and character. It might be described as seaside parkland with stands of trees and flowering bushes giving perspective to a site that, in keeping with the region, is flatter than your average kitchen floor.

It was laid out in 1922 by a local architect with some in-put from James Braid, whose distinctive bunkering is readily recognisable, particularly the fore-shortening cross bunkers that became popular in that era.

The renowned greens are of modest size and generally flat so plainly the priority is putting the tee shot into the required position for the approach. The fairways are generous but miss one of them and, more often than not, you can forget about par.

Hit the greens in regulation, though, and if you can putt at all you'll be in seventh heaven, as Justin Leonard discovered in final qualifying for the 1996 Open. Justin, a sublime putter, shot a course record 64 and was granted honorary membership in consequence.

The par of 74 owes much to five par 5s, four of them on the back nine including a closing run of 5-5-3-5. The better player in full fig will reach most of them in two but normal mortals with anything like a short game will have a grand day if they keep their wits about them and temper ambition. Fairhaven is one of the unsung gems of English golf and not to be missed.

There's little we can tell readers about Royal Lytham that they haven't seen for themselves, in person or via television. Access has been somewhat restricted in recent years but a new policy has opened the door rather wider.

Mondays and Thursdays are assigned to corporate groups but some tee times have become available through the week, and even on Saturday afternoon and Sunday. In keeping with demand, the costs are not cheap (see the information panel elsewhere) but playing this great links is an imperative when visiting the town. Make up a four ball for 36 holes and have lunch in the grand old clubhouse. It will be the highlight of your golfing year.

UPON REFLECTION, A MISCELLANY

Memo to the critics of Augusta National: get lost!....

The over-blown row about the all-male Augusta National Golf Club generated almost as much editorial mileage as the Masters' Championship staged there. Candidly, it gave me a pain where I should have pleasure: political correctness always has that effect on me. I tend to switch off when misguided campaigners use major events to ride a fashionable hobby horse but in this instance, because golf is involved, a response is appropriate.

Doubtless I'll be contravening some newly-designated law or other and will probably find myself prosecuted or ostracised but, having been thrown into jail for journalistic activity, I'm impervious to crooked cops, insults and threatening letters....

So here goes. My message to the do-gooders is simple: don't try to tell the Augusta National members how to run their club: it has nothing to do with you so mind your own bloody business! There. That feels better already.

The essence of this is quite simple, really. The club in question is a private members' club, indeed membership is by invitation only. How the members run it is their concern. It has nothing to do with outsiders who are permitted onto the premises once a year to cover an event for which the course and the club were founded back in 1934. We should be grateful they stage the Masters, not critical of them for no good reason.

Over my 57 years in the golf writing business I've been a member of ten golf clubs around the world, from Bermuda to Britain to Australia, so I believe I speak with authority on the subject.

Here's the crux: With each acceptance I promised to abide by and honour the constitution of the club. Implicit in this, was that I wouldn't campaign to change the club's rules on a whim, or even with good intent. That was the deal and I lived by it. Still do.

Such rules were written for good reasons, mainly involving tradition and sound management. In many cases the rules have achieved their aims for upwards of a century. Fiddle with them and you'll have no complaint if you're requested to resign. That's the way things work.

So if individual members are bound by such rules by what right do outsiders perceive they can rip up a club's constitution on a politically correct whim? In essence, their ramblings on the subject were so much editorial bull dust.

This point was endorsed for me by one self-righteous, non-golfing commentator, for *The Times* of all journals, who referred to the championship as "hitting a ball the size of a champagne cork around a field." Which says everything about his knowledge of a game that dates to the early 15th century, to say nothing of recent golfing history and the beginnings of Augusta National. With luck this character won't be invited again next year. Doubtless he will be pontificating at length if this proves to be the case... Poetic, what?

I would love to become a member of Augusta National but my chances are comparable to a snowball in hell. That said, I would have no wish to campaign editorially or harangue the club president in public to achieve my goal. To do so would be both ungentlemanly and insulting.

I recall an Open Championship at Royal Birkdale some years ago when a female reporter, pursuing that unending campaign for "equality", complained bitterly because, unlike her male colleagues, she wasn't allowed into the players' locker room to conduct interviews. One leading player, holding his daily post-round conference in the media centre, said he'd be comfortable with that if the lady didn't mind seeing him in the buff as he walked out of the shower....

The potential problems in such a scenario were obvious. Good sense prevailed then. It should in this case. Leave well alone. It's a storm in a T cup that should be ignored. There are more important campaigns waiting to be activated out there....

It's the ball, stupid! Reflections by Pete Dye

At 78 years of age Pete Dye has been around the block a few times. As an amateur he once played 72 holes in the US Open, out-scoring Arnold Palmer in the process, so he knows a thing or two about our game.

As an internationally acclaimed course architect he has been plying his trade since the 1950s, has seven designs listed in the leading 20 US courses and 14 in the top 100, plus a couple at Casa da Campo in the Caribbean that most knowing folk reckon are among the finest in world golf

He's not reticent about voicing an opinion so when he cuts loose on the subject of the current state of golf a scribe could learn a lot in a hurry by sharing a golf cart with him over 18 holes. That's personal experience speaking.

On the grounds of propriety I'd better modify his response to my question concerning the effect of golf ball technology on course architecture. Let me interpret his answer to read that while the game is not about to go to hell in a handcart if the Devil came along he could probably load it up without much opposition from the governing bodies.

"Their response to the problem has been disgraceful. They should have taken action years ago but they buried their heads in the sand. Now the problem has been compounded to the point where they have to trick up courses to contain it."

He was referring, you'll gather, to the inordinate length of shot that has become the norm in professional tournament golf, where the longer hitters can reduce the most demanding par four to a drive and a flick and there's virtually no such thing as a par five. Hence, many great courses have become redundant as championship venues unless their set-up borders on the penal.

Mind you, the USGA and the R&A are not his only targets. The golf manufacturing industry is equally culpable, he says.

"The average golfer with a standard swing speed gains little or nothing from this constant development of the golf ball. Take the lady golfer who hits the ball 130 yards off the tee. She gets no benefit at all because her swing speed is too slow."

What's more Dye says he can prove it, or rather Beth Daniel can prove it for him. This former US Champion and leading LPGA Tour money winner has tested every new ball on the market. The result: "She finds that by using the latest ball she gains four yards with her tee shots: four yards! That's only because she swings at 100 mph, far faster than the average lady golfer and most male amateurs, too."

Meanwhile, says Pete, the Tour pros have forgotten what it's like to hit a four iron approach to a par four. "There's no such shot for them these days. It's quite ridiculous."

Most golf course architects would have a personal view on the subject but Dye takes it a stage further: he has a solution, one that has long been available to the governing bodies, hence his chagrin at their inactivity. It is this.

"Some years ago, back in the 1970s I think it was, a far-sighted US Baseball Commissioner saw the potential problems with the emerging technology in sports goods manufacture. He could see that if the major league ball players were allowed to use hot bats (of man-made substances) there wouldn't be a stadium big enough to contain them. The consequences were obvious to him.

"So he used his political connections in the US Senate to have the law modified as it related to commercial responsibility and activity in this area. There was opposition, predictably, but he made his point. The law was modified. Then, with the protection of the law, he decreed that all major league baseball would be played with equipment comparable to that used in a mutually selected year, circa 1950.

"That decree holds good today. The big hitters are still setting records in home runs but they're keeping the ball in the park. The traditions and history of the game have been saved and nothing but good came of it all."

So why, Dye asks, can't the governing bodies of golf take similar action? "Why can't they rule that all Tour players use balls of say, circa 1980? They could fulfil their contractual obligations to the manufacturers, who in turn could reduce their investment in development and the ball market sales would be just as buoyant, probably more so because golf balls should be less expensive."

It's difficult to refute such an argument, or deny the effect it would have on golf courses, their construction and maintenance costs. This is another subject that gives Dye heartburn.

We were playing the New Course at the San Roque club in Sotogrande, a course designed by his son Perry, and Pete had just putted out for par on another immaculate green. I commented on the quality of the putting surface and wondered aloud about the grass Perry had used.

It's Bermuda Tifeagle, I gathered, a new strain and ideal for the climate in Southern Spain. It thrives in the heat, has a smooth matt and a nap that is just strong enough to demand attention. It also gives a true, medium-paced roll that can be a tad sharp down-grain.

"A good choice," said Pete. "I think the new nap-less grass strains produce crazy speeds. In the 1950s the greens on Tour, even for the Majors, would be running at what would now be about six on the stimp meter. These days 12 is considered normal. On certain courses with the modern ball this diminishes the tournament, turns it into a putting contest. It's another aspect of tricking up courses to combat technology.

"Then there's the cost factor. I estimate that such grass adds in excess of $100,000 to a club's annual course maintenance costs because the greens have to be verti-cut and groomed on a regular basis or they develop problems."

Like most forthright men Pete Dye has the courage of his convictions, a trait common among those who are innovators. And some of his innovations have become the norm in golf.

Consensus says it was Dye who introduced multiple tee placements at different angles, to give an easier or more difficult line of shot according to handicap. Instead of simply adding forward tees he varied his strategy in placement, angling the teeing grounds so that fairway hazards would be less severe for the higher handicapper. In effect he created several courses in one. Certain US resorts now produce scorecards for each course or set of tees and request that visitors play from the one dictated by their handicap. It creates a more enjoyable experience and also helps speed up play.

Dye also introduced island greens, now a penny a dozen, and also the use of railway sleepers as bulkheads in bunkers. He cracks a joke about this.

In 1963 he was touring Scotland with Alice, his wife who is also a golf architect, and gaining inspiration from the classical links they played.

"I first saw railway sleepers at Old Prestwick and liked the idea. I thought, if it was good enough for Queen Victoria it was good enough for me! So I introduced sleeper bulkheads at my next suitable design opportunity.

"Pretty soon there were lots of imitations and now whenever anyone sees a sleeper bulkhead they say it's a Pete Dye course. There are dozens of them, but do you want to know something? I only ever did three!"

His work has been described as uninhibited and wildly creative in its use of mounding, humps and hollows and steep-faced bunkers. He frequently integrates classical links qualities into a variety of settings and was one of the first architects to balance a course, with an equal number of holes bending left and right.

His contribution to golf has been immense but it may be that his greatest is yet to come. If his solution is acted upon he will have solved arguably the biggest problem ever to face the Royal and Ancient game.

How to write up a storm, politically speaking....

It's not often that a golf writer provokes a political storm, bringing red faces and pointed questions in high places, but I managed it on one of my trips.

The year was 1997 and I'd gone to the Costa del Sol for *Golf Monthly* to preview the Valderrama course for the up-coming Ryder Cup and, having completed the project, I was pottering around the region to review developments since my previous visit some years before.

That's when I popped into the El Paraiso club to see Chris Christoferson, the golf director at this Gary Player-designed course, and virtually fell into a major story.

After our chat Chris invited me to play the course and arranged for me to join a trio of visiting players from England's West Country. It proved a pleasurable experience: good company on a sound, well-maintained course and, thanks to an efficient marshalling system, we completed the round in a tad over four hours, which was pretty good for a four ball in a holiday situation on an unfamiliar course.

"Just shows what can be done when folk know what they're doing," said one of my playing partners. "This was our fourth round this week and it's the first time we've managed to finish. Yesterday we walked off at the 9th after three hours and until today we hadn't reached the 15th on any course."

At three different courses in three days, it transpired, there had been no sign of course marshals and slow play had backed up to the first tee, bringing long delays to pre-booked tee times. The cause: slow players who were obviously beginner golfers with no experience and little knowledge of etiquette.

For a golfing holiday destination it was the poisoned chalice, once the word reached the UK clubs whose members were the major market audience for the region. A little research seemed apposite: my chum's assessment proved correct. I visited several clubs along the coast and discovered long queues on the first tee of each. Visiting Brits I found echoed the complaints of my chums: there were some very unhappy golfers hanging around the club bars.

So I wrote the story (see page 56) warning our readers to book the earliest possible tee time or be prepared for a frustrating time on-course.

I thought that would be the end of it but the repercussions quickly followed when the magazine hit the shelves. Fearful of visitor response and its effect upon the economy, the powers that be in government called a conference of resort owners to rattle their cages and solve the problem. I wasn't a popular amigo in Espana....

One resort owner even wrote to my editor and accused me of fabricating the facts! He was given short shrift. Whether the problem was resolved is open to question. I didn't return to the region for some years.

A few weeks later I was in Tenerife and witnessed the antithesis: course marshals at the Golf del Sur club were not only in evidence; they were repairing pitch marks on the greens as they patrolled the course.

Conclusion: golf resorts should employ staff who understand the game and, better still, play it. Simple.

There's trouble brewing on the Costa del Golf

If you're a first timer planning a golfing holiday on the Costa del Sol, be warned: don't do it yourself; use an established golf tour operator and request early morning tee times, as close to dawn as possible.

If you're lucky, and with an early start, you could be first off and navigate the course in reasonable time. The alternative is likely to be rounds well in excess of five hours or, if you're an independent traveller, the reverse, no golf at all.

The fact is that the Costa del Golf, as they like to call it, is enjoying a boom that makes a Wembley cup final crowd look like a family gathering. At most clubs I visited recently car parks were over-flowing, tee times were like gold dust in the streets and the courses were populated by Northern Europeans who regard 18 holes as a day's excursion and whose interpretation of course etiquette is, like their knowledge of the Rules of Golf, at best fleeting.

I heard of one British foursome who walked off in frustration after nine holes; another group had called it a day after 14 holes had taken five hours. I heard of a German who, offered a 2 pm tee time, complained that his group couldn't possibly finish in the time available.

Told that the light would be playable until at least 7.30 pm, he replied: "We need minimum six hours for 18 holes." They were directed elsewhere....

Their number is legion and, what's worse, growing apace. According to a report in a local golf newspaper two German tour operators, new to the region, will be bringing an additional 20,000 players between October and April.

It was a source of rejoicing for the local authorities and golf associated operators. But with courses already crowded to the point of claustrophobia in all but high summer I would suggest that it should instead have been a cause for concern. (It would be educational for someone in authority to visit Majorca, to see how the Germans now dominate most aspects of daily community life to the point where the locals have finally started to protest.)

"Generally speaking we have to take what's available," said one British golf tour operator. "It's the same at all of the good quality courses and it is reflected in the prices. Candidly, it's a nightmare."

Such news will be anathema to 476,000 Britons who took world-wide golfing holidays last year and spent £480 million in the process. A goodly chunk of this will have dropped into Spanish pockets because Brits are the dominant national grouping among golfing visitors and Spain is their first choice in short haul destinations.

They voted with their feet ten years ago when green fees on the Costa spiralled in a display of greed without comparison in the industry. They went instead to Florida and the Carolinas where good value and quality service are common and course rangers pounce on dawdlers. There were mutterings in the tapas bars recently that it could happen again, that once more there will be hundreds of empty hotel bedrooms, bars and restaurants and idle rental cars.

Consider this: In 1998, 430,000 visiting golfers played 1.3 million rounds over the region's 33 courses and contributed 45,000 million pesetas to the local economy (that's about £185 million, give or take). And such is the boom that owners of the more popular courses report a steady growth, in the order of ten per cent per annum, of rounds played in the shoulder seasons. Saturation is nigh. And this covers only eight months of the year: there is minimal play in the summer season, which operators are now trying to market as a viable alternative.

Consider also that golf tourism in Europe has doubled in the past five years and it will be obvious that additional courses would be the solution. Several are mooted but we've heard that song before and generally speaking they're property-driven, relying for their profit on villas sales.

More, what little suitable land is available is prohibitively expensive to purchase and develop properly — a couple of lay-outs in hill country are best described as scenic — and even if the proposals were to reach fruition it would take the better part of five years for all to come on-stream. By which time supply will lag even further behind demand and the golden goose will have flown.

There's plenty of construction under-way, but of the wrong sort from the golfing view point. The skyline has a permanent backdrop of cranes and the place is virtually a building site once more, recalling the first property boom of two decades ago. There are clusters of villas and apartment blocks rising at every turn, many alongside the beach, and the motorway linking Malaga with Sotogrande and beyond seems to have been under construction for ever — they started at either end and the gap in the middle is now about ten miles.

While the family beach holiday industry makes a vital contribution to the local economy it has a limited season in terms of the mass market. Golf is far more viable, on several counts. Its season is virtually year-round, bringing much full-time employment where once it was only temporary; in fact golf has created 30,000 permanent jobs on the Costa in the past three decades.

More, its per capita ancillary value is such that one golfer is reckoned to equal a family of five in terms of holiday spend and affluence. They require rental cars and fuel; they investigate the local restaurants each evening, and they frequent the clubhouse dining rooms and bars, as well as the pro shops.

The latest campaign is to tempt golfers into summer visits, to prolong the golfing year and to ease the strain on demand caused by the northern winter. So what began circa 1962 as an adjunct to the beach package market, extending the holiday season by a couple of months at either end, has turned full circle.

In fact there is already a summer market; July and August are when Spanish golfers descend on the Costa from Madrid and other major cities. It's not a huge market but it's lucrative; they keep the tills ticking over. And while their numbers are increasing there's plenty of capacity on the courses, although accommodation is usually at a premium because of the family package market.

To combat this, some country clubs have added hotels to their facilities and, in the reverse, certain hotels have acquired land and have golf courses under construction or in the planning stages, the latter to guarantee tee times for guests, the former to attract golfing guests who are offered greatly reduced summer green fees, plus a shared cart.

It's a feasible option in either case, particularly where the course has some elevation and is open to sea breezes. I think immediately of Almenara, Mijas and La Cala as examples. By taking a cart and playing early morning the shade and the breeze created by the movement of the cart would make golf a pleasurable experience in the low golfing season from June to late September.

It's a popular concept in Florida where resorts such as Daytona Beach offer free summer golf to guests of specific hotels, simply to have a cash turn-over at their other facilities.

Getting flights in what is the peak travel season would be the major problem on the Costa, to say nought of the drive from Malaga in bumper to bumper summer traffic and unfamiliar conditions.

An appealing alternative is to fly into Gibraltar and play the four clubs in and around Sotogrande, only 20 minutes away. The courses are of the top echelon, they're generally less busy anyway and would be delightful for summer golf.

A minor hiccup comes in the shape of the bad tempered Spanish border guards who scowlingly delay traffic on a whim as it leaves the Rock. Smile at them: it's a small price to pay for the pleasures in store. The gates are 100 yards from the airport and the trick is to walk through and be collected on the other side. It takes five minutes. (Avis now have a rental car pick-up there, too.)

The region is perfect for short breaks and even longer holidays, although you'll need to book accommodation and tee times well in advance.

But those contemplating a holiday in the main golfing season, from early autumn to spring, had best be on red alert if looking further east, towards or beyond Marbella. It's a jungle out there. Go loaded for bear.

Creating the perfect links: the inside story.

Those golfers aspiring to a deeper knowledge of course architecture should read what will probably become the Golf Book of The Year for 2012. It's a visual and intellectual delight that will open the eyes, lift the spirits and bring a new interpretation to what most players regard as golf course management.

Entitled *"The Perfect Golf Links"* and written by Pat Ruddy, Ireland's foremost golf writer and course architect, it provides a technical insight into his design masterpiece that is the links of The European Club at Brittas Bay, near Dublin.

This is a unique book that will become a collector's item: large-format, hard-cover and brimming with sumptuous full-page photography complemented by Ruddy's equally enticing writing. Its 144 pages cover a discursive journey, from the first tee to the 18th green, during which the author muses on golf course architecture generally while explaining some of the design concepts he has installed at The European and revealing a few of the secrets to playing this majestic links.

Not the least of the disclosures is that Ruddy has rejected an offer of 40 million Euros for the links he self-financed and built from scratch after discovering the site 25 years ago! It's his legacy, he says, to leave for his family who maintain the links and run the club. Aside from which, he hasn't finished it yet! He's still tinkering with the design that most knowledgeable golfers would regard as perfect....

Of the project beginnings and his philosophy, Ruddy muses: "I didn't want to borrow much and I didn't want to take partners. So I decided to proceed in the old fashioned way, of growing things and improving things over a period of years. The acorn to oak tree principle, if you will, spreading the investment and allowing income to help with onward improvements."

So how good is it? Suffice to say that five years after completion it was ranked among Ireland's top ten courses (it's now number four) and among the top 100 courses of the world in the rankings of Golf (USA) magazine. More, in Golf magazine's 500 Greatest Golf Holes Pat Ruddy's creation has three entries, one of them, the par four 7th, being voted one of the world's 100 best holes.

Which prompted this gem: "If people thought we were that good we had better do our best to honour their beliefs. The pursuit of excellence continues...." Hence his tinkering, his search for perfection...

A consummate gentleman and a golf architect extraordinary, Pat Ruddy is also a great Irishman. The preface to his book includes the line: "Come with me for a stroll around my links and a wee chat."

You should take up his offer, pronto. You won't believe what you'll see or hear, and your golfing dreams will be realised....

*   You may order a copy of The Perfect Golf Links via Mastercard or Visa by fax to 353-404-47449; or by telephone on 353-404-47415. The cost is 30 Euros per copy plus 7.50 Euros p&p.

A suitable case for uni-lateral disarmament?

This may put me OOB with some sporting goods folk I'm acquainted with but I often wonder whether all this fancy hardware we buy is absolutely necessary. Most of us wander onto a golf course packing more artillery that an SAS hit squad but how often do we use all the weapons we have at our disposal?

Think of it this way: there are certain clubs the average golfer couldn't use in a fit but he carries them around because they are part of the set. They come under the classification of excess baggage and have little but nuisance value, particularly when he's tempted to use one of them to hit a career shot.

The thought struck me recently when playing with a delightful character whose equipment consisted of a derelict three wood, five rusty irons and a putter that may have seen action when Old Tom was strutting his stuff. He carried the lot in an old canvas bag that sagged in the middle and probably weighed in about ten pounds complete with ironmongery.

Despite this, and the fact that in age he is closer to 70 than 60, he plays to a handicap of eight and can navigate most courses put in front of him in better than 80. His rationale is that because he has so few clubs he has learned to finesse a variety of shots with each to suit the demands of the occasion. There's no doubt he's a better golfer as a result, as he proved against yours truly whose bag weighs in at around the half ton, complete with rain suit and spare balls.

Then there's the chum in Bermuda with a handicap of six who regularly gets around his par 71 course in the mid-70s. That's with a full set of clubs. Given the right inducement (a bottle of something aged in wood for ten years would suffice) and he'll take only his putter and hack it around in maybe 78 or so.

It gets a tad tricky if he finds a bunker but he can knock it 220 yards-plus (I should add that he's a gent of ample proportions) and from 50 yards in his putter becomes a magic wand.

Lee Trevino calls his putter the Texas wedge because, used to playing in high winds common to Texas, he often uses it with telling effect from off the green.

Bob Charles, arguably the finest putter the world has seen, gave me a tip on this subject. He said that for really long putts he used the normal Vardon grip instead of the reverse over-lap that is standard among leading golfers. Seems it imparts a little extra club head speed required for putts beyond, say, fifty feet.

That's versatility for you and I think it illustrates the point I'm making. If it's good enough for world-class professionals it should suit you just fine.

But I've long had a theory about putters. They're more humanoid than mere golf clubs with minds and characters of their own. How else to describe their foibles and downright unpredictability? Some of the things they do simply defy logic. They cannot be inert, soul-less masses of steel or brass or whatever.

I know folk who have names for theirs. They talk to them and swear that often reply, usually sardonically. There's one fellow who swears he heard his putter scream! It happened during a nightmare of putting horrors which saw him three putt the first four greens and four putt the fifth.

Without further ado our tormented friend wrapped the offending stick around the nearest tree. He had second thoughts about leaving it there when he heard the scream and after unwinding it as best he could he set about straightening the shaft. He managed to remove most of the kinks but the last one defied all coaxing, so he left it as it was...The odd thing is that since then he's putted like Ben Crenshaw: anything under 20 feet is conceded, unless it's a medal event.

"I reckon Mabel learned her lesson," he said (he named her after his mother-in-law who had a similarly perverse personality) "and she behaves much better with a bend in the middle..."

Needless to say, he wouldn't part with her now: he's had several new sets of clubs over the years but he and Mabel have lived happily ever after

Another character I know was so tormented by his putter that he would leave it in his locker and putt with his one iron. He said he'd tried talking to it without response but this was understandable: he had a broad Scots accent that only his dear mother could love and understand and when we checked out his putter we discovered it was an American model. So he did a crash course in that language and since then his relationship with the putter has become a thing of beauty, much discussed at the 19th.

In fact she's a sister to Betty, the love of my life, an old centre-shafted implement with a brass head that I've used for twenty years or more. They look so alike that we suspect they're twins, although the strange thing is he doesn't get on with Betty and in my hands Mabel feels like a broomstick.

I'm getting new clubs soon (with a swing like mine you'll try anything once) but Betty will stay. She's seen four new sets come and go and we've been together too long to part now.

Apart from which I hate to hear a grown putter cry...

PEOPLE IN GOLF

The Urchin Caddies Who Reached For The Stars...

It was more money than Teddy Halsall had dreamed of in his 14 years and his hands trembled as he clutched it and ran, fearful of being robbed, from the Royal Birkdale links to his home on a council estate a mile away.

"It was £50 and when I put it on the kitchen table my mum couldn't believe I'd earned it just for carrying a golf bag. I thought I was about to get a thick ear and be marched to the police station.

"When I convinced her that it was my caddies' pay her eyes misted over and she gave me a big hug. It was very important money for those times, particularly for a family of ten, with jobs hard to find and the average man's wage about £5 a week."

The year was 1954 and Ted's reward was the climax of a week that had started unremarkably. It had brought the first Open Championship to be staged at Royal Birkdale, where local men and boys had long supplemented family incomes by humping members' golf bags around the course each weekend. Ted, already a seasoned caddie with a voluminous knowledge of the links, had been awarded a professional's bag in the great event.

"He was an unfancied Frenchman, but he not only made the 36 hole cut he finished 25th and won a sizeable cheque. Even so, I couldn't believe it when he gave me £50. It was a fortune in those days, really serious money."

The incident was the bridge that transported Ted from that Southport council estate to the world's most exclusive golf clubs and five star hotels, on first name terms with famous players and witness to historic events in major tournaments. He still pinches himself when he recalls how it all began.

From the Royal Birkdale Golf Club to Suffolk Road is about a mile as the sea gull flies. In reality they are worlds apart. One is the playground of the wealthy in the Lancashire resort town of Southport; the other is on a council estate, literally and metaphorically on the wrong side of the tracks.

It's an unbridgeable chasm, ostensibly, and yet a quartet of youngsters once vaulted it with improbable results. From being boy caddies on the venerable links, venue for this week's 127th Open Championship, they became the first of the new breed of professional caddies and over the years found modest fame and security undreamed of by their neighbours.

Sadly, sickness and death have left Ted Halsall as the only active survivor in golf. No longer a caddie, Ted is a businessman of some substance with his own transport company. He happily admits that he owes everything to golf and the opportunities it brought as on-course mentor to Johnny Miller, the former US Open champion whom Ted helped win the 1976 Open Championship, fittingly at Royal Birkdale.

Teddy was six years old when he first caddied there, earning five shillings a round for carrying a bag bigger than himself. Frequently, too, it was heavier but by the age of 12 he was happy to walk five rounds – close to 30 miles — each weekend, gathering the expertise that was to change his life.

There were 100 men and 50 boys competing for the work. Among them were Jackie Lee, Ted's young chum; Alfie Fyles, older by ten years, and Albert, Alf's sibling. They all lived on Suffolk Road, a little cluster of twenty or so houses in the back streets of Birkdale.

Like contemporary life, the street was tough but respectable and not over-endowed with privilege. Inseparable by circumstance and calling, the boys' careers in golf were to run parallel for the next four decades. They couldn't have guessed what lay ahead.

The immediate post war years had brought a flurry of major events to the club and the Suffolk Road lads were in the thick of things: the Brabham Trophy, the Walker Cup, the English Amateur, the PGA Championship, the Ryder Cup, the Open Championship, all brought opportunities, and vital income, for aspiring caddies.

Alfie, the senior, set the pace with an unsurpassed record from the 1950s to the 80s. He carried for the winner at six Open Championships, five World Match Play Championships, two Alcan World Championships and a host of other major events, initially with Gary Player, later with Tom Watson. And this mainly in the days before yardage charts, when a caddie clubbed his man using personal judgement of distance and how the shot would be affected by the wind and conditions. Eye balling, Alfie called it.

Jackie, too, achieved great things, first with five times Open champion Peter Thomson, later with Greg Norman. Cumulatively, the group would notch up 11 Open Championships, three of them at Royal Birkdale. Their other victories are countless.

Albert's big moment came with Tom Weiskopf in 1973 at Royal Troon where Johnny Miller was runner-up with Ted at his side. This was fortunate for Albert: a leg injury had threatened to leave him sidelined for the final round, missing his moment of glory — and a handsome cheque. But Ted stepped in and wherever possible he carried the two bags. "Albert would have done the same for me," he said simply.

The Miller-Halsall pairing was a consequence of the 1969 Ryder Cup at Royal Birkdale when Ted had caddied for Brian Barnes in his match against Billy Casper.

An impressed Casper asked Ted if he'd like to work with a rising young protégé due to make his Open début the following year. Ted agreed. It was the birth of an alliance that endured for 17 years and matured into friendship which continues, even though both have now retired from tournament golf.

"John was a marvellous player, the best in the world for some time" Ted recalls. "He could have won the Open twice before he finally did it in 1976."

Coming as it did at Birkdale, it was almost worth the wait. Miller shot a final round 66 to win by six from Jack Nicklaus and Seve Ballesteros. "The finest round of golf I've ever seen," said Ted.

The previous year at Carnoustie Miller had ignored Ted's advice on the final tee and paid the penalty.

"I wanted him to hit the three wood, to lay-up short of the bunkers, but he took the driver and found sand. It was a costly mistake. After Carnoustie he said: 'This is your course. Just give me the club you think and tell me what to do.' It worked like a charm."

Birkdale is a cerebral links that favours the greatest players, as the roll call of Open champions proves. But as Peter Thomson, Tom Watson and Johnny Miller will concede, a local caddie is invaluable. And if he comes from Suffolk Road that's all the better...

*   Sadly, Ted has passed away too. He died in Southport on 15 December 2005.

Pat Ruddy, architect of a legend

Spot a Dublin taxi in a golf club car park 40 miles south of the city, its driver dozing as he waits for his passengers to complete 18 holes on a wind-swept links, and you'll be safe in betting that his fares are tourists who flew in that morning and couldn't wait to get at it.

Such a sight is common at The European Club, Ireland's major new links where the visitors include Australians, Canadians and the ubiquitous Japanese. Even in a land where tall tales are ten a penny they're part of a remarkable story.

Only a year after its opening in May 1993 it was ranked seventh of Ireland's top 30 courses. Now, two years on, it is maturing with the predictability of a vintage champagne, a legend in the making.

Remarkably, The European is the realisation of one man's dream, nurtured since his youth, of owning and designing a world-class links. It's a classical example of a lifetime of preparation bringing over-night success!

Pat Ruddy is the two handicap visionary, a golf writer turned architect, who discovered the 200 acres on the shores of Brittas Bay. He raised an initial Euros 1.5 million and then spent six years moulding the wild duneland into a links that's guaranteed to make the heart sing, one that perpetuates many of the old-fashioned values, encompassing simplicity and an observance of the natural order of things, albeit with a modern flair.

Thus, blind shots are anathema: the green is visible from 14 tees and the landing area is in view from the others. But all is not what it appears. Illusion is rampant, deception the norm, uncertainty the consequence. This is white knuckle country, even on a still day.

From some tees, for instance, a protruding sand hill will hide one half of the fairway; on the other side a lone tree or a bunker will catch the eye and squeeze the target area still further. There's precious little to aim at, it seems, and yet many of the fairways are up to 80 yards wide.

Most meander between soaring dunes, converting them visually into narrow corridors and exaggerating their length, a ploy compounded by placing the green side-on to reduce the visible target area. Imagine looking through the wrong end of a telescope and you'll get the picture.

The greens, invariably slightly elevated, may be angled a touch and tilted slightly, with a guarding hummock or a distracting bunker cutting into a narrow entrance. So what in reality is a mid-iron approach to a large green appears a three wood to a small one. Such examples are legion. Duplicity, the good architect's stock- in- trade, is part of the equation on every hole.

"It's all about imagery and the fear factor," says Ruddy. "I've placed one bunker 170 yards from the tee with rising ground beyond. It narrows the perspective, although there's plenty of space behind. Someone complained, until I proved it could be cleared with a 7-iron."

The European has a dozen holes that will stay in the memory: 18 of them — make that 36 for the true believers — would be a matchless golfing adventure. And the scenery will stop your back-swing!

Carlos Franco: living the dream

It would stretch credulity to the limits but there's a novel waiting to be written on the golfing life of Carlos Franco. Hollywood, that home of dreams and fantasies, would probably snap up the story line.

Just imagine how they would treat a tale about a boy born to impoverished parents in a mud hut in far-away Paraguay, who learns to play golf with a club carved from a tree branch but who eventually turns pro, though he's never had a lesson, and within a few years is beating the best in the world, becoming a millionaire in the process.

I ask you, outside of Hollywood who would swallow such a load of old tosh?

It's no fairy tale, though; it's all true. It's a story that began 30 years ago: Carlos, then three years old, shared a one-roomed mud hut with his parents, five older brothers and a sister on the edge of the Ascuncion Golf Club. They had a rudimentary outside toilet, their water came from a well. With twice as much they would still have been destitute.

Father scratched a living as greenkeeper and caddie; the boys followed suit, earning a dollar here and there to help feed the family. Carlos tagged along, learning the trade, playing when he could with a hand carved club and an old ball.

He had his first set of proper clubs when he was 15, the gift of a member grateful for his expertise as a caddie. Within a year he was playing off scratch. Two years later he was caddie master; at 20 he followed his brothers and turned professional, all without benefit of a single lesson. Plainly, he was a natural and touched by the golfing gods. Little did he know they had set him on a pathway to the stars.

It was, though, an incongruous launch pad. There are only four golf clubs in Paraguay and so few professionals that there are no tournaments to speak of. But Carlos had dreams to sustain his burning ambition and they started to come true in 1993.

The scene: the Old Course at St Andrews, the home of golf. Carlos and brother Angel had been invited to play for Paraguay in the Alfred Dunhill Cup, the international teams' event. Drawn against Scotland, Carlos beat Sam Torrance, ranked in Europe's top 10, as Paraguay caused the major upset of the tournament in winning 2-1. The fuse had been lit.

His win over Torrance brought Carlos an invitation to play on the Asian Tour. He promptly won the Philippines Open and went on to collect the Order of Merit. He was the top man in Asian golf. That brought an exemption to the Japanese Tour and he took to it like a duck to water.

In five years he won five times and had 39 top ten finishes. In other words, like many other now famous players, he had paid his dues. He was ready for the big time, the USPGA Tour.

Flash forward to 1999. In only his fourth US Tour event he finished 15th. Two weeks later he was third; three weeks after that he was sixth in the US Masters.

It gets better. Returning from Paraguay, it took Carlos three flights and 14 hours to reach New Orleans. Despite this he shot 66-69-68-68 to win the Compaq Classic by two and take a cheque for $468,000.

It didn't end there. Eight weeks later he won the Greater Milwaukee Open by two shots from Tom Lehman, the US Ryder Cup player and former Open Champion. His reward: a cheque for $414,000. In the process he became only the fourth US Tour player to win more than once in the season: the others were Tiger Woods, David Duval and Payne Stewart. All are ranked in the top five. Carlos Franco had signalled his arrival; Paraguay was finally on the golfing map.

By season's end Carlos, now 33 years old, was ranked 18th in the world with official winnings of $1.6 million. He's also hot favourite to be voted Rookie of the Year, an award which usually goes to newcomers ten years younger.

No other winner of the award has been totally self-taught and it's a gold plated bet that none of them was born in a mud hut. Some rookie. Some year.

Just imagine making a film about that. Whoever would believe it?

Bobby Jones: an extraordinary human being

There will never be another sportsman quite like Bobby Jones. Let's amend that: there won't be one remotely like Bobby Jones. The epitome of the true blue amateur; modest, gracious and totally unassuming, he garnered more honours and admiration in his all-too-brief career than any athlete, male or female, before or since.

He was loved by all who knew him, revered by those who saw his peerless, graceful swing and idolised the world over, long before the age of television, that ultimate marketing machine to which many modern stars owe so much.

As an amateur he dominated what became known as The Golden Age of Golf, winning thirteen major events in seven years against the world's leading professional players. Many still consider him the greatest golfer who ever lived. With nothing left to prove, he retired at 28 to return to his Atlanta law practise. Bernard Darwin, the doyen of British golf writers, recorded that "he left trailing clouds of glory."

His record will never be equalled, simply because it would be impossible for a modern amateur to emulate the man whose career created the phrase The Grand Slam. In one unforgettable year, 1930, he won the Amateur and the Open Championships of both the United States and Britain, setting standards that transcended anything seen before or since.

Born in 1902, Robert Tyre Jones won the junior championship at his club, East Lake, Atlanta, at the age of nine and the club championship at 14. That year, too, he won the Georgia State Amateur title and was leading qualifier for the US Amateur Championship, an event he was to win five times between 1924 and 1930. In 1923, at 21, he became US Open champion and between 1922 and 1930 he only once finished out of first or second place, winning it four times, losing two play-offs and coming second in another.

He seldom went to Britain outside of the years of the Walker Cup, the bi-annual teams event between the amateurs of Britain and America, but he won the Open Championship in 1926, 1927 and 1930, when he also took the British Amateur Championship en route to the Grand Slam. Those are bare statistics that only hint at an exemplary sporting career and a life of almost magnetic achievement.

Because in between all of this Bobby gained first class honours degrees in Law, English Literature and Engineering at three different universities! He was truly a one-off, a role model without equal.

When he retired from playing he realised a dream of building the ultimate golf course. With his great friend Clifford Roberts and aided by Alister

Mackenzie, the renowned British golf architect, Bobby converted an old fruit farm into the rolling acres we now know as Augusta National Golf Club.

Just for fun, he invited a few friends down in April 1934 for an invitational tournament. The friends just happened to be some of the world's greatest golfers and the event became The Masters in 1938. Since then it has been regarded as one of the four major championships that now comprise The Grand Slam.

After a crippling illness that confined him to a wheelchair for much of his later life, Bobby Jones died in 1971. But the course and the tournament he created will forever be a living memorial to a career and a life of which lesser mortals can only dream ....

Billy Hume: still larger than life

We were pondering the identity of the oldest golfer to better his age when we ran across Billy Hume. End of quest.

"When did you last beat your age, Billy?" I asked the 81 year old former Irish international.

"Twice last week," was the prompt response. "Shot 75 two days running at Warren Point."

Seems he does it most weeks: he's had a bad round if he doesn't!

Indeed, Billy was a bit miffed recently when his handicap was increased to eight. He was a category one player for 57 years and two years ago he birdied all five par threes at Warren Point en route to a gross 69, two under par and ten shots better than his age. Which must be a hat-trick of world records.

Still 6ft 2 ins tall and 17 stone, Billy has long been an outstanding character on the Irish golfing scene, which is never short of characters.

Also a member of Royal County Down, he was a scratch player at 15 and played 28 matches for Ireland alongside Tom Craddock and J.B.Carr. He won national and major regional events and once reached the final of the Irish Amateur.

There's more! In 1939 he beat Willie Nolan in the final of the Warren Point President's Cup and 40 years later he beat Frank Nolan, Willie's son, for the same trophy!

To complete his golfing CV, Billy has had 19 aces! "Should have had 20 but one stopped on the lip a couple of weeks ago," he said, somewhat crossly.

Irrepressible Leslie is still on-course!

Golf writers report the news, they don't make it. But one of our number will be a focus of attention when the 100th Amateur Championship is staged at Royal Liverpool next month. Join me in a salute.

For Leslie Edwards, now 88 and one of only two surviving founder members of the Association of Golf Writers, the championship will stir a lifetime of memories, of playing and reporting.

Leslie covered his first Open at Hoylake when Walter Hagen won in 1924 and until 1972 only war service kept him from his appointed rounds at the major British championships.

The 1927 Amateur Championship at Hoylake was his first at what was to be his home club — he began as a member of neighbouring Wallasey — and in time he was to make news as a player. A member of Royal Liverpool for almost four decades and a scratch man for many years, Leslie regularly played in both the English and the Amateur from 1933, reaching the fourth round of both in the 1950s.

He's been beating his age since he was 71 and shot a gross 78 at 83, when he played off nine. That year, 1987, he won the club's Spring meeting in a gale force wind, carding 82-9-73 when the scratch prize was won with an 85!

Leslie frequently wins his age section at the Seniors' Championship — he was 72 when he shot a 70 at Formby and won his division by five strokes at Prestwick at the age of 75.

Club colleagues say he's still a fierce competitor and though now off 15 he still has the occasional purple patch in his thrice-weekly round at his beloved Hoylake where he first saw the great Bobby Jones.

His memories would fill a book, in fact they have. It's entitled *The Game That Was Golf*. It's required reading for any student of the game, an account of a life-long romance with golf and of the great players Leslie has known over the decades.

Still an active writer, Leslie has penned a ruminative chapter for the commemorative book being produced by the club to mark the 100th playing of the championship it founded in 1885.

He'll be on-course again next month watching the world's finest amateurs grace the Hoylake fairways, compiling more memories, re-living old ones....

Battling Bill beats the odds

Raise your caps to Bill Kirkland, the first nomination for our Club Golfer of the Year competition. His story is an inspiration to the incapacitated, indeed anyone who plays golf.

Bill was a nine handicap member of Effingham GC, Surrey, when in 1991, at the age of 52, he suffered a stroke that left him speechless and paralysed. Hospitalised for almost a year, and for six months was unable to move or talk. Recovery was slow and painful but eventually he was able to go home, into the care of his wife, Jennie.

Little by little his mobility and speech returned, although for months he could only slur his wife's name. A walking frame and unwavering courage extended his mobility from two steps to 10 to 20....

Then, a year later and with a view to further rehabilitation, Jennie booked him a series of golf lessons with club pro Stephen Hoatson as a 54th birthday present.

"Bill had no feeling in his left arm," Stephen said, "and he couldn't walk far but he wanted to play a bit of golf. We got him going again, swinging right handed. I had to create a bit of width in his back-swing. His courage did the rest."

The club presented him with a single seater caddy car and soon he was back on the course, playing two holes with one club, then four, then six... Eventually he completed nine holes and was re-handicapped at 26.

"I still get very tired," Bill said. "I can hold my putter with two hands but no other club. When I try, my left hand just flies off the grip. But it's smashing to be playing again. I'd been thinking about it for two years but having no feeling in my left arm I didn't think I'd be able. Until Stephen helped me."

Then last summer, by now able to play 18 holes, came two highlights to crown a remarkable fight-back.

Firstly, Bill and his son Geoffrey, a 24 year old 11 handicapper, placed second in the club's Father and Son foursomes tournament.

"I cocked it up," Bill confessed. "I put our tee shot out of bounds on the 18th. We were second by a stroke."

And in August he scored a hole in one at Effingham's 167 yard 4th.

"I usually use a 3-wood at the long holes," he said, "but on this tee I hit the 5-wood. It bounced once and trickled in."

In January, because of a trolley ban, Bill actually played nine holes on foot, a blazing example of one man's will power in the face of seemingly insurmountable odds.

John Sheridan, a club pro *extraordinaire*

The item on Tom Lynch, a club pro for 45 years, 37 of them at Langlands Bay GC, brought a response that will be difficult to better. Tom, 63, may be the longest serving club pro in Wales but not in Britain, as I wrote.

At 75 years of age, John Sheridan is in his 61st year in the pro ranks and with an unbroken spell of 49 as head professional at Denham GC, Bucks!

"He has hinted at retirement," says my correspondent, "but the club doesn't want to let him go"

Young-at-heart John spoke of his "long-suffering wife" but was otherwise non-committal on the subject. We suspect he'll see out his golden anniversary at the club.

A member of the PGA since 1939, John's first day as an assistant was at Swinley Forest GC in 1935. He moved from there to Sunningdale and thence to Denham in 1946.

He doesn't play much these days but enjoyed his moment of fame in a 1952 PGA event when he carded 29 for the opening loop at Moor Park.

"My father, James, was the famous one of the family," he said. "He was known as Sheridan of Sunningdale, where he was the caddie master for 56 years."

John has vivid memories of Sunningdale, where he was brought up. As a schoolboy he saw Bobby Jones play there in his Grand Slam year of 1930, and frequently watched James Braid play.

And later, as a young assistant there, he several times caddied for the great Joyce Wethered, described by Bobby Jones as the world's finest player of the age.

"Those were the days," John said. "Golf's not what it was but I've enjoyed every minute."

Tim Hutton gets his just rewards

It was a routine press announcement but it caught the eye and the response was to fire the imagination. It came in a note from the Golf Foundation bearing the news that Tim Hutton had won the Sir Henry Cotton Award for Meritorious Services to Junior Golf.

When we followed it up Tim won our vote as the Golf Club Professional of the Year. It's a warming story of endeavour and dedication, of a man's love for teaching youngsters and how he found his Field of Dreams.

Tim, now 43, was for 12 years the professional at Sleaford Golf Club, Lincs, and in 1986 he bought a 20 acre field, complete with a barn, at the village of Carlton Scroop, six miles from Grantham. He had retirement in mind and a place to continue teaching youngsters, something he'd enjoyed at Sleaford where the club had a strong youth policy — Walker Cupper Andrew Hare was a pupil.

The grassy field had an interesting shape, albeit somewhat flat, but Tim sought out six amenable spots, mowed them tightly and converted them into greens. Not expecting too much, he then nailed an honesty box to the gate and a notice inviting anyone to play for £1 a go.

The results were astonishing. So much so that he and his wife Judith decided to move there full time, converting the barn into a home and an old pig-sty into a make-shift locker room.

In 1990 a farmer sold them an adjoining 20 acre field and Tim went to town. In short order he'd created a 2,283 yard, par 33, nine hole course, planted 1,000 trees to give definition to the fairways, and built properly constructed greens and tees.

Then he added a small clubhouse, with changing rooms, toilets, catering facilities and dining accommodation for 24 at a push. He named it Sudbrook Moor Golf Club.

Now he has EGU affiliation and 500 members, including a strong junior section and an equally active senior section, which last year took the honours in their inter-club league.

"Like most professionals, I'd always dreamed of owning my own course," Tim said. "It seemed as though this one was just waiting for me to come along. It simply took over our lives."

Note the use of the plural there: Tim says he couldn't have done it without Judith, who runs the clubhouse, and their sons, Ben, 15, and Simon, the joint head green keeper at 16!

"Simon's a whiz with all the machinery," Tim said, "and he has a sound practical knowledge of green keeping. Soon he'll go away to learn the theory. It's his life."

The course is in a valley with a stream running through and two feet below the top soil Tim struck sand that's at least eight feet deep. So water is no problem, nor is drainage: the course is very seldom closed. He and Simon believe in natural conditioning, using the minimum of fertilisers for what has been described as an immaculate course.

"It keeps down costs and our prices," he said. "We want our course to be accessible to anyone."

To that end, consider the fees: Full membership is £65 annually, seniors £55, intermediates £15 and juniors £10. The adults pay £2 each time they play, the juniors £1. That's for a day ticket. The growing number of casual visitors pay £5 for a midweek day ticket, £7 at weekends.

If you're a youngster eager to learn, Tim gives free tuition every Saturday morning for 45 or more youngsters, some of whom didn't miss a morning in that last rain-swept winter!

It's golf tuition at the grass roots by a dedicated man with a vast enthusiasm for the game, one who has for years been deeply committed to the young.

That's why Tim Hudson has won the Sir Henry Cotton Award. And thanks to his remarkable accomplishments and his service to golf he could be our first Club Professional of The Year.

Dorothy is our first lady of golf

The search has ended: we've traced arguably the oldest active golfer in the country. As you read this Dorothy Huntly-Flindt will be celebrating her 98th birthday, probably on the golf course at Barton on Sea, Hampshire.

This remarkable lady, born on 19 June 1898, plays at least three times each week, summer and winter. Over 18 holes, too. In fact the day we spoke she was about to play in the monthly medal.

"I'm the only club member over 90 who still plays 18 holes," she said. "The others have given up. Ridiculous!"

Dorothy first played in her native Edinburgh as a child — she can recall saving up the penny green fee for Braid Hills — and took the game seriously in 1922 when she moved with her late husband to Thurlestone in Devon, where she won her first trophy in 1938.

"I've got the maximum handicap now," she said, "but in those Thurlestone days I played to 12."

The Barton ladies' captain in 1973, Dorothy has another claim to fame: a place in the Guinness Book of Records as the oldest lady golfer ever to hole in one, a feat she performed in 1989 at the age of 90. That was her fourth ace.

Dorothy, still trim at 5ft 4ins, says golf helps keep her fit, plus her ballroom dancing and keep fit classes, of course!

You'll gain an idea of her mental attitude when you learn that she frequently joins the inaugural flights of Virgin Airways to such far-flung destinations as Tokio and Hong Kong. That's thanks to her grandson, Richard Branson, who keeps a loving eye on her.

The daughter of a clergyman, Dorothy served as an Army driver in both world wars and met her husband, a staff officer, when he was a passenger in her car.

"It was a bitterly cold night and when he climbed into the back of the car he commented upon the temperature. I suggested that he sit in the front, with me, where it was warmer."

The temperature obviously rose higher when he switched seats and eventually they married.

He was a keen golfer and together they joined the Thurlestone club when they moved there between the wars. So one love affair led to another and though her husband has gone both romances live on for our young-at-heart First Lady of Golf.

Dorothy is revered at the Barton club and the members are already anticipating her centenary. It will coincide with that of the club. Now that should be a party to remember!

* Sadly, Dorothy didn't see her centenary: she passed away in August 1997.

The McKie brothers: victorious in adversity

Modern golf course development is a killing field for beginners with starry eyes and hard-hearted bank managers. Such people are legion, victims of over-enthusiasm, bad advice or avarice.

It is warming, then, to tell of two non-golfing brothers who have emerged from the mine field not merely unscathed but victorious.

Their names are Stephen and Philip McKie, now the proud owners of Blundell's Hill Golf Club at Rainhill, near St Helens, in Lancashire. It's a region more renowned for rugby league but only two years after the course opened a full membership bears testimony to the demand for good golf at affordable fees. That it's a first rate course with top class facilities helps a bit, needless to say, and the fact that an adjacent motorway provides easy access from several nearby towns.

The brothers became involved almost by accident. Philip lives locally and owned seven acres of woodland and a quarry that's now the site of the elevated, two storey clubhouse. A friend who owned the adjacent 120 acres said he was contemplating building a golf course and the brothers, successful in the engineering business, offered to become partners.

Development was a long, slow process, the original owner withdrew and Stephen and Philip took the project to a conclusion, although, as Stephen said: "If we'd known what we were getting into we may have had second thoughts."

But four years and a considerable investment later the club prospers, the course is maturing, and both brothers have been bitten by the golf bug, in the normal sense of the term.

As beginner players they've got another tiger by the tail: their course is one that demands considerable accuracy, off the tee or to the green and frequently both. Nobody's murdered it yet and as thousands of new trees mature the going will become tougher with each passing year. It's good now, it's going to be a cracker.

It was laid out by Stephen Marnoch of Glossop, an architect of the old school, a minimalist with strong beliefs in the traditional virtues of golf course design. He used the lie of the land to perfection, moving earth only where necessary and then sparingly, shaping fairways around the stands of mature trees that abound, bringing eight ponds into play but resisting the temptation for water carries.

Part of the site was a turf farm when he first saw it, flat as a board but with excellent grasses, mainly fescue. The remainder was gently undulating farmland with only one incline of note.

If your eye is attuned it has a links look about it, one encouraged by the fact that much of it is laid on sand-stone. So it drains well but the brothers didn't leave it at that: a comprehensive drainage system is only a part of the expansive infrastructure that indicates there's been no skimping. They say Tim Harrison, the greenkeeper, is there all hours God sends and the signs of that are everywhere.

Even after a soggy winter the course had a look that belied its lack of years. There's irrigation and no shortage of natural water so after a warm summer they'll be queuing down the motorway.

It's a pretty course with a lovely tempo, a gentle start with everything in view, becoming progressively tougher with lovely par threes and a couple of short straight-away holes to counterpoint demanding dog-legs.

Holes 4, 5 and 6 present a combination the equal of most and a couple of others in the run-in aren't so shabby, either. The par five 18th is close to being a classic.

So the brothers McKie have cracked it, as they say, and it couldn't happen to nicer people. When completion of the clubhouse was four months behind schedule they gave the 500 members sub-free golf until it was opened. Integrity in golf course development? What is the world coming too?

James Braid: requiem to a giant of golf

IF you're a devotee of James Braid with a dream of tasting all the fruits of the great man's architectural talents you'll face a marathon project that should occupy your annual holidays for years to come. You'll spend a pretty penny in travelling expenses, too, and it would help if nomadic tendencies run in the family.

Britain's most prolific designer was responsible for in excess of 160 courses between 1902 and 1950 and was arguably the nation's most influential architect in the 1920s and 1930s.

In those two decades between the wars the five times Open Champion designed six or seven new or reconstructed courses each year and he was still going strong only months before his death in 1950. All this is discounting the minor works on established courses, the extensions and bunkering made necessary by the improvements in equipment.

His annual mileage must have been astronomical in that era. For someone who abhorred travelling he did an awful lot of it! From his home near Walton Heath he covered the country, from Budock Vean in deepest Cornwall to Brora in the Highlands, invariably by rail because he was a constant victim of car sickness. In consequence, he had memorised many of the principal train timetables .

"James had the most prodigious memory," wrote Bernard Darwin in his biography of him, "and a great visual memory for courses, an invaluable gift for a golf course architect. He could play a course he hadn't seen before and afterwards draw plans of each hole, as they were or as he wanted them to be."

He also had that matchless capacity for an architect, "a good eye for country." He could immediately identify the principal attributes of a virgin site and almost instantaneously devise what today is known as the route plan, the direction and playing order of each hole.

This combination of eagle-eyed observation and memory enhanced his reputation for precise drafting, just as the demands of his duties as club professional at Walton Heath contributed to his alacrity and the brevity of his on-site inspection visits. He travelled by rail where ever possible, completing all but the longest return journey within a day and taking the overnight sleeper when he couldn't.

His "land-devouring stride" would cover any site within a couple of hours, in his view ample time to get the lie of the land, select the salient features to be utilised, stake the positions of greens and tees, in relation to the wind and sunrise, and devise the likely order of play.

This done, he would whisk back to the railway station in short order, submitting detailed plans by mail for consideration by the club committee. A year later, weather permitting, the course would be open, an occasion frequently marked by an exhibition match involving Braid and one or other of his great contemporaries, Vardon and Taylor.

All this, of course, was in the age before golf course construction entailed moving thousands of tons of earth. Not that Braid would have contemplated such action, even had the machinery been available. In the modern idiom, he was a minimalist, a course designer of the old school who preferred man-made contouring only on and around the greens.

"He worked hard to make the course fit the ground," said J. Hamilton Stutt, the eminent architect whose father was Braid's long-time confidant, collaborator and course constructor.

"James and my father worked as a team on 60 or so designs between the wars and he would frequently arrive to view a new project to find father waiting at the station with a survey map of the site."

This saved precious time for Braid and allowed him to concentrate on the creative aspect of his inspection visit, the detailed plans that were renowned as models of clarity and precision. Braid's original plans for the Gleneagles courses, for instance, are a mass of numerals indicating the rise and fall of the land, the topographical elevations. They could have been drawn by a surveyor.

So finely tuned was his perception that he designed several courses — most notably one in New York and another in Singapore — purely from survey maps.

"His precision was such that even minor amendments during construction were quite exceptional," said Hamilton Stutt, who as a boy frequently travelled with his father and Braid in the days before joining the family's Paisley-based company as a young man.

Thus did Braid leave construction in the safe hands of John Stutt, seldom visiting a new course again until the project was near completion "to the satisfaction of both the club committee and Mr. Braid," as the contracts stipulated.

The accord between the two men meant that satisfaction was never less than absolute. It was a rare partnership of kindred spirits. Hamilton Stutt recalls them gently chiding a committee rash enough to alter a bunker they'd placed many years earlier!

The young Stutt has fond memories of Braid, "a great big, kindly man who always had a bag of sweets in his pocket to mollify a small boy while travelling."

At 6ft 2 ins in height, Braid resembled a beanpole when at the peak of his playing powers but became somewhat rotund with the passing of the 46 years he spent at his beloved Walton Heath.

Born in 1870 at Earlsferry, near Elie, young Braid was a carpenter in his early years and became a professional golfer against his father's wishes. Unusually for that time and place, Braid senior was not a golfer. For James, no other game could compare. He played to scratch and held the Earlsferry course record at the age of 16. Three years later, with a handicap of plus three, he began winning senior amateur tournaments. The seed of ambition was sown.

He turned professional in 1893 when invited to become club maker to the Army & Navy stores in London. The following year he made his debut in the Open Championship when it went to Sandwich for the first time. He placed 10th. In 1896 at Muirfield he was sixth and the following year at Hoylake he was runner-up to Harold Hilton by a stroke. The age of the Great Triumvirate was about to dawn.

By that year, too, James had become green keeper and professional to the Romford Golf Club in Essex. It was here that he took his first steps into golf course design by up-grading and lengthening the Romford course, a project he completed in two stages between 1896 and 1899. Romford, founded only in 1894, was soon to earn a reputation as "perhaps the best course in Essex , if not in the whole of the Metropolitan area," according to *The Victorian History of the Counties of England.*"

Little is recorded of Braid's early progress in the field but that began to change in 1901 when he won the Open for the first time and, following the trend of the era, came into demand as an architect.

His first known design commission came later that year and it was historic in more senses than one. It involved Royal Blackheath Golf Club and the wife of Mr. Christian Gray, a future club captain. Ladies were not allowed on the course and, eager to play with the other "golfing widows", she persuaded her husband to build a course for them. The dutiful spouse bought the land, called upon Braid for the design and in 1903 it opened as Barnehurst, arguably the world's first ladies' golf club.

A wooded parkland in the grounds of Mayplace Mansion, the course suffered various vicissitudes in consequence of the two world wars but nine of the 18 holes are still there. Braid's signature is evident in some of the bunkering and several holes, played down avenues of stately trees, are obviously original.

The circumstances surrounding that commission generated considerable publicity and, as it coincided with the golf boom encouraged by the arrival of the rubber- cored Haskell ball, it proved to be the first of many. Braid, now a household name, moved to Walton Heath Golf Club in 1904. The stage was set for the next act in a remarkable life.

Braid dominated the Open for the first decade of the new century. He won five championships — all in Scotland — between 1901 and 1910, four of them in six years. Thereafter, beset by eye problems, he faded from the limelight, at least in the Open. Then came 1914 and the first world war. By the time the troops returned home the great man was in his 50th year.

He continued to play exhibition matches and had at least one round of golf virtually every day of his life — he was still bettering his age at 79 — but his club duties aside, his full attention now turned to course design.

He worked his magic in all the classifications, links, parkland, moorland and heathland and his name is forever linked with a multitude of renowned courses: Dalmahoy, East Renfrewshire, Hilton Park, Irvine, Lanark, Orsett, Southport & Ainsdale, Taymouth Castle and Stranraer, to name a few.

The latter was his final work, designed in 1949 but not completed until after his death. A seaside parkland, it is one of the unsung gems of Scottish golf and is a fitting monument to a marvellous career. The 18th is known as Braid's Last. Its impossible for the knowing to play it for the first time without feeling a lump in the throat....

While Braid didn't discover heathland golf it would be true to say that he created more heathland courses than any other architect. Rosemount at Blairgowrie, Parkstone and Sherwood Forest are only three considered in the top echelon but the name which made Braid's reputation was Gleneagles, Britain's first custom-built golfing resort.

Braid surveyed the 830 acres before the first world war and had designed 27 holes by 1914. For obvious reasons the project was held in abeyance and those 27 holes — the King's course and nine holes of the Queen's — were not constructed until 1919. By 1924 Braid had completed the project, adding the second loop to the Queen's. Such is the stature and international renown of Gleneagles that it may be Braid's most significant contribution to British golf.

The innovations that were to become the hallmark of his artistry were all displayed here: the distinctive, mounded bunkering, the ingeniously constructed greens, the instinctive design strategy that rewards concise analysis and execution of shot.

"James wasn't a penal architect," wrote Darwin. "He didn't lie in wait for every bad shot — but he wouldn't let an errant player 'get away with it' and now and then would take malign satisfaction in blocking the easy road."

Contrary to opinions held by certain players of the age, Braid didn't care for penal bunkers. Study his designs and you'll see that he frequently used fairway bunkers as beacons, indicating the correct line for the tee shot. Skirt a fairway bunker and often as not you'll have the best line to the flag, down the green's opening and between two sentinel bunkers. Be off-line and you'll be required to lay-up or fly those sentinel bunkers with a teasing recovery, usually a chip to a down-sloping green, for those who played safe and took the extra club.

He didn't care for acres of sand, though. Often just a crescent moon of it is visible, below the guarding hummocks that signal their position. The hummocks have other purposes, too. They act as windbreaks, to prevent the sand being blown out. But primarily they're designed to deflect a slightly mis-hit shot over or away from the bunker or down the grassy slope towards the centre of the bunker. You'll be penalised but at least you'll have a shot from a level lie on sand. There are no perpendicular walls on Braid bunkers, obviating a situation where the wall becomes excavated by players attempting shots from impossible lies. He considered such a situation not only unfair but ridiculous.

His greens are equally distinctive in configuration. Several of them on each of his courses are humped at the rear, calling for imagination and a sound short game. He may also have been the first architect to create multiple flag positions on greens of modest size, creating level areas guarded by gentle undulations which also act as drainage channels for rain water. He didn't believe in excessive rolls and while most of his greens slope up from the front, he wasn't averse to introducing the odd one that runs away, from front to back, where the design called for a short iron approach or a long, links-style pitch and run. The 14th hole at Gleneagles is the most notable example.

In the days before artificial watering Braid devised the dew pond system of irrigation for greens, laying a layer of clay in the foundations to act as a reservoir for the grass roots in dry spells. He also introduced what today is recognised as graded rough, abhorring time lost searching for balls only marginally off-line.

There's an interesting tale apropos of this which involves Gleneagles where nature, usually the ally of the architect, has become the enemy. Over the years bracken has engulfed the heather in several areas, squeezing some fairways and green surrounds to the point where the holes have changed character. The change went unremarked until recently when Braid's plans were discovered and now a project is under way to re-introduce the original concept.

It's a programme Braid would have appreciated. He was frequently called upon to modernise the work of other architects and thus do two of the world's most venerable links bear his stamp..

Shortly after the first war he made adjustments to Old Prestwick and among them was the introduction of a bunker on the 4th, a dog-leg of 382 yards. Previously a generous fairway that curved with the Pow Burn, Braid placed a bunker on the turn, at driving length. This reduced the target area but left just sufficient space between bunker and burn for those brave enough to take the short route, "a narrow and tempting enterprise," as Darwin wrote, with the option of a longer second shot on the safe line, left of the bunker. There's no finer example of strategic bunkering.

In 1926 Braid also remodelled Carnoustie where he effected a similarly strategic situation. It became known as Hogan's Alley, so christened during the 1950 Open Championship when Ben Hogan four times threaded his drive down the short routé on the way to becoming Open Champion at his first and only attempt.

Those who know the present course will be agog to learn that Braid removed several dozen bunkers, perhaps as many as 80, according to Hamilton Stutt. But he introduced a new one, known forever since as Braid's Bunker. It lies waiting just left-centre of the fairway 222 yards from the medal tee on the 432 yard 2nd hole. Recently introduced bunkers 40 yards further on to the right pose greater problems these days but for many years it influenced the tee shot by reducing what had been a magnanimous target area.

Unless a gale blows up it should pose few problems for competitors in the Open Championship but it will catch the eye and play on the mind, a mental nudge in the ribs by one of the Great Triumvirate from the Golden Age of British golf.

SCOTLAND, WHERE THE PAST IS EVER-PRESENT

Golfing history revisited at the home of the game...

Just as it is impossible to play golf on a Scottish links and be unaware of the history of the game, so it is incongruous to write about Scottish golf without reference to its past. At the Home of Golf, history is part of the fabric of every-day life providing a rich vein of tradition and culture that is unique in international sport. There's barely a Scottish links that's not a century old or more, and rare is the clubhouse that doesn't have history leaking out of its wood panelling, its trophy cabinet and the fading portraits on its walls.

Many medals and other treasured baubles dating to the early 19th century are still played for each year in clubs up and down the land, their long-departed donors still revered. Thus is the history of Scottish golf kept alive, in word and deed, over links which frequently evolved through usage long before the first architects came along to add a final polish.

It is here, on the course, that golf has its most palpable ties with the past: here an average golfer can tread the greens where Young Tom Morris and his father putted out for the Open Championship. At St Andrews he can play over a links that has been extant since the mid-15th century, long before the game assumed its present form. So much earlier, indeed, that its origins have been lost in antiquity.

The Old Course has no known architect, although it has been refined over the past century, since Old Tom Morris, for many years its professional and green keeper, laid out the adjacent New and Jubilee courses.

There's much conjecture about how the first links came into being, how St Andrews became the home of golf when it might have been the equally venerable Leith or Mussselburgh or Prestwick. That, as they say, is a long story.

How did the game of golf begin at St Andrews? The commonly accepted theory is that the sparsely grassed dunes, left exposed when the sea retreated during the Ice Age, were used for grazing sheep and that the shepherds invented the earliest form of the game to while away the hours, knocking pebbles with their crooks to mutually agreed targets. There were no greens, of course, and it's unlikely that there were any holes, simply a succession of natural object at which to aim across country.

In time, the targets became permanent, as did the first bunkers, scraped out of the dunes by sheltering sheep and incorporated by their minders for use in their pastime. So appeared the first rudimentary hazards and greens, but even then there were no tees: the ball was put back into play close to the hole.

As the game became marginally more sophisticated, holes with markers were introduced, the route of play was from the town to the river mouth and back and thus evolved the first double greens for which St Andrews was to become famous. There was no specific number of holes until about 1760 — at one point the Old Course had 22 holes — and a round became 18 holes in an almost accidental manner in the mid-19th century.

Many links were laid out on common land used for grazing and games. Some had five holes, some six and others seven. At Prestwick, where the Open Championship was inaugurated, there were 12, following a roughly circular route. Three times around became recognised as a good day's sport, so when the Open was first staged there in 1860 the event was over 36 holes.

At St Andrews the number of holes had varied over the years from five to 22, and it was partly because of the Prestwick format that 18 became standard. In fact the Old Course had 11 double greens laid out in a strip along the shore and ending at the river. Players teed up near the home hole, played out to the far reaches of the course and then played in the reverse direction to different holes on the same greens. Hence the expressions 'out' and 'home', to indicate two halves of a round.

When the Open Championship was first staged at St Andrews in 1873 four of the greens were adapted to house single holes, thus creating 18 holes and setting the format that was to become recognised as standard. Tom Kidd, a local professional, won with a 36-hole score of 91-88-179 and the 18 hole round was established: Prestwick, then of 12 holes, became an 18 holer for the championship of 1884 and when Muirfield staged its debut Open eight years later the great event was staged over 72 holes for the first time. Thus, 1892 signalled the birth of the modern era of championship golf.

So St Andrews set the standard, as it has in so many aspects of the game. From course design to playing equipment, the influence of the Old Course, and those who played it in the formative years, has been deep and far-reaching. Mysterious, ethereal, frustrating, awe-inspiring, uplifting, it has made a contribution to every course built since, although no designer could replicate it *en toto*. If he tried, sad to say, his clients would probably demand their money back!

It was the training ground for Old Tom Morris, one of the first course designers to operate on a commercial scale, creating links now regarded by the purists as models. And it had a major influence on one of Old Tom's proteges, too, and through this are extended the historical links to the modern era.

His name was Donald Ross and for some years as a young man he was assistant to Old Tom at St Andrews, before moving to Royal Dornoch to become head green keeper and professional. Tempted to America a few years later, he became the doyen of golf course architects there, designing some 600 courses between 1898 and his death in 1948.

He lived in Pinehurst, North Carolina, and his memorial is Pinehurst's No.2 course, venue for the 1999 and 2005 US Opens. Another of his famous creations was the Scioto club course in Ohio, which also was to earn a place in history: it was the home course of a powerful, fair-haired boy who launched a glorious golf career from there. His name was Jack Nicklaus.

And so a link is established between Old Tom and Big Jack, two of the dominant figures of golf. When Nicklaus turned naturally to course architecture in the autumn of his career his knowledge of design, forged on the Ross courses at Scioto and Pinehurst and honed by constant visits to the Home of Golf, where he twice won the Open, became the bedrock of his philosophy.

Tastes and fashions may change but every architect worth his salt has made a bee-line for the Auld Grey Toon, to stand and marvel at the most famous course in the world.

In truth, there's not much for the unknowing to see. First-timers need a caddie or they'll be lost within minutes. The odd gorse bush aside, there's not much to aim at, there's little definition, no perspective. Flatten the rippling fairways and the course would resemble a biscuit-coloured floor stretching to the horizon, broken only by devilishly hidden pot bunkers — 'just large enough for an angry man and his niblick' — waiting to ambush the unsuspecting.

It's an original combination of the strategic and the penal, the ultimate test of golf when the weather is fractious. More, it's a course which can change every day, according to the wind and the placement of the flags on the huge greens where 30-yard putts are common and 50-yarders not unusual.

Similarly, most of the classical Scottish links had simply evolved and, when the founding architects came along to cater for the first golf boom in the 19th century, they adopted this natural philosophy, using the existing land form with the prevailing wind as the major hazard.

The 19th-century golf boom? That came about when the old feathery ball, hand-stitched and expensive, was replaced in 1848 by the gutta percha ball. The moulded, rubber-type 'gutty' was much cheaper to produce and attracted vast numbers into golf who previously could not afford the featheries that had been in vogue since about 1618.

The reuseable gutty lasted in various improved forms until the turn of the century and the advent of the Haskell ball, the first with a rubber thread wound under tension over a solid centre and with a balata cover. Much livelier than its predecessors, it was the first ball to be mass produced, which not only lowered its cost but attracted even more aspiring golfers, particularly in America, whence it came.

In commercial terms it had the perfect launch. Using it, Walter Travis won the 1901 US Amateur Championship. The following year it reached Britain and Scotland's Sandy Herd, initially opposed to it, had a last minute change of heart and used it in the Open Championship at Hoylake. He won by a stroke from Harry Vardon who played a gutty. The age of commerce had taken its first tentative hold on the Royal & Ancient game.

Golf was played on quite an informal basis until the mid-18th century. For 200 years or so there were no organised clubs as such, no recognised rules or format, not even an agreement upon how many holes constituted a round. Several societies staged regular meetings and private matches between individuals, often for heavy wagers, all in matchplay format with the minimum of local rules.

But the principal attraction appeared more social than sporting: the highlight of such meetings was dinner at a favoured hostelry and the consumption of copious quantities of claret, the subject of the wagers.

This began to change in 1744, the date of the first recorded official open competition, an event that was to have far-reaching implications.

The golfers of the Society of Leith petitioned the Burghers of the City of Edinburgh to donate a trophy for annual competition. The elders agreed and donated a silver club as a permanent trophy. Ten years later the 22 Noblemen and Gentlemen of Fife, the forerunners of the Royal & Ancient Golf Club, followed suit, providing a silver club, financed by private subscription, for an annual competition open to members of other societies. But realising that in an open event visitors would be playing under unfamiliar local rules they adopted the 'Articles and Laws in Playing the Golf' devised by the Leith Society ten years earlier.

They were thirteen in number and simple in the extreme and they were the foundation for the Rules of Golf we know today. In that era, though, there was no such thing as stroke play; all competition was in match play and the rules reflected this. The first recorded mention of stroke play was dated 1759 at St Andrews, and in the fullness of time the rules were amended to cover unplayable lies — a situation that didn't exist in those days of match play where the rule was "play as it lies or concede the hole.'

So the two competitions, and the silver clubs which were their trophies, brought about a formalisation of the game through the instigation of official rules. Important as that was, they achieved far more: they caused a chain reaction which, in effect, is still felt today.

In 1764, because of the legalities concening ownership of the original silver trophy, the Leith Society became a club, thenceforth known as the Honourable Company of Edinburgh Golfers. It was the world's first golf club and the example was soon followed by the golfers of St Andrews, then in steady succession by the Aberdeen Golf Club (1780), Crail (1786), Bruntsfield (1787) and Burntisland (1797) until the chain reaction assumed the proportions of an avalanche.

The Prestwick Golf Club was founded in 1851 and nine years later its members subscribed to a Moroccan leather belt in-laid with silver as the prize for an annual competition for professionals. It was won by Willie Park and in the following year it became 'open to the world'. It was won for the first time by Tom Morris Senior, and thus was born the Open Championship.

Its initial history is somewhat chequered: in 1870, at the age of 19, Young Tom Morris won the belt for the third time in succession, thus making it his own property. There being no trophy, the tournament lapsed, to be revived a year later when the present trophy, the famous silver Claret Jug, was donated jointly by the Honourable Company and the clubs of Prestwick and St Andrews.

The new rules called for the event to be played in rotation over the clubs' three courses, including Musselburgh to where the Honourable Company had moved in 1836. As was his habit, Young Tom won again, at Prestwick, setting a two round record score of 149 to win by 12 strokes. It was a 36 hole tally that was never equalled in the era of the gutty ball: Willie Park Junior shot 155 at Musselburgh in 1889 but, that apart, no one got within 10 strokes of it until Harold Hilton had opening rounds of 80-75 in the 1897 Open at Hoylake.

By this time the championship was well established. It became a 72 hole event when it moved to Muirfield, by then the home of the Honourable· Company, in 1892, and was staged in England for the first time in 1894.

Those two championships signalled the start of another era. The first was won by Harold Hilton, the great Hoylake amateur, who thus became the first Englishman to win the Open — John Ball, his club colleague, was runner-up — and the second saw the emergence of the Great Triumvirate. J.H. Taylor took the title at Sandwich, with a young Channel Islander named Harry Vardon in sixth place.

The second major era of golf began when the Open returned to St Andrews in 1900. Taylor, Vardon and a young Scot named James Braid took the first three places. It was Taylor's third victory, a feat already achieved by Vardon in the space of four years.

But it was the closest Braid had so far come to winning the championship he was to dominate between 1901 and 1912. The Great Triumvirate was complete. The Golden Age was born. Collectively, Vardon, Taylor and Braid won a total of 16 Open Championships and in doing so elevated the lot of the professional golfer from humble artisan to one of stature. They were among the first popular sporting heroes. In time, all three became golf architects, feeding the insatiable demand their popularity and fame had created and which the mass-produced Haskell ball encouraged.

All three held positions as club professionals, of course: the era of the tournament player was still eons away, not even a pipe dream. But such was their stature they all had senior assistants, allowing them considerable latitude to pursue other interests.

None pursued them more avidly than Braid. Born in 1870 at Elie, not ten miles from St Andrews, he became the most prolific course designer in Britain, of that or any other era. For a man not fond of travelling—because he was prone to travel sickness—he obviously ended up doing an awful lot of it! In all, he laid out or remodelled close to 200 courses between 1910 and his death in 1950 and covered most of Britain in the process.

Golf architecture these days is a heavily populated profession and I find it amusing that certain tour players are denigrated for turning their hands to it, often while still playing. In fact, all the earliest designers were Scottish players, active in their sport; there were no professional golf architects until the era of Harry Colt, a Cambridge graduate, English solicitor and scratch player, which began in the 1890s and lasted until the 1940s.

Old Tom Morris was the trail blazer. He was designing courses long before others knew enough to do so. And his original designs, still extant and based on the natural principles which influenced the Old Course, are revered today. His most famous course is Royal County Down, without doubt one of the world's great links, run a close second by Lahinch, known as the St Andrews of Ireland. At Machrihanish on the Mull of Kintyre he created a jewel of a links with arguably the most spectacular opening hole in golf He also designed the New and Jubilee courses at St Andrews, the exquisite Tain, near Royal Dornoch where he laid out the original course, and a dozen others worth a pilgrimage.

Not surprisingly, several of his Scottish contemporaries followed Old Tom's trail: Willie Park, Willie Fearnie, several of the Carnoustie Simpsons and Sandy Herd all became architects whose work is still admired and loved.

By this stage in the history of golf two important developments had2 taken place, both frequently overlooked but of comparable importance to the foundation of the rules and of organised clubs: mechanical grass cutters had become common and the teeing ground had become formalised.

Oddly, the former happened first. In the early years of the game, course maintenance was at best rudimentary and the results rustic. Scythes and sickles had replaced rabbits and sheep for grass-cropping purposes but the length of grass on the fairways still served to shorten shots and stretch courses, and even the best greens were uneven in both surface and response.

To exacerbate these problems, until the 1870s there were no tees as we know them today: the ball was teed up on the green, close to the hole, using a handful of sand. The Articles of Golf devised by the Honourable Company referred to teeing up within a club's length of the hole and, though this progressed over the years to 'no less than four club lengths and no more than eight', then to 'no less than eight club lengths and no more than twelve', the consequences to even the best kept greens can be imagined.

The first mention of a formal teeing ground was recorded in 1875, and in 1882 the Rules of Golf first referred to a tee rather than simply the distance from the hole. The basic components for golf course architecture were thus established.

In 1893, the teeing ground was accurately defined as 'two marks in line at right angles to the course to a depth of two club lengths'. The game's architecture took a giant leap forward. The modern golf course began to emerge. By this stage, too, hand-pushed grass cutters had become more readily available: putting surfaces assumed a consistency previously undreamed of, thanks to Edwin Budding. He was a Gloucestershire man who produced what was the world's first lawn mower. Aside from committing future generations of men to an unending weekend chore, he changed the concept of golf course maintenance. The gang mower was not far behind.

It is not known precisely when Budding unveiled his first lawn mower but the patent was taken up by Ransomes, then manufacturing ploughshares, who in 1832 obtained a licence to build the first commercial model. Within two decades, their promotional literature proudly announced they were turning out around 70 to 80 such machines annually, complete with rollers–a vital component — and catch-boxes.

By the time the teeing ground was introduced in the 1880s, it's fair to assume, most golf clubs would have availed themselves of this revolutionary invention which would transform their courses beyond anything previously imagined. The two developments merged into common usage to initiate another upsurge in course construction.

Architects began to have a field day and James Braid was at their head. None could match him for the sheer volume of the designs he produced, among them many of Britain's finest–Rosemount at Blairgowrie, the Kings and Queens courses at Gleneagles and the two at Dalamahoy, to list only a handful of note in Scotland. To these can be added some of the little-known gems I visited in the course of this research: Boat of Garden, Brora, Forfar, Irvine, Lundin, Powfoot, Taymouth Castle and Stranraer. The latter was Braid's final creation, completed in 1951, a year after his death. It's a fitting monument to a golfing giant.

Braid built most of his courses from scratch but a small proportion were extensions from nine holes to 18, or adaptations and revisions where more length was required due to improvements in equipment and playing technique.

When Old Tom began plying his trade few courses were above 5,000 yards in length but the equivalent of today's par 72–the consequence of hickory shafts, unmown fairways and primitive balls which made 170 yards a long drive. The Haskell ball began to change all that, and when steel shafts arrived in the early 1930s many courses required modernisation to cater for the greater length of shot which had become common.

But the ancient Scottish links have retained their intrinsic character. Thanks to modern agronomy, they have improved with age and are a daily reminder of the great players-turned-architects who gave the Royal & Ancient game to the world. Those shepherds of St Andrews could never know what their pastime had set in motion.

GOLF RESORTS: FOR HOLIDAYS TO SAVOUR

Family fun at a golf resort? You'd better believe it!

When the subject is travel and holidays we golfers have the best of all worlds. Not for us the frantic annual crush most families associate with summer package holidays, with bulging airports and interminable flight delays, dubious hotels and questionable food. We golfers may select our exclusive destination and choose our time to escape, eschewing the heaving Costas for the more sedate ambience of an exclusive golf resort far away from the madding crowds. It's all very civilised.

The only fly in the sun cream is the bewildering choice of destinations. As the world continues to shrink there's simply no end to the possibilities as new venues compete for our custom with the venerable resorts, some almost a century old, where tradition and quality are paramount.

There is one aspect of golf-travel that shouldn't be overlooked because it holds the key to successful holidays. It is this: the golf travel season is unending. No matter the time of year you'll find an agreeable venue for a golfing holiday with weather that's sure to please. Whether you're an all-male foursome or a couple seeking a romantic get-away you'll find total flexibility in timing and choice. So you can avoid excessive summer heat, for instance, by going in the shoulder seasons at a time convenient for that wedding anniversary or the annual thrash with the club bandits. Flights are cheaper then, too, as frequently are resort rates.

Even better, golfing parents plotting to indulge themselves on a guilt-free family holiday have discovered how to have the best of both worlds. They take the tribe to a golf resort!

This may sound incongruous, and a little fast talking will be necessary to convince the youngsters, but it's a fact: golf resorts are not just for golfers. No matter their age or interests everyone will have a ball; every day will be full of activities.

The fact is that the resort operators know a thing or two about marketing. They realise that to fill their villas, hotels, clubhouse bars and restaurants they also have to cater for the needs of non-golfers and the youngsters.

So they lay on oodles of alternative attractions, every sport and pastime from blue water fishing and horse riding to tennis, bikes and disco dancing. Non-golfers can do as much or as little as energy dictates, switching activities as the mood takes them.

If the Significant Other requires a little pampering, there's sure to be a spa, plus a health and beauty clinic and a hairdresser. She'll return feeling like a million dollars and Senor Smoothie will have a stack of brownie points in credit.

That's merely an over-view of what's available at many resorts, and we've barely touched upon the golf! Most resorts have at least two courses, many have several, with others nearby. Some are world class, the venues for major events, all are to a high standard of design and presentation, frequently with state of the art teaching and practice facilities.

The golf is the focal point of such resorts, the *raison d'etre*: the courses dominate the vista from virtually every viewpoint and bring an ambience that is at once serene and picturesque. They offer a glorious holiday setting, a communion with nature. A family, even one with non-golfers, would be enchanted with the ambience and the off-course facilities.

In the US, where it all began at the famed resort of Pinehurst, North Carolina, such choice has been par for the course since 1895. Set in 5,000 acres of pine-covered sand hills, Pinehurst has been the model for every resort built in the past century. And they're still making additions and improvements.

These days it has eight golf courses — the 2005 US Open Championship was staged on its revered No. 2 course — plus a 50 court tennis facility with a 10,000 seat tournament stadium, a croquet club that is the headquarters of the game in America, a new, $16 million state of the art health spa and a man-made beach alongside a 200 acre lake for fishing and all forms of water sports that don't involve an engine.

There are horses, bicycles, nature trails, you name it. The great hotel, its façade of painted white timber and with a gleaming copper roof, is justifiably known as the Queen of the South. The Carolina dining room is an imperative experience.

There are perhaps 1,000 similar resorts scattered around America, and as many again around the world. All are open year-round, all are eager for your patronage. Go once and you'll return.

Most resorts have a central hotel, although there's usually a choice of accommodations. Depending upon the size of your group, and certainly if there are youngsters, you may prefer a fairway villa, a beach side cottage or a spacious apartment. Eating out? You'll be spoiled for choice there, too, with a different venue every evening.

Many resorts are close to the ocean and so the beach plays a major role in daily life. Frequently, too, there'll be a town nearby, perhaps even a city of some charm, often historic and with countless attractions.

Because of competition the value is exceptional, the standards high. And declining costs of long haul flights, particularly in the shoulder seasons, put such a holiday within reach of any family or group with a sense of adventure. And for golfing youngsters it will be a preview of Heaven!

Turnberry and Gleneagles: a glittering duo steeped in history

All-inclusive holiday resorts are somewhat thin on the ground in Britain, doubtless because of our climate and the appeal of exotic alternatives to be found in sunnier climes.

It may appear a little incongruous, then, that two of the finest resorts in the world are to be found in Scotland, not a country blessed with a sub-tropical climate and even more so in that they are, relatively speaking, almost neighbours.

Perhaps it's not so odd, upon reflection: both have long had golf as the major attraction, their *raison d'etre;* in fact if they had nothing other than golf to offer they'd still be world famous. Gleneagles and Turnberry are names to conjure with, part of the golden history of our game.

Both were founded in the age of steam and their hotels were built by the railway companies of the day, mainly to generate business. Turnberry, indeed, was one of the first custom-built golf resorts in Europe and its neighbour was not far behind. James Braid, the venerable architect and great Open champion at the turn of the last century, surveyed the 830 acres of Gleneagles before the first world war and by 1914 had designed 27 holes.

For obvious reasons the project was held in abeyance and the construction of those 27 holes – the King's course and the first loop of the Queen's – was delayed until 1919. By 1924 Braid had completed the project, adding the second loop to the Queen's course, by which time the new resort hotel was ready to open for its first guests.

Since then, Gleneagles has gone from strength to strength. From a small hotel attracting discerning golfers and shooters it has developed into a full-scale resort establishment offering every imaginable sporting and social facility, all allied to a sumptuous elegance in a supreme lowland setting an hour north of Edinburgh. Not for nothing is it known as the Gateway to the Highlands.

These days, since Jack Nicklaus worked his architectural magic in 1993, it has three golf courses which collectively have been the stage for a series of events of the top rank, most notably the Scottish Open Championship.

Golf aside, the resort has won a swath of international awards for excellence from the tourism and hospitality industries. In 1986, for example, Gleneagles was awarded the Automobile Association's supreme accolade of Five Red Stars, which it has retained every year.

By the 1950s the resort had become an annual fixture on the social calendar. After the London "season" it was yachting at Cowes, polo at Deauville and golf and grouse shooting at Gleneagles.

Until 1982 the hotel opened only during the summer months but within four years more than £11 million had been spent on a total renovation and restoration, so that the elegance and traditions of Gleneagles could be enjoyed year-round.

Capital investment since 1982 now totals more than £46 million, the bulk of which, since 1998, has brought the total renovation of all the bedrooms. The most recent project, the building of the hotel extension known as Braid House, was completed in December at a cost in excess of £10 million. The Old Master would be mightily proud to see how his fledgling resort has blossomed.

There has been even more activity at Turnberry, much of it recent, and those who knew the resort in its early days wouldn't recognise it now. The supreme quality of service and accommodations is unchanging, although these days there's rather more of both!

The resort is world-renowned for its golf in that spectacular setting along the Ayrshire coastline, thanks in large part to the Open Championship of 1977. No one who saw it will ever forget that epic Duel in the Sun between Tom Watson and Jack Nicklaus, arguably the greatest finale in the history of the event. It couldn't have been stage-managed any better! Mere mortals playing the course now still marvel at the scores returned by those two great players.

There had been a private golf course on the 800 acre site since 1901 but then in 1906 the Glasgow and South Western Railway Company opened the de luxe Turnberry hotel and a railway station, thus creating the first golfing resort of its kind. Three years later the forerunners of the Ailsa and Arran courses were opened and in 1912 came the first major golf event, the Ladies British Open Championship.

Since 1977 the Open has become a regular event on the Turnberry calendar, a far cry from the second world war when, incredible to believe now, the site was a base for RAF Coastal Command and several fairways of the Ailsa course were concrete runways!

Oddly, this may have been a blessing in disguise. The hotel that still dominates the skyline was then owned by British Transport Hotels, an off-shoot of the railway conglomerate, and a new business plan saw Mackenzie Ross, one of the renowned golf architects of the day, commissioned to transform what was then a desolate site into a golf facility of the top rank.

The project occupied him for six years but the result was the Ailsa course, reopened in 1951, and the Arran, which followed in 1954. The first chapter in the modern story of Turnberry was written in 1961 with the staging of the Amateur Championship. Two years later came the Walker Cup match and the rest, as they say, is golfing history.

In 1997 the resort was acquired by the Westin group, a subsidiary of Starwood Hotels which in the year 2000 announced a £21 million programme of investments covering a range of activities on the estate.

Much of the project is now complete. It includes the Colin Montgomerie Links Golf Academy, an outdoor activity centre and a collection of lodges and cottages offering alternative five star accommodation for long or short stays.

The lodges, sumptuous in the extreme, have six to eight en suite bedrooms, spacious lounges and a private dining area, with catering available from the hotel. They are ideal for business groups or families who may book an entire lodge, but are also available to individuals who may reserve a single bedroom.

The cottages, ideal for small family groups, have two bedrooms, one fitted with bunk beds, and all the usual facilities you'd have at home. Like the lodges, these are also to five star standard.

This was a radical departure for Turnberry but there was more to come. It arrived in the shape of the Kintyre links which opened in July 2001 and was immediately acclaimed as one of the leading new courses in the UK.

Accolades aside, it has also been recognised by the Royal & Ancient in being named as one of the four venues for final qualifying for the 2004 Open Championship to be staged at Royal Troon.

It was designed by Donald Steel and encompasses part of the Arran course and an elevated stretch of land that extends along the cliff tops. The Kintyre matches the Ailsa course in its spectacular coastal scenery and gives views of Ailsa Craig and the Isle of Arran.

Like its equally historic neighbour at Gleneagles, Turnberry is a joy to play for the scenery alone. The rest is a memorable bonus.

You'll be King of the Castle at Glorious Bovey

Describing Bovey Castle requires barely a moment's reflection. It may be the finest resort of its kind in Britain. In an age when crass is considered the norm and style is a rapidly vanishing quality, Bovey Castle is a *tres elegant* example of impeccable standards, the stage for a by-gone era revisited.

It has every facility and attraction; its accommodations are opulent; it has peerless cuisine and incomparable service and the ambience is redolent of another, more gracious age. All this in a setting of natural beauty, viewed from a building that oozes elegance and good taste. You'll gather from all this that Bovey Castle is rather special...

Set on the edge of the Devonshire wilderness that is Dartmoor and formerly known as the Manor House Hotel at Moretonhampstead, it was once the country seat of the W.H. Smith family and latterly an hotel that had seen better times. Then along came Peter de Savary, fresh from similar endeavours at various fleshpots around the world, who set about a miraculous transformation that saw the huge estate converted into a oasis of opulence and lavishly orchestrated service. He re-named it Bovey Castle. The lovely old place has never looked back, nor been in finer fettle.

The objective, happily achieved, was to create an ambience synonymous with the 1920's, an era of prosperity, happiness and optimism that became known as the Jazz Age: Scott Joplin's music is top of the hit parade in the hotels' music system, the décor throughout is art deco, highlighted by oak panelling, hand painted silk wallpaper and ornately framed posters from a by-gone era. They come in every size and shape, from early holiday resort posters to Vogue-style covers and old railway, airline and tourist posters from all points of the globe. There are hundreds of them and they decorate the walls in a ubiquitous art gallery that's said to have cost upwards of £500,000.

The public rooms, once tired and well-worn, have been transformed into havens of style. The 65 guest rooms and suites are simply sumptuous; the Palm Court dining room is a visual delight, the stage for a celebration of the culinary arts that is enhanced by views across the terrace to the golf course and the wildly beautiful countryside of Dartmoor beyond.

Needless to say, the transformation wasn't achieved cheaply. A reported £30 million was spent on refurbishing the hotel, its estate and its gardens, including £2 million on up-grading the golf course. No corners were cut, no expense spared. The end result is a romantic retreat that is a joy to behold.

Aside from the venerable golf course, there are 25 miles of salmon and trout fishing in the River Bovey which winds its way through the estate; there's an equestrian centre, with lessons and trekking for all standards of rider; there's falconry, two all-weather tennis courts and a grass court; there's croquet, archery, clay pigeon shooting, quad biking and driving, nature trails for hiking and bird watching and a local crafts barn where ingénues can try their hands at cider making or fish smoking.

Services of a less esoteric nature are available in the spa, which offers holistic therapy in private treatment rooms; there are sauna and steam baths, a Jacuzzi, a hair dressing salon, indoor and outdoor swimming pools, a gym, and a sun deck for alfresco relaxation

Those with youngsters will have plenty of time to themselves: there's a children's club, known as the Bovey Rangers, that offers day-long activities and outings supervised by various experts; there's a dedicated club room, child-special meal times and there's even a baby sitting service.

The golf course too, is a feast for the eyes and the senses. It dates to 1930 and was laid out by J.F. Abercromby, one of the lesser-known but highly respected names in the golden age of British golf architecture in which James Braid, Alister MacKenzie and Harry Colt were the figureheads.

It was designed as a resort course with no ambitions beyond offering guests a modicum of fun and relaxation. But it was always renowned for its condition and Henry Cotton described the long 14th as one of the finest par fours in British golf, with a couple of other holes not far behind in terms of challenge.

Piecemeal modifications in design were effected over the years but in 2003, when de Savary took the reigns, Donald Steel and Tom Mackenzie were commissioned to undertake a major overhaul, to restore the course to its former eminence. Referring to the original plans by Abercromby, they succeeded admirably.

The River Bovey contributes nuisance value on the first eight holes but it's a pretty nuisance, only a few yards wide in places. It may also be the longest ball washer in the world of golf and anyone who negotiates his round without raising a splash deserves to win the drinks and probably will. It's sheer bliss, a preview of golfing heaven and a golden bonus to an outstanding hotel.

Location: Bovey Castle is 15 miles south of Exeter, which is some 170 miles from Central London. Exeter has an international airport which accommodates private jets by arrangement.

Leave the M5 at Junction 31 and take the A30, sign-posted Oakhampton. Then take the first exit off the A30 onto the B3212 for Moretonhampstead (10 miles). Go through this town, keeping the White Hart Inn on your left, towards Postbridge. Bovey Castle is one mile further on.

Home away from home at the Old Course Hotel

Imagine the end of a perfect golfing day. You've bettered your handicap, won your match and now, in the same agreeable company, you're dining in some style in a restaurant overlooking the most famous landscape in the world of golf.

Below, the Old Course is resplendent in the late evening sunshine, shadows dappling the fairways beyond the window at your elbow. In the distance, the Bay of St Andrews is an azure backdrop, diamonds glinting from water frolicking in a gentle breeze.

Dinner in such a setting is the stuff of dreams for any golfer with an ounce of soul and a taste for the finer things of life. For this is the real McKay; this is the Old Course Hotel.

It stands in regal splendour alongside the Road Hole, the 17th, the game's Bermuda Triangle, for a century or more the stage for famous triumph and disaster. In the living theatre that is golf there can be no more envied seat in the house than the one you have chosen for dinner tonight.

So a word to the wise. Demand predicates that you advise Pierro, the *maitre d'* of your requirements well in advance. The elegant and welcoming fourth floor Grill Room has only 88 covers and most tables are some way removed from the views.

Once the meal begins, though, you 'II be sufficiently distracted no matter where you're sitting. In my experience, de luxe hotels of such elevated standards are seldom renowned for their dining rooms. On the other hand, the cuisine of this Grill Room merits a detour, as M. Michelin would say.

Like the expansive wine list, it is international in style, although the national allegiance is, not unnaturally, Scottish. East Neuk fish, Angus beef, Sutherland lamb, Highland game and local cheeses illuminate the disparate menus. Most ingredients, not least a variety of scrunchy vegetables and salads, are locally produced and as fresh as can be.

Being in an area rich in primary produce you'd expect this, of course, but it's not universally guaranteed. Here, by repute, it is the norm. Hence the AA Four Red Stars rating and a commendation from Relais du Golf.

It was not always thus: the hotel has a history best described as varied. Only .in the past four years, since a change of ownership brought total renovation and a new management style, has it achieved its present eminence. The story deserves recounting because the site has long been part of the ancient history of the Home of Golf.

For a century or more there was a collection of smoke-blackened railway sheds nearby, alongside the line which passed through St Andrews en route to Leuchars. The embankment is still discernible but chopped off just short of the hotel's main gate. Climb it and you'll see that the line ran through what is now the hotel's pro shop, the library and the gift shop. Nearby is the Jigger Inn, once the station master's cottage.

The sheds, used for coaling, created the corner at the dog leg of the 17th hole and were a landmark. This began to change in 1968 when, following the infamous Beeching decimation of the railways, British Rail recognised the potential of the site once the line had been removed. So, just as it had done at Gleneagles, it built a hotel.

Several metamorphoses later the sheds are still there, at least in spirit. Replicated in size and profile but of a more fetching material and hue, they are used by hotel staff as stores and offices. Gifted players must still hit over them from the 17th tee: we hackers hoik it left and play, hopefully, for a bogey.

Such is the proximity of tee to hotel that, despite the toughened glass, replacing broken windows costs £10,000 a year and a guest once achieved his 15 minutes of fame by plopping his tee shot down the main chimney. Legend has it that the ball ended its descent on the carpet of the Road Hole Bar and when the player asked for a drop he was served a small whisky! Rules are rules, after all.

The hotel itself has changed dramatically in appearance over the years. Once described as "looking like a chest of drawers with the drawers open", it now projects a modern elegance that, oddly, is in total sympathy with its historic surroundings. It also contains all the good things that guests now expect of a world class hotel. There's a spa with heated swimming pool, a health and fitness centre with steam rooms and sunbeds.

There's a choice of rooms for private or corporate dining, a ballroom, conference rooms, one of the finest pro shops in Scotland and a golf office where George, the steward, will arrange your golf and transportation. Plus the inevitable helipad.

Not least are the 125 executive bedrooms and suites, most with golf course views, that offer every comfort and facility. All this is complemented by warm but unobtrusive service that enhances a relaxing ambience rare for a setting of such formal luxury. The place is popular in corporate circles but goodness knows how they get their work done! With difficulty, obviously, but the holiday-maker can do as much or as little as he desires.

The hotel is a magnet for golfing celebrities and others on the Grand Tour of Scottish golf. Prince Andrew and Clint Eastwood, who both wield a mean three iron, were recent visitors. Neil Armstrong, the astronaut, drops in from time to time and even Ol' Blue Eyes, Frank Sinatra himself, was a guest during the Open Championship, although he doesn't play golf.

Not all guests are golfers, you see: hence Pierro's rare gaffe.

"Do you play golf?" he asked one diner, obviously an Australian.

"Hmm ... a little, not too much," said Peter Thomson, the five times Open champion.

Which leads nicely to the latest development. The Old Course Hotel now has its own course .. a recent event of particular interest on two counts: it is the first parkland course to he built at St Andrews. and it is the first in Britain designed by Peter Thomson, now an internationally acclaimed golf architect.

It came about as the consequence of need. Because of demand. access to the Old Course is the subject of a daily ballot and of late only thirty per cent of applications have been successful.

So to guarantee golf for guests, in 1992 the hotel management took the bold step of buying 330 acres of land in nearby Craigtoun Park and commissioning the great Australian and his company to lay out a course. It is now completed and opens for general play next spring.

It will be an event of considerable significance, perhaps the major course opening of the year, one to set new benchmarks in quality and innovation based on traditional values.

Thomson has produced a jewel of rare lustre, a course of inordinate rhythm and playability that could stage international events and yet be accommodating to the average player. At full stretch it will measure 7.110 yards but multiple tees on each hole will offer various options relative to ability and the degree of challenge required.

Consider that in Britain a site of 150 acres is considered ample for a golf course and the 330 acres available at Craigtoun could have housed 36 holes. In fact. the original intention was to build 27 but Thomson opted to eschew quantity for quality and utilise the best features to create a classic 18. The consequence of such largesse means that while in clusters the holes are individually isolated and generally hidden from their neighbours. The serenity is total.

The munificent site also gave him scope for landscaping and the creation, through the usc of a variety of indigenous grasses, of wild life habitats on land that had for many years been farmed. Deer, red squirrel and badgers have already made themselves at home and water fowl have been investigating the newly established wetlands.

Thomson's philosophy has equally natural roots. He spent most of his playing life in Britain and knows and respects the old traditions of our golf. So there's nothing contrived about his courses. Craigtoun exemplifies this.

In style his fairwavs are based on those of the ancient links nearby, punctuated by hummocks and swales and dotted with clusters of small bunkers, often built into the base of mounds. Golf should be a game of strategy, he says, played along the ground, not in the air.

"The real challenge should be getting to the green, not just landing on it. Once there. putting should be fun on generally flat surfaces."

The consequence of Thomson's philosophy is a course of infinite grace and charm, one that perfectly complements the hotel it is designed to serve.

Golf launches a bloodless revolution

There's a revolution under-way in Southern Turkey but it won't alarm the United Nations. There's no bloodshed, indeed no victims at all, in fact the populace is delighted. Because this most ancient of lands has discovered the Royal & Ancient game, with gratifying results.

With acres of marble and wall-to-wall luxury the clubhouse had all the ambience of a five star hotel, with service and cuisine to match. The setting was equally impressive: a pristine golf course whose fairways were splashes of emerald just visible through the pine trees. On the horizon, snow-capped mountains completed a picture that could have come from a travelogue. The air was vibrant with the sounds of nature, the serenity was tangible.

It was early December. The day before, London had been marrow-chilling cold, with snow confirmed in the Highlands and down the east coast. It was winter's nadir and escaping it was a welcome prospect.

Now, only four hours away by air, we were lunching on the clubhouse terrace in short sleeves, basking in sunshine that had coaxed the temperature into the mid-70s.

Lunch took an hour and in that time the 18th green below us remained undisturbed, a golfing still life. The rest of the course appeared equally under-populated and in impeccable condition, despite the season, the bent grass greens striped and glinting.

"It's not always like this," our host admitted. "Only at this time of year, and in the summer months. In spring and autumn we can be quite busy, but even then it's millionaire's golf."

The flying time gives a clue to this Utopian destination, but despite the mention of pine trees it's not Portugal or Spain or even Italy.

It's a region that carries the hall marks of being the next major destination for British golfers seeking outstanding courses and fine hotels at reasonable cost. We're talking Turkey, more specifically the Turkish Riviera, the coastline that rims the Mediterranean.

Our focus is on the Paradise Beach region of Belek, a small municipality only 25 minutes' drive from Antalya airport. If you follow news of the senior tour you'll maybe have heard of Belek. Tommy Horton and his chums stopped off there again last year. They rave about the place.

At first they played their championship on the National course, then the only one open. Now there are three more, Gloria, Tat Beach and Nobilus, and a two others will open this summer, with another in the pipeline. All this within five miles of where only seven years ago there was but one hotel and the National Golf Club was only a pipe dream.

The innovation was the consequence of an urgent need to promote up-market tourism and attract desperately needed foreign capital, both to boost the sagging economy and bolster local employment. Fortunately, some one on high did his homework and came up with a one word solution: golf.

He wasn't the first to discover that our game can be a central plank in tourism strategy, bringing financial rewards and a buoyant economy through mass employment as it attracts multitudes of addicts who be-sport themselves in odd seasons, when everyone else has gone home.

Given a brace of sound courses, an agreeable hotel with good dining and something decently drinkable, it was found, and golfers are not too fussed about unending heat. Warm and dry is just fine, and that nicely sums up the Turkish off-seasons.

Well, the courses are rather better than sound, as we will reveal, and the hotels — there were 24 at last count — are all sumptuous. Most of them are five star, or to de luxe standard, and all are individual in style and design.

More, the tower block syndrome that has blighted Iberia is anathema at Belek. Here most hotels are low profile; each is set in 25 acres or more of gardens running down to a private beach; all are gated, with stringent security the norm. For those who want privacy and a little extra luxury, most have rental villas in the gardens.

All hotels have a full complement of sporting and leisure facilities, and internally they want for nothing: concierge services, daily laundry, air conditioning and satellite television are standard, as are shops, beauty parlours, health and fitness centres and entertainment for the children.

Meals, generally, are carvery-buffet style offering multiple choices and unlimited quantity to appeal to every taste, with wine included. Most hotels offer an all-inclusive package but for those seeking the exclusive in apres golf cuisine, a la carte dining is readily available in hotels and clubhouses.

For the adventurous, too, there's a selection of beach-side restaurants in nearby villages, or a 40 minute drive will take you to the ancient city of Antalya (population 1.5 million) whose picturesque harbour is a venue for first rate cuisine and evening entertainment.

It doesn't end there: Antalya airport has a new terminal and a new motorway system has reduced the drive to the coast to about 25 minutes. It all adds up to a Utopian situation for the golfing holidaymaker. Iberia had better get its act together, is the unspoken message: the Turks mean business, and there's more to come.

The Belek resort currently has two pairs of courses at each end of its beach and separated by a 10 minute drive with most of the hotels in between. This brings another bonus: there's no need for a rental car, thus further reducing costs. Most hotels have an airport bus service but a shared taxi will cost no more than £20 and, once in situ, getting to the golf courses is simply a matter of picking up the 'phone and requesting transportation.

Getting onto them is not difficult, either, although it's advisable to have hotel reception telephone for a reserved tee time and to establish your discounted green fee (US$50 is standard, about £30), although your tour operator's package should include golf.

The courses are eminently playable, with nothing to choose between them. Each is marginally different from the others and it's generally accepted that the National and Nobilus may be three shots more difficult from the back tees.

National, twice the venue for the PGA Seniors' Belek Open, was designed by the Irish duo of David Feherty and David Jones and a cracking job they made of it. Transforming heavily timbered swamp land into a rolling course evocative of the Carolinas, they drained the water into lakes which influence six holes and retained most of the pine and eucalyptus trees that are a feature of the region.

It's a big site with lots of traditional touches where every fairway is hidden from its neighbours but wide enough to forgive the odd indiscretion. The greens are modestly sized, some are elevated, most tightly guarded.

The par threes will have you salivating and a couple of the two shotters are as good as most. You'll need to drive it passably well, particularly on the par fives but a sound short game and some imagination are prerequisites here. From the back tees this is one the low markers will love, although it won't scare the rabbits up-front.

There's a rambling, traditional-style clubhouse overlooking a lake by the 18th green. Nearby is an open air waterside restaurant that's just the spot for a 'tween-rounds lunch. For more formal occasions the clubhouse restaurant offers a la carte dining each evening, although you'll require reservations.

The course at Gloria GC was designed by an architect new to me, but one whose work I'll search out in future. His name is Michael Guyen, he's French and an exceptional talent. He has created a big course, albeit one requiring finesse and imagination, although built-in options await discovery.

The course is flat, lush and moderately tight, with major trees dominating critical points. It was formerly a pine forest but my guess is that Michael didn't move too many trees!

As with most inventive architects, his signature is evident mainly around the greens. Most are flat, by which I mean level with the fairway, in the traditional style. This creates problems of judgement and perspective and makes them small targets, even though some of them are huge — shades of the Old Course, one is 95 yards long!

They're angled disparately and protected by hummocks and vast saucer bunkers, similar to the waste bunkers common to the Carolinas. The greens ripple like badly laid carpet, some are gently shelved to boot, and with a response akin to putting on marble.

There's one double green, serving the 2nd and the 5th, the like of which I've never seen, in size or configuration. It has a bottle-necked junction, more rolls than an incoming tide and what appear to be about 100 potential pin positions, most of them devilish.

Gloria may be unique in another respect: it has five par threes and five par fives and with the exception of the 9th and 10th, both of which are par four, no two successive holes are of similar par. The tempo is a delight.

It's a well-named course, too; ravishingly beautiful and, like the others, built to USGA specifications. It is owned by a major Turkish building company and no expense was spared. The clubhouse described in the introduction is the one at Gloria. It alone is worth a detour. The course is a bonus.

Like Gloria, Tat Beach is part of a hotel complex with its own stretch of beach, several swimming pools and multiple sporting facilities for all the family. In the case of Tat Beach there are 27 holes of golf, designed by Martin Hawtree. It's a classy piece of work.

This one is more coastal in style, in fact two holes run by the beach and several others are within an 8-iron distance of it. So there's a touch of links here, although much of the remainder involves woodland. Stands of timber form a backdrop to many holes and major trees dominate the second shot but generally speaking the course is receptive and forgiving from the tee.

It's a natural course that already has a venerable look about it. Hawtree discovered a site that required little excavation and he used it admirably, giving Mother Nature only a gentle nudge along the way.

There's a river frontage and a series of lakes and waterways come into play on all three loops, but with only a couple of exceptions the carries are minimal. The water is largely peripheral, although we played it on a windless day. It may prove lethal under adverse conditions.

Those familiar with the re-designed Royal Birkdale would recognise Hawtree's style. Moderately-sized greens are ringed by gentle hummocks and swales that meld into the surrounding terrain, creating a look in sympathy with the setting. Few have more than one bunker, in fact all 27 holes are conspicuous for the paucity of sand. Hawtree is a minimalist of the first order and his skills are evident in abundance at Tat Beach.

David Thomas, one of the world's pre-eminent architects, was unrestrained in his appraisal of the site he was given at Nobilus Golf Club. It opened two years ago and has grown in beautifully.

"The whole region is perfect golfing country," he said, "and the site at Nobilus is spectacular, with 80 foot pine trees, sandy soil and a high water table. I was thrilled with the result."

It helps that he was given virtual carte blanch by the owners, who have also built an opulent clubhouse and clusters of de luxe rental villas on the perimeter, with a de luxe hotel now nearing completion.

The course, which Thomas regards as the equal of any he has designed, could best be described as rural wooded parkland with a hint of links, particularly on open land where six holes run down to a river which he dammed at one point to create a lake.

The principal feature, major trees aside, are the greens, Some of them 700 square yards in size, the Thomas signature. At Nobilus, though, they are more undulating than he usually creates and place an emphasis on approach play and a sound putting technique.

Four courses of such stature, and some cracking hotels, add up to a golf destination of the first order. But there's more. The new courses are coming along nicely and they'll be on-stream before you know it.

David Jones is building a second course at the National, scheduled to open in May, and at the vast resort known as Sirene City they're pulling out all the stops to get a piece of the action.

Within a couple of years the Sirene Hotel group will have two courses, one for club players and another, of 7,000 yards plus and par-72, for championship play. And that's not the cliché commonly associated with such new projects: they mean it. In time they'll be bidding for something big on the European Tour and make no bones about the fact that they have what it takes to achieve their objective.

The major course is now under construction and should open in the autumn; the club course will come on-stream 18 months later to complete a five star complex with a palatial clubhouse and a golf academy.

Set in 230 beach-side hectares with a de luxe hotel and several hundred apartments and villas already in place, they are even building a 250 roomed five star hotel specifically for golfers! This will open in the summer of 2001 just as the first course, being built by European Golf Developments, is bedding down.

The opening promises to be the apogean point of the Paradise Beach success story so far. But it won't be the climax. There's much more to come.

When to go: The climate is comparable to Iberia; summer temperatures hover around 95F (35C) and in winter they average 59F (15C). Early Spring is high season for golf when tee times must be booked and June to mid-September is peak season for hotels, although courses then are virtually deserted. Best period for golf is late-April to May and September to early December when courses are less crowded and temperatures are moderate.

Money matters: Such is inflation in Turkey that many prices in Belek are quoted in US dollars or Sterling. At 950,000 Turkish lira to the £ Sterling you'll become an instant millionaire but wait until you reach Belek and change only sufficient cash for tips and taxis. To avoid confusion and additional exchange costs, pay golf club purchases, including green fees, in Sterling or US dollars. Charge hotel extras to your account and pay by credit card when leaving.

Tips: A vital source of income here and usually well-earned by obliging staff. Rule of thumb says tip roughly half of UK city rates.

Dining out: Antalya has some sound restaurants, particularly around the marina which is 40 minutes away. Most Belek hotels offer buffet/carvery dining for guests on half board but others have a la carte restaurants for those seeking exotica. A gourmet meal for two will cost about £30, including a local wine.

Where to stay: The choice is large but the following are best suited to British guests. All are to 5* standard and warmly recommended.

* Belpark Hotel. Part of an international chain, the Belpark is a three storey de luxe hotel in 20 hectares of gardens with a private beach. Only five years old, it has 160 rooms in the hotel and 320 rooms in a villa complex in the grounds. It sounds large but it has an intimate atmosphere with a cosy lobby and the hotel rooms overlook an indoor atrium-garden. Very romantic and ideal for couples. It has a variety of sporting facilities, a health and fitness club, beauty salon and swimming pools. Golf may be arranged at the nearby National GC for which there's a shuttle bus, also available for airport transfers. Reservations are vital, particularly for the 30 suites. Pleasant, attentive staff enhance a delightful hotel.

* The Gloria Hotel & Golf Club. A lavishly appointed 5* hotel with every facility, including its own golf course, the venue for the PGA Seniors Belek Open. The Gloria has 420 bedrooms, including 80 units in villa-apartments in the expansive gardens that run down to a river and, via a bridge, the beach. There's a health and fitness centre with gymnasium and sauna, a Turkish steam bath, a nightly disco and a piano bar. Classical concerts are staged twice weekly in the summer. A large swimming pool complex has an area for children. Ideal for couples, families and groups, there's a choice of restaurants in the summer months when two outdoor dining areas come into their own. An imposing hotel that sets local standards of excellence with a high guest-staff ratio.

* The Sirene City Hotel & Resort. This is a remarkable resort in 250 wooded, beach-side hectares that has every luxury and service. There's a seven

storey, 300 roomed hotel overlooking a pool complex and the sea and another 240 rooms in low profile apartments in village clusters, each with its own pool, bars and restaurants, mainly open air. Another 250 room de luxe hotel, exclusive to adult golfers, is almost complete overlooking a golf complex. There's a clutch of restaurants and bars, nightly discos and cabarets and every type of entertainment and sport, on water and land. Ideal for all classes of holidaymaker, from couples to groups, and it attracts guests from around the world. It is first class in every respect and may be unique in Europe.

Casa de Campo, the Jewel of the Caribbean

To say that Casa de Campo is an all-inclusive resort is rather like saying that Jack Nicklaus plays golf or that Warren Beatty likes ladies. Located at La Romana in the Dominican Republic, the owners describe it as the most complete resort in the Caribbean and while I've seen several such establishments over the years I've never seen one that ranks higher And that's discounting the world-class golf. You'll gather I'm enthused.

Think of amenities and you'll find them all here. Like a skeet gun club of international repute with a sumptuous new $3 million clubhouse; an equestrian centre with 300 horses, for trail riding or staging rodeos or polo matches or show jumping; and a world class, 13 court tennis club.

There's charter boat fishing, a health and fitness centre with all mod cons, a covey of swimming pools, a necklace of beaches and a smorgasbord of bars, night clubs and restaurants.

Several of the latter are in an authentic replica of a 16th century hill-top village known as Altos de Chavon. It has narrow cobbled streets lined with art galleries, museums, a variety of shops and a tiny church, plus a 5,000 seat amphitheatre, opened by Frank Sinatra, that's a regular venue for concerts, both classical and pop. Evenings here are magical.

Accommodations? You can pay from US$150 to $1,500 a night, depending upon taste, budget and season. There's no hotel as such: there are 280 apartment-style suites, four to a two storey cottage, some large enough for a family; or you could rent one of the 150 luxurious villas with up to four bedrooms that come with maid service.

Or you could push the boat out and have a palatial Excel Club villa that's the last word in exclusivity, with daily maid and butler to serve meals, a private garden, a swimming pool, a bar, a golf cart and everything that opens and shuts.

So throw in the golf and you'll see that here's a place that caters for everyone, no matter their age, style, interest or social standing. It offers a holiday that's sound value or one in the lap of luxury with no expense spared.

It's also a year-round resort and though hot in the summer it's never excessively so because of the cooling sea breezes. And they say the temperatures seldom vary more than 10F summer and winter. The only noticeable difference is that you might need a sweater when you dine by candle light on winter evenings at the lovely restaurant on the beach.

If your geography is fallible, the Dominican Republic, roughly the size of Switzerland, shares an island with Haiti about two hours south of Miami. Its capital, Santo Domingo, was the first city of the New World, with the first cathedral and the first university, both influenced by Christopher Columbus who popped in around 1492, en route to you-know-where.

It's a sprawling island whose five million population is not over-privileged, as you would gather on the 90 minute drive from Santo Domingo airport to the gated estate of Casa de Campo that reclines over 7,000 acres in the south east corner.

The resort began in the 1970s when a sugar company built a collection of villas for its expatriate staff and added a golf course as a recruiting attraction. It has simply grown from there.

Now there are three courses, all designed by Pete Dye who is building a fourth on high ground with dramatic views beyond the River Chavon to the sea, and with a fifth in the planning stage.

The story is a common one in international tourism: a summer resort becomes year-round when the owners realise the demand for golf extends beyond the normal seasons, bringing vital revenue and employment to a needy populace.

And what golf this is! The first course, known as Teeth of The Dog, is ranked by America's leading golf magazines in the world's top 25. Another is its equal, says consensus, and the one under construction appears of comparable quality.

Not far behind in terms of quality is what's known as The Links, a pretty but deceptively demanding resort course stretching to 6,460 yards, that opened in 1974. It starts in benign fashion, becomes successively more challenging and includes a couple of white knuckle holes over the run-in.

It has a pleasing tempo but though more accommodating than its neighbours it's no push-over: some tight driving, evil bunkers and generally small, elevated greens see to that, plus Bermuda rough that's common to all three courses. Find it, hack out, pay your dues and smile. There's no alternative.

Play the Links first, and don't be bashful about using the forward tees (5,590 yards) to test the water. Further advice: even though carts are included take a caddie. They're inexpensive and most are worth their weight in golf balls if only for their ability in reading the Tifdwarf greens that to the uninitiated are an open invitation to blasphemy.

After a couple of holes your man will club you accurately, help keep you on the straight and narrow and find your ball when you stray. When you get to play Teeth of The Dog he'll enhance your enjoyment of one of the great days you'll know in golf.

Pete Dye reckons he's responsible for only 11 holes of the Teeth, that the Good Lord created the seven strung along the rocky beach. He's being too modest. The Lord may have lent a hand here and there but there's no mistaking the Dye hallmarks on a succession of majestic holes, among them three one shotters that maybe without peer.

The ocean is in play on all seven holes — four going out with the Caribbean on the left, three coming home in reverse— but it dominates the three par threes with tee shots that must fly the pounding waves crashing onto rocks — the Teeth of The Dog — planted to protect the course from erosion. Here's a stretch to test your nerve and technique to the limit.

After a tough start into the prevailing wind the fun begins at the 5th, which is 155 yards from the back tees to a green that appears the size of a pool table. It continues on the 7th, all of 225 yards from where the tigers prowl but with a sympathetic gathering bank to the safe side of the tilted green. The 6th? That's index 1; the 8th is index 3, of 449 and 417 yards respectively with carries that could turn your hair white except that outward-bound from this point the prevailing wind comes from behind and across the left shoulder, giving a gentle push to safety.

Coming home is another ball game. Those on a roll who draw or hook have to aim in the general direction of Bermuda and hope the wind co-operates.

Faders love this stretch, holes 15, 16 and 17, par fours of index 4 and 2 which sandwich another pulsating par three, of 185 yards, whose green is out on a headland with sand all round and a stand of trees behind. You could go left and play safe but that would be limp-wristed in the extreme and there's no telling what your second shot might be. You simply must have a crack at the green in what may be the most spectacular hole in golf. Take an extra club and try to hit a high fade, it says here.....

The holes that Dye claims as his own encourage the shakes, too, particularly in the approaches. Most of the greens are off-set and turtle-backed, reminiscent of those by Donald Ross but much more severe. So severe that the pin positions can be downright wicked.

The fairways generally are magnanimous but you can hit two good shots, sensibly laying-up, and walk away with a double bogey before you can blink. Be only a whisker off-line with your pitch and the ball will run off or be kicked away, leaving you another uphill pitch with little or no hope of stopping it close.

Then, like as not, you will have a 30 foot putt which breaks two ways across a green that imitates a marble staircase. That's where your caddie will be invaluable.

Good advice is to use the white tees (6,057 yards) on your debut, simply play the percentages and have fun, with no regard to the score. In fact take it easy and you could score well. Go the other route and you're on death highway, with the coroner waiting around the next bend.

On the other hand, if you have a short game worthy of the name and can stop a four iron where you want it on demand you'll know one of golf's great journeys. This is a course for the strong player in that it may be slightly easier from the back tees (6,888 yards). Patience and imagination hold the key here, plus soft hands and a watchmaker's touch. As our American friends would say: Enjoy!

You'll no doubt want to play the Teeth every day but take a tip: do everything, anything, to have a round on La Romana. It's a private course only five minutes away but if you ask nicely and say you don't mind playing after noon you'll find there are slots available.

The card for the blue tees reads 6,661 yards, par-72. I must presume that someone measured the course at night using an elastic tape measure. I have never hit so many long irons in one round, and I was driving well.

The par fours seem like par fives, the fives were just wishful thinking. Nothing penal, you understand: there's nothing hidden, no vast man traps of bunkers. It's not as complex as the Teeth, either, and although their configurations will give you the vapours the greens are easier to find and hold. It's simply that you'll be hitting lots of shots up-slope, frequently into a breeze, and most of the greens are elevated.

Generally speaking you can open the shoulders, in fact it's necessary. There's no holding back here. Brace yourself! It completes a marvellous combination, the equal of any I know, on a resort that will win a permanent spot on top of your holiday list.

Getting there: American Airlines fly from Heathrow via Miami, and British Airways from Gatwick via a 50 minute flight from San Juan, Puerto Rico. The former requires an overnight stop in Miami and both services fly directly into the resort's airport at La Romana.

Best for golf: October and November offer premium golf and slightly cooler weather. April and May are also appealing but the two resort courses may be closed in sequence for annual maintenance during the last week in April and the first week in May. One course is always open and possibly one loop of the other. Best tee time: afternoons, because most want to play at 8.30!

Climate: The annual temperature range is 75F to 85F, though winter evenings can be chilly. In April I found temperatures between 80-85 with low humidity. Sea breezes and cart (with ice box) made for pleasant golf.

Currency: Local currency is the peso but take US dollars for tips and small purchases at the shopping mall. Use your hotel card to charge anything else to your account, paying with your charge/credit card. All major cards accepted. There's an airport tax of US $10 per person payable, in US dollars only, upon arrival.

Gourmet Golf in La Belle France

It was, in retrospect, a *faux pas* of the first magnitude. A late lunch at the Royal Mougins Golf Club followed by dinner at the exquisite Palme d'Or restaurant would have been an adventure in excess for a starving gourmet. After two days spent sampling the delights of Cannes we should have read the clues, should have guessed that the highlights were still to come.

If you're familiar with such exotica you'll doubtless know of the Palme d'Or. M. Michelin has graced it with two stars and has placed it at the pinnacle of French *haute cuisine*. It is a temple of the culinary arts where the devotees come to worship. Part of the sumptuous Hotel Martinez on La Croisette, the famous beach-side boulevard, it has the Bay of Cannes as a glittering backdrop. Dining here is a celebration of the culinary arts.

There are no black ties or tiaras. Style is the key here, not fashion. The waiters wear lounge suits, like supporting actors in a play with the diners cast as the central characters.

"Champagne blanc or rose, madames et monsieurs?" was the opening line of dialogue as we gathered in the reception lounge. Decisions, decisions... There were more to be come. It proved to be an eight-act play as course followed course, a succession of vintage wines playing counterpoint in the culinary symphony. With lunch still fresh in the mind, we responded manfully but with barely restrained delight.

Our table was six strong and included four nationalities. Conversation sparkled. It was an event of sheer bliss. I will refrain from reciting the menu: it would only induce disbelief tinged with jealousy...

The dinner occupied three hours and was, consensus had it, the finest in our collective memories. A twelve hour fast would have been a more apposite preamble but we, unknowing golfers, had been ambushed by le chef at Royal Mougins, although being gentlemen golfers we blamed our tardy arrival on a late tee time and a demanding course.

In retrospect, if our dinner was unforgettable the lunch was almost as memorable, albeit of simpler fare and style. Give the French their due: when the subject is food they hold top spot on the leader board. Here in the UK we eat to live: in Europe they live to eat and in La Belle France it is a pastime at which they excel. *Formidable!*

So an exclusive golf club is also a magnet for gourmets. If they are golfers too they have the best of both worlds at Royal Mougins. The lunch was a concerto of delights, three courses with a choice of wines, served by multi-lingual staff in a setting that was a feast for all the senses. Heck, you'd want to be a member simply to have entrée to a weekly lunch!

The elevated terrace at Royal Mougins is an integral and much-used accoutrement of the Provençal-style clubhouse and a focal point for the club's social life in a climate that, for much of the year, is close to perfection. Set on the highest point of the wooded estate, it overlooks rolling emerald fairways glimpsed through tree tops and is a natural habitat for *al fresco* diners.

We were there on seniors' day and 40 or so resident ex-pats were lunching after their competition. It was a happy occasion, bubbling with laughter and ribaldry at the prize giving. You'd kill for membership but don't make plans: it is by invitation only and is limited to 700, comprised of 32 nationalities, we gathered. We viewed them with green eyes.

The course, open since 1993, reposes in a secluded valley near the town of Mougins a short drive from Cannes. It is a serene Provençal landscape dominated by a river, venerable trees and ancient stone-wall terracing. You'll deduce it is not displeasing to the eye and the course melts into it in a masterpiece of design and routing. It was laid out by Robert Von Hagge and like his creations at Golf Nationale, Les Bordes and Seignosse, was acclaimed the nation's best new course at its opening. The Peugeot Golf Guide, the game's equivalent of Le Guide Michelin, has it in the nation's leading five courses and among the finest in Europe. Few would debate either ranking.

To extend the culinary theme, this is a main course par excellence, at once tantalising, robust and fulfilling. But it should carry a health warning: I would suggest it is not for those with handicaps in excess of 20. It is too tough, at least at first sighting. The Cannes Open has been staged here. The Tour pros were suitably impressed. They didn't murder it.

It is a par-71 with a card reading from 6,600 yards (SS72) to 4,930 yards (SS69) for the ladies. Most holes have five tees, some have six. So options abound. It is never less than undulating, is hilly in parts with a flatter forest area on the valley floor. You'll face lots of awkward stances and devilish bunker shots.

So variety is the keynote, topographically and technically, too, with a mix of holes ranging from the demanding to the relatively genteel. It calls for every club in the bag and some shots you may not yet have invented.

There are two split-level fairways: the par four 9th, which is index one, and the 18th, a gorgeous par five. The lower levels, where danger lurks, are for those feeling frisky but they'll need to nail the tee shot and find the correct spot. This is a general rule of thumb on most good courses and an imperative here.

From the back tees all but the longest hitters should contemplate a lay-up on certain holes. Risk and reward is the name of the game. It's basic course management and, as always, it adds to the enjoyment of a delightful course where the flag positions on large greens, most of which undulate generously, can accentuate the challenge.

Eight lakes are linked by a river system, with waterfalls and streams to distract, and in a setting of such natural splendour you'd expect a few spectacular holes. You won't be disappointed.

A highlight comes early in the round: the par three 2nd is a wondrous hole played from a vertiginously elevated tee via a sheer drop to a green guarded by a lake and with a waterfall to the left. Depending upon which tee you select, it can measure anything from 140 to 184 yards. The flag position here can be a killer, although the large green offers options as well as the opportunity to take three putts! The hole is named Angel's Dive. A few have no doubt invoked the devil but it's an outstanding one shotter. Take three or better and you'll be off to a flying start.

Big hitters who have breakfasted on red meat will relish a couple of the short par fours. The 12th and the 14th are right-angled dog-legs with hidden greens but drivable for those capable of cutting the corner over towering trees. A playing partner eagled the 12th after a 275-yard tee shot to 12 feet. Mind you, he plays to a handicap of one!

You'll gather we had a fun round but even if you play like a goose (and many do on their debut here) you'll have a round to remember in a lovely corner of France. It's a grand way to develop an appetite. But a word of caution: don't over-indulge at lunch, eh?!

Unless you are familiar with the locality Cannes wouldn't leap to mind in terms of a golfing holiday. The world knows it as the natural habitat of playboys, film stars, beach bimbos, million dollar yachts and stretch limousines and while it offers all the known pleasures of the flesh golf has been somewhat low on its list of hedonistic pastimes.

Not that it's a closely guarded secret, far from it. In keeping with world-wide trends, the number of golfing tourists is increasing annually, drawn by the 18 golf clubs strung along the Cote d'Azur, four of which are within a short drive of La Croisette, the boulevard that is the main artery of Cannes and the home of several of the world's most luxurious hotels.

The crown jewel, the focal point of the necklace, is the Hotel Martinez, an extraordinary hotel of exemplary standards, taste and service. Those who know it, and they include the leading lights attending the annual Cannes Film Festival, would consider no alternative.

Recently refurbished with a seemingly unlimited budget, the Martinez is seven floors of sheer opulence, largely in the art deco style. Even the standard rooms are sumptuous. Its first floor is the natural home of the aforementioned Palme d'Or, there's a less formal pool-side restaurant and another, more casual, on the hotel's private beach, just across La Croisette. Fine food is a pre-occupation in Cannes, you'll gather. All manner of hedonism may be enjoyed at the Martinez; there is every diversion you'd expect of one of the world's great hotels.

A gentleman of a generous disposition could win serious Brownie points by inviting his best beloved to share the pleasures to be found on the seventh floor. Here, in a major consequence of the recent cost-no-object refurbishment, will be found two penthouse suites, the ultimate in luxurious living, each spread over some 500 square meters, each with a huge terrace giving views over the Bay of Cannes. A monarch would feel quite at ease in such regal surroundings. A butler is provided, of course.

Nearby are a number of junior suites, smaller but of comparable quality and, most significantly, the now-acclaimed Givenchy Spa. This covers 900 square meters and offers every facility for pampered good health and beauty. It has been rated the finest in France, a unique haven that has become an imperative for many guests of the female persuasion.

And while your best beloved is becoming even more beautiful you could slip quietly away and avail yourself of the delights at Royal Mougins. Yes, the Martinez offers golf packages. Here, nothing is overlooked except the glittering Bay of Cannes.

Golf finds a natural home in Brittany

Flashing swords and thundering hooves are not usually associated with golf, even though the game is both royal and ancient, but take a golfing holiday in France and with a hint of imagination the connection is easily established for those of a romantic disposition.

The reason: castles and medieval châteaux abound here where knowing golfers congregate, particularly in the south and near the channel coast where in the Middle Ages rival kings of England and France spent their lives knocking seven bells out of each other in pursuit or defence of empires.

An example: see the great castle that is the focal point of the golf resort of La Bretesche and if you've an ounce of soul you can almost hear the hoof beats and the clanking armour and visualise the knights riding off into the woodland mist rising from the lake that was the castle's main defence. It may be the most distinctive landmark in French golf and it helps to draw thousands of visiting holiday makers to this enchanting region of Brittany. There's another castle, even bigger, not too far away at Nantes.

It's some way removed from a golf course, being at the hub of this ancient and charming city, but there's a connection, nonetheless. Because thanks to its airport and a newly launched service by GB Air, Nantes has become the gateway to a golfing destination *par excellence*, the centre piece of the region known as the Western Loire Valley.

It's only two hours flying time from London Gatwick but in terms of ambience it's another world. Once the capital of Brittany — the Breton flag still flutters in profusion on the castle ramparts — parts of the city date to 200 BC and while there's no evidence of that by-gone era history permeates what may be a model conurbation.

It has a population of 600,000 these days, a high tech city with a university that is renowned for its research into subjects esoteric. And even though it is 40 miles from the Atlantic coast its port is still the fourth largest in France, thanks to the great river that once encircled it.

Thus it was an island, which must have presented a major logistical hiccup for aspiring invaders, and it remained that way until early in the last century when one arm of the river was filled in, allowing the city to burgeon. Where once the river flowed is now the principal boulevard and tramway, a source of considerable surprise when you learn of this while sipping a glass of Chablis *al fresco* on what was once the river bank.

Some traditionalists of a certain vintage still mourn the change, it seems; modernists laud what must have been a considerable feat of engineering which has brought an expansive aspect to the newer section of the city where imposing buildings line broad, tree-lined avenues tailor-made for pavement cafés and promenading.

'Tis a handsome place indeed, with a host of attractions, historical, gastronomic and cultural, to enchant the thousands of visitors who discover the place each year. Golfers are joining their number and soon they will be legion, drawn by a collection of courses of the first order.

Some will prefer to base themselves in Nantes, to enjoy the charms of the city, and sally forth each day for golf. Four courses, L'Epinay, Vignen, Nantes-Erdre and Pornic, are within a short drive. Somewhat further afield are Savenay, about 45 minutes, St Jean de Monts, about 70 minutes, La Bretesche, about 80 minutes and La Baule, about 85.

The development boom that a decade ago put France to the fore of European golf has virtually run its course but the end results are now part of the tapestry of French life and a magnet for golfing tourists.

Consider that 15 years ago there were 93 golf clubs and 43,613 registered players in a population comparable to Britain's but with a land mass three times as large. In mid-1990 the statistics were 355 clubs and 173,700 registered players. Now there are 514 courses and the French Golf Federation is contemplating a membership of 300,000 by the end of the decade.

What's more, unlike the majority of British clubs, many of those in France are dedicated to pay-and-play, commercial ventures combining private housing and extensive facilities for visiting golfers.

One such organisation is Formule Golf, a subsidiary of the French Water Board, which manages, among others, seven courses on the Brittany coast and 11 on the Vendee, the Atlantic coast.

These clubs have limited local membership and rely heavily for revenue on visitors and their use of clubhouse facilities such as the restaurants, which, without exception, offer admirable and inexpensive fare as well as good value green fees. Or there are all-inclusive packages offering golf and accommodation at selected hotels and inns. The value is astonishing for the quality.

Formule Golf has two clubs in the Western Loire region, both deserving of investigation. One is Golf de Nantes-Erdre, which is only 10 minutes from the Place Royale in the centre of Nantes. It would be an admirable starting point for your stay in the region.

The course, set in 50 hectares of parkland with three lakes as garnish, is an equable lay-out, as pretty as can be with a variety of flora to admire. The high water table brings lush fairways that stretch a course of 6,600 yards, par-71, from the back tees but there are options further forward for those past the first flush of youth. For those who decide to linger hereabouts there's a surfeit of attractions in terms of golf and accommodation relatively locally.

Firstly, you should tarry for 18 holes at L'Epinay, a course designed by Britain's Martin Hawtree. Its name derives from the château that is its centrepiece. It's no great distance at all: you'll find it at Carquefou just off the A11, the road to Angers.

L'Epinay is first class in every respect, a course whose technical demands are not reflected in a seemingly modest card of 6,370 yards. It's huge fun, the presentation is excellent and the facilities are first rate. Upon reflection, forget my remarks apropos 18 holes: take a long lunch and stay for 36!

Not too far away is Golf de Savenay, another property of Formule Golf, an outstanding course of some challenge designed by Michael Gabon in 1987.

Equidistant from Nantes and Saint-Nazaire on the RN165, Savenay runs close to 7,000 yards from the back tees, a par-73 that overlooks the River Loire and winds its way between lakes and woodlands on the edge of the Briere marshes.

We're talking serious golf here, and to complete an appealing picture the acclaimed Manoir du Rodoir, offering all the good things in a picture postcard setting, is close to hand and convenient for the other courses. It's a blissful prospect.

Unlike the centres of golf in Spain and Portugal, the French resorts are geographically widespread, although the more renowned are within sniffing distance of the sea, particularly in this region. Which brings me to introduce La Baule.

The course, designed by Peter Alliss and David Thomas, opened to great acclaim in 1976, with a third loop, designed by Marc Guignon, being added seven years ago. The new loop is now being extended to 18 holes and with a superb practice facility designed by Jack Nicklaus you'll understand why La Baule is recognised as the premier golf resort in France. It is outstanding by any criteria, a total resort with every amenity.

And then there's the new Hotel du Golf International Le Saint-Denac. Located in the heart of the La Baule course and two minutes from the clubhouse, it is owned and managed by the esteemed Lucien Barriere group.

There are 145 luxurious rooms where guests enjoy free access to all the facilities; the casino and nightclub, the golf, tennis and bicycles to investigate the generously endowed estate. There's a shuttle coach to the golf club and into the town of La Baule, a famed beach-side resort that is a year-round magnet for tourists from all over the world. It has most of the facilities of Cannes but without the commercialism and with rather more charm. The climate, too, is comparable.

The weather, indeed, is one of the aces up the local sleeve. The tropical plants and palm trees to be found at the gateway to the Loire Valley endorse claims by the natives that their climate is some way removed from that further north. It's a boon to golfers seeking an alternative winter holiday destination or simply a short break, which the new air service now allows.

The summers are a delight — although France generally should be avoided in July and August when the natives holiday en masse — but those who visit in late autumn or early spring would have it no other way. Prices are lower, the golf courses are under-populated and good accommodation is more accessible.

Golf aside, the scenery is worth any drive: a succession of well endowed villages with neatly trimmed hedges, flower pots in profusion and no signs of litter or graffiti. One suspects that vandals receive short shrift hereabouts, such is the obvious civic pride, and crime seems minimal.

Which succinctly describes the region known as the Western Loire Valley. One could drop anchor anywhere hereabouts and savour the rich variety of life that is the essence of France at its best.

Easy to see, then, why monarchs would fight to their last breath to claim it as their own.

How the Iron Duke became the father of French golf

The Duke of Wellington was not noted for his associations with anything so frivolous as sport, least of all French golf. Indeed, he was probably blissfully ignorant of the game which until recent times in France was comparable in popularity to alligator wrestling, perhaps, or underwater ballroom dancing.

But although he may not have been aware of it, the Iron Duke made a considerable contribution to the French version of the Royal and Ancient game, albeit *en passant*. It seems that during his Spanish campaign the Duke occasionally withdrew with his officer corps to France for a spot of rest and recreation: more specifically, he took them just over the border to Pau, in the Bayonne district.

There, at the foot of the Pyrenees, in the enchanting little town that was the birthplace of Henry IV, he laid the foundations of an Anglo-French association that was unique in its time and which, 160 years later, is still thriving. There's an exclusive English Club originally patronised by his officers and which remains in daily use by expatriates and the local gentry possessed of English cultural and business associations. There's a casino, reputedly the oldest in France, which owes its origins to the Iron Duke's men, as does the golf club, formally founded in 1856 and thus the oldest in Europe..

Its headquarters, not two miles from the town centre, is a lovely old farmhouse, all creaking timbers and mellowed stone, with a splendid dining room and irrepressible hospitality. A bubbling river winds its way around the lush, tree-lined golf course that is endearingly rustic in its design. The mountains, often snow-capped, form a backdrop. It's not difficult to become enthralled.

Pau is typical of French golf: providing one observes the etiquette and books a tee time — and a table for lunch — a welcome is assured. France is the most egalatarian of countries but in golf they are sticklers for form, if only because of the increasing demand.

And if that last phrase has raised your eyebrows, obviously you are not aware that the game in France has not simply blossomed, it has boomed to the point of explosion. Indeed on a pro rata basis France leads the world in the phenomenal expansion of the game at club level.

Consider these facts: in the late 1980s there were 93 golf clubs and 43,613 registered players in a country with a population comparable to Britain's but with a land mass three times that of ours.

In the mid-1990s the statistics were 355 clubs and 173,700 registered players. (The UK, in contrast, has some 1.5 million members of 2,100 clubs.)

Such is the rate of growth that it is difficult to establish the precise figures on a monthly basis, but it's reckoned that there are now 410 clubs in operation and that the figure will reach 500 within the year. These are projections confirmed by the news that when the last count was made there were 100 additional courses under construction, 68 in final planning stages and literally hundreds of others pencilled in for feasibility study. The French Golf Federation is contemplating a membership of 500,000, perhaps before the turn of the century.

The significance of this in terms of golfing holidays is that because of the country's egalitarian nature the vast majorty of these new clubs will come on-stream as tourist attractions: the facilities of French golf clubs, even in exclusive residential areas, such as Mougins near Cannes or Hossegor near Biatritz, are readily available to visiting golfers prepared to observe etiquette.

What's more, unlike the majority of British clubs which are based on private membership, a large percentage of those in France are dedicated to 'pay and play', commercial ventures combining private housing and extensive facilities for visiting golfers. They have limited local membership and rely heavily on visitors for revenue, through green fees and the use of clubhouse facilities such as their restaurants which, almost without exception, offer admirable and inexpensive fare.

All good news for British golfers seeking holidays of quality and variety: Indeed, there are those Francophiles among us who aver that in terms of convenience, cuisine and quality of accommodations France has no equal. The golf is a glorious bonus and it abounds, from the Alps to the Riviera, from the Normandy coast to the Spanish border.

Unlike the centres of golf in Spain and Portugal, the French resorts are geographically wide-spread, although the more renowned are within ozone sniffing distance of the sea. The coastal regions of Brittany, Normandy, the Cote d'Azur and the Cote Basque may be regarded as the principal centres and, discounting Pau for the moment, the latter is certainly the spiritual home of French golf.

Dieppe, whose golf club was founded in 1887, Le Touquet (1904), Deauville and Hardelot, all resorts with casinos, abundant de luxe hotels and within a brief journey time of the Cinque Ports, were where French golf tourism took a substantial foothold before and between the wars.

The present boom has widened the selection almost beyond credulity. The region now has so many superb courses, all with agreeable accommodation nearby, that one is totally spoiled for choice and it is impossible to even attempt to list them. Instead, you are referred to a splendid map, available from the French Tourist office in London, specifically designed with the visiting golfer in mind.

From Normandy, the golfing Francophiles moved down the coast, via the ports of Cherbourg and St Malo, to savour the multifarious delights of Brittany and to consolidate the ancient Scottish one founded at Dinard Golf Club in 1887. Here, too, new courses dot the lovely countryside where driving, in a region redolent of the West Country of which it was once a part, is such a delight.

With such a generous foothold, the French game began to attract visitors prepared to travel further afield in this vast and beautiful country and soon the Cote d'Azur and the Cote Basque, for long sub-tropical winter retreats for the seriously wealthy, fell willing victim to the golfing invaders.

There has been a golf course in the hills above Monte Carlo since 1911, and at Cannes the Mandelieu club, one of several in the locality where a course by Robert Trent jones has just opened, dates to 1891. But it is the Cote Basque, with the exquisite old resort town of Biarritz at its epicentre, that has long been regarded as the spiritual horne of the game in France. Once merely a fishing port until discovered and made famous by the patronage of Empress Eugenic, wife of the Emperor Napoleon, it has been the winter playground of European nobility for the better part of a century.

Doubtless prompted by the influence of the ancient club at Pau, about an hour away by road, golf has been played at the Biarritz Golf Club since 1888. And in addition to the several new courses in the region there are three other long-established clubs in the immediate environs of the town: Hossegor, a fourth and of world class, is a short drive away, with a fifth just over the border in Spain. Plainly, then, this beachside community, a pleasant 150 mile drive through wooded country south from Bordeaux, is a major attraction for international golfing visitors who delight in the picturesque courses, their facilities and the welcome extended.

There is, though, more significance to Biarritz than its prominence as a tourist centre. The town has produced a succession of the country's most gifted players whose accomplishments have helped raise the profile of the game domestically, encouraging its popularity and contributing in no small way to the present boom.

Why it should be so is a matter for conjecture, but the fact is that with one notable exception all the great French players have been women. Four of them, indeed, would be numbered among the greatest ever and of those three came from Biarritz.

The most renowned, without doubt, carried a famous name before ever she picked up a golf club. Catherine Lacoste, now Prado, once the world's greatest woman golfer, learned the game at the La Nivelle club. I first saw her play in the 1964 Espirito Santo, the world's amateur teams' championship for women, at

St Germain, near Paris. At 19 years of age, against the very best field then ever gathered in international women's golf, she took the individual honours and swept the French team to a famous victory.

It was obvious, as time was to prove, that here was an extraordinary talent. By the time of her premature retirement from international golf she had re-written the history book. In 1967 at the Hot Springs Golf Club, Virginia, she became the first amateur, the youngest player and the first foreigner to win the United State's Women's Open Championship.

In 1969 she won the British Ladies' Open Amateur at Royal Portrush, and in the same year took the United States Women's Amateur to complete an historic hat-trick within two years. Almost en passant, she won the French championship four times between 1967 and 1972.

One of her team mates in those historic times was Brigitte Varangot, who was French champion on six occasions, the first in 1961 at 21, and was the British champion in 1963, '65 and '68. These two precocious talents were part of a succession of great French women players: Cecilia Mourgue d'Algue and Lally Vagliano, later the Viscomtesse de St Sauveur, were both British and French champions and the figureheads of their respective national teams which enjoyed unprecedented success. They were the trail-blazers who set unimagined standards in international golf, and whose banner has recently been passed to another remarkable girl, also from Biarritz.

Marie-Laure de Lorenzi had an outstanding early career but since leaving the amateur ranks in 1986 has turned the European LPGA Tour on its ear. She won professional tournaments almost immediately and in 1989 topped the Order of Merit with ten victories and winnings of £77,000. It reached the stage where the rest were virtually playing for second place each week; and they're not eagerly anticipating her recovery from the elbow injury that plagued her last year.

Although Catherine Lacoste's great record was a landmark in French golfing history, the first great Gallic victory in Open events predates hers by 60 years! It was a remarkable story.

Arnaud Massey left France for Scotland at the turn of the century as a left-hander but once there was persuaded to switch to the orthodox. That the transformation was a success was proved in the 1905 Open Championship at St Andrews when he placed fifth in the great event won by James Braid. He repeated that feat the following year at Muirfield and at Hoylake in 1907 he became the first continental player to win the championship, beating J.H. Taylor, Ted Ray and James Braid in the process.

It goes almost without saying that Massey, too, was a native of Biarritz! Like Catherine Lacoste 60 years later, he played much of his early golf at La Nivelle CC.

His male successors in the French professional ranks have enjoyed only limited success over the years, but with the expansion of the European Tour — this year's 38 tournaments offer a total of £20 million in prize money with several events due to be staged in France — more of their leading male amateurs are taking the plunge. The Swedes have shown it can be worthwhile.

More, the growing stature of French golf has been recognised in a most tangible fashion: each November the European Tour Academy stages its annual tournament for aspiring professionals at La Grande Motte near Montpellier. If your geography is rusty, that's in the Languedoc region of South Eastern France, just north of the Spanish border.

En route to his first summer camp at the foot of the Pyrenees, the Duke of Wellington would have passed close by. Doubtless the present-day burghers of Pau and Biarritz, golfers all, are eternally grateful that he turned left and not right.

Praia d'el Rey: finding gold on the Silver Coast

Journalistic scoops are rare in my line of work. Occasionally my colleagues will discover a new resort or perhaps a golf course with hitherto hidden qualities, but finding something to grab the headlines and send ripples through the industry is so unusual as to be unique.

Which nicely places Praia d'el Rey into the perspective it merits. You'll not have heard of it yet because, completed two years ago, it opened only in June and few British golfers wander as far as the Costa Prata (the Silver Coast), north of Lisbon.

So unless you've stumbled across it, as I did, the name won't ring any bells. Rest assured it will, in time, and if you're prepared to drive the extra hour from Lisbon airport — a new motorway helps — you'll be rewarded beyond imaginings. The contributing factors are three-fold: it's that *raris avis*, an Iberian links; it has a setting of great beauty, and its design will quicken the pulse.

The architect is the expatriate American Cabell Robinson, a name familiar to those who relish Moroccan golf. His work graces every major city in that golf-mad kingdom but I'll wager none fulfilled him as did the jewel that is Praia d'el Rey.

It hasn't been placed in the national rankings yet, simply because it's not been inspected. When those who indulge in such activities get around to it they'll face a simple exercise: to install it at the top of the pile and shuffle the others down a peg. That's not mere hyperbole: Praia d'el Rey is the finest course in Portugal and some way beyond.....

Its style and character apart, it has something lacking at both Valderrama and San Laurenzo, by consensus the two leading courses in Iberia. It is not merely open to the public, visitors are warmly welcomed at fees which mock the quality. And such are the options that it is eminently playable no matter what your handicap.

I discovered it on a perfect summer's evening, the loveliest time of day on any links, to find the lowering sun glinting off the bent grass greens and decanting shadows into the undulations on rolling fairways replicating the restless ocean in the background. I could barely believe my luck, or my eyes.

Four holes are strung along the edge of cliffs overlooking the Atlantic; another six are adjacent, with the remainder a touch inland, four of them lightly wooded and with a hint of heathland.

No two holes are remotely similar, and I dare say that the knowing golfer could play here for a week and face a different challenge on every shot.

He'd finally get it right, no doubt, and have the time of his life analysing the architectural nuances.

They are at once numerous and subtle: the rye grass fairways are generous in width but don't always appear so. Here a sand hill obscures part of one, ostensibly narrowing the tee shot target, while a tree on an up-slope serves a similarly distracting purpose on another. Hummocks on the front edge create illusion on a long narrow green, while mounds and swales and gently rising ground confound any approach shot lacking precision and judgement. Illusion is rampant; imagination, authority and confidence are the keys.

And yet it is far from penal, unless you step out of your depth on the back tips and here even the scratch man will need to keep his wits about him. There are hidden depressions and diagonal ridges to obscure, deflect or gather and pot bunkers to guide or ensnare, depending upon ability and ambition. Precise clubbing is imperative and you'll use your full armoury here.

The options include at least five tees on each hole and I'm not referring to those boring airport runway jobs. All are islands, isolated and staggered and each offers a line of shot commensurate with its ranking.

The greens range from small to expansive, as strategy demands, and are frequently on the diagonal with artfully-placed bunkers creating nuisance value. Some greens are markedly elevated, pulpit-style; others are only slightly raised, their up-slopes a counter to the weak approach, and one or two are flat, or appear so from long iron range. But nothing is as it appears here.

A purist could simply walk Praia de'l Rey for a week, drinking in all the architectural expertise and natural delights that Robinson has recruited. For above all, like all the great old links the architect has sought to emulate, Praia de'l Rey is essentially a product of Mother Nature. Robinson, spoiled for choice in potential green sites, simply lent a hand here and there, highlighting the salient factors and polishing the gems he found along the way. He must have whooped for joy at first sight of it. The result is obviously a labour of love, one that took ten years to reach fruition from his first sighting....

"The combination of cliffs, dunes, extraordinarily rich ground cover vegetation and pine forests ranked this site somewhere between a nine and a ten," he said. "The only sites I'm familiar with that have this combination of features, especially the cliffs and dunes, are places like Cypress Point and Pebble Beach, and that's not bad company."

Not bad indeed. Those were the names that sprang to mind when I first saw the gem he has produced.

The course measures 7,113 yards from the tiger tees and 6,144 from the most forward men's tees, with a par of 72. Unusually, all four par fives are single figure index holes, as much a tribute to their lay-out as to the constantly-shifting Atlantic breeze. The 17th is stroke one because at 627 yards it may be the longest three shotter in Europe. It's a dog-leg, right to left, and uphill after the turn. A heroic hole....

It's part of a four hole finishing stretch that from the back is as tough as any, wind or no wind. But the counter-balance comes with some lilting par fours, including a brace that are drivable when the breeze and form are conducive. The rest are simply unforgettable — the par threes would collectively grace any course you'd care to name.

Great sites merit great courses but successfully converting one into the other is never easy and not always achieved. In this instance Robinson has created a monument to flair, setting standards to which others can merely aspire.

To compliment such a masterpiece there's a clubhouse and practice facilities of the first rank. So nothing has been overlooked, nothing skimped. Go there, play it, take your camera. You won't believe your eyes, or your luck.

Fact file:

> Praia d'el Rey Golf Club, Vale de Janelas, Apartado 2, 2510 Obidos, Portugal.

Location:

> From Lisbon take Highway IC 1 north, heading for Torres Vedras, or the new motorway. Just south of the town of Obidos turn left in the village of Serra de'l Rey and follow signs.

Maldonaldo and Montenmedio and a tale to warm the heart

The name Alejandro Maldonaldo will mean nothing to you unless, that is, you've been to Montenmedio and if I have to qualify the latter with the appendage "golf club" then you won't know that either. If the names are familiar you can probably guess what comes next. If neither rings a bell, you have a treat in store simply reading what follows. In this age of the bottom line it's a tale to warm the heart.

It's about an uncommonly altruistic Spanish tycoon who decided that 300 hectares of coastal wilderness he owns in the region of Cadiz was too beautiful not to share. So he set about creating a low key resort on part of it, fencing off the rest as a nature reserve that was to become a major attraction.

A lover of horses and carriage driving tournaments, he then built an equestrian centre, an arena and a museum guaranteed to delight the aficionados of his sport. He followed that with an 18 hole golf course that will thrill anyone who has ever teed up.

That's where Alejandro comes in. No, he's not the owner, who insists upon remaining anonymous. He is the course architect.

Let me amend that. Alejandro designed and built the course, virtually by hand. Now, five years after the opening, he's the greenkeeper, his original calling, who lives and breathes for Montenmedio. He probably sleeps there.

It's the only course he's ever laid out and, a man of simple origins, he claims to know little of the intricacies of design. Called in by the owner from another club, he says he merely did what comes naturally. He paced the land for weeks, searching out green sites, then he shaped each one by hand after clearing a path for the fairways between the umbrella pines and cork oaks to link greens and tees.

Bunkers came later, when all else was completed. Earth movement and excavation was virtually non-existent. He worked hand in hand with Mother Nature, just as the first great architects did more than a century ago. The end result is a jewel of rare lustre, a glorious addition to Spanish golf and a memorial to integrity and flair.

It doesn't end there. While perforce a commercial venture, revenue appears of only passing interest. More important, according to the new manager, was to create a first class course with the emphasis on service and enjoyment. To this end the tee times, of 15 minute intervals, will be restricted to 60 players a day!

A realistic green fee of 5,500 pesetas will give access to a course of only 6,500 yards but which, because of the rolling terrain, offers a considerable challenge with its subtle dog-legs and small, cunningly contoured greens. The rough is minimal, the bunkering astute and limited. So the essence is on strategy, with options for all classes of player.

A sumptuous clubhouse is now fully operational and there are plans for a small de luxe hotel. If you're any where in the vicinity you should make every effort to play Montenmedio. It will lift your spirits. It's off the beaten track but easy to find, being 40 minutes north of Sotogrande on the main Cadiz road, and 50 minutes south of Jerez, which is 10 minutes from Montecastillo.

You'll have heard of the latter, naturally. It's been the venue for the Volvo Masters and in terms of architectural pedigree it occupies the other end of the spectrum from Montenmedio.

It's a Nicklaus design, a big, muscular course that demands total golf: strong driving, sound course management and imaginative approach shots. Then comes the difficult bit.

The greens hold the key to scoring with their subtle breaks and slopes and intimidating size and speed. Miss the hole and you'll have a ten footer back: three stabs. Do that a couple of times and your stroke will become tentative, compounding the problems.

But it's great sport in a spectacular setting, a course that's improving with maturity after ten years or so. Play it on wheels, though: like most American architects, Big Jack used the site to its best advantage and that often brings long walks between green and tee with few short cuts on foot.

Stay at the Hotel Montecastillo which overlooks the course and you'll double the treat. It's five star with every creature comfort. As a guest you'll find the green fees most agreeable at 3,300 pesetas, or about £15, and a shared cart is 4,000 pesetas.

That's outstanding value for one of Spain's premier courses. Couple it with Montenmedio and you'll enjoy a holiday to dine out on at the club.

Golf Resorts in the Good Old US of A

Pinehurst: where a golfing holiday is an annual pilgrimage

Pinehurst is recognised as the cradle of American golf. It ranks alongside St Andrews as the place most golfers hope to see, in fact 'tis said in US golfing circles that you don't go to Pinehurst on vacation; you go there on a pilgrimage. Some families have been visiting for generations.

This North Carolina resort is more than merely venerable and historic: it is the oldest in the world, the template for every golf resort built since it opened in 1896. From small beginnings it evolved into the ultimate resort with renowned accommodations and an all-encompassing infrastructure with incomparable facilities, activities and service.

Initially it was a rudimentary holiday destination attracting New Yorkers escaping their harsh winters. Golf was a secondary attraction, catered for by a rustic nine holes created by a friend of owner James Tufts, a Boston pharmacist who discovered the site in 1895. Nearby was a halt on the Boston-Miami railway line and that was the key to success. Tufts called in a Boston architect to replicate a New England village and named it Pinehurst. It had a small hotel (the Holly Inn, now beautifully restored), two boarding houses and cottages and a general store, all edging the village green. Then Tufts met a young Scottish immigrant named Donald Ross. Tufts hired Ross on a handshake and the direction of US golfing history was changed forever in what may have been the most fortuitous meeting in international sport. Formerly assistant green keeper to Old Tom Morris at St Andrews and then professional at Royal Dornoch, Ross converted the nine holes into a quality course of 18 holes. Then he built another, and another, until there were four. Pretty soon, Tufts needed more accommodation and in 1901 opened what would become the most famous resort hotel in America. From that point the project expanded beyond imaginings.

The original village remains largely unchanged and although it has grown to encompass a cluster of restaurants, a variety of shops and several boutique hotels it is still true to the original concept, formulated when electric lights were a novelty and the pace of life was unhurried.

Now Pinehurst caters to every imaginable individual sport that doesn't involve an engine, it has eight golf courses served by three club houses. Its famed Number 2 course has a permanent place in America's top five and has become a regular venue for the US Open and the stage for every major golf event, amateur and professional, in the United States.

Thousands flock there each month, pulses quickening as they turn into the driveway whose terminus is the regal Carolina Hotel, known for a century as the Queen of The South. Colonnaded, pristine white and with a gleaming copper roof, it oozes the style and the aura that is the very essence of Pinehurst and yet it is as homely and welcoming as your granny's parlour, with an ambience enhanced by the aroma of millions of pine trees that form the backdrop to this all-encompassing resort.

Some say that if Pinehurst had only one golf course the world would still beat a path there, week in and week out. As the great Jack Nicklaus has it: "Pinehurst is more than good golf courses. It's a state of mind." James Tufts would be delighted.

For most golfers a dream would be to stay at Pinehurst for eight days and play each of the eight courses in turn. For those to whom such a dream is beyond imaginings, here's a hint of what you'll be missing. Try not to cry!

The courses have been a century in the making and so cumulatively they show the many styles of architecture that have evolved over that period, from the ancient to the modern.

The first four were laid out by Donald Ross, who learned his craft while assistant to Old Tom Morris at St Andrews. So although they have been up-dated over the years the Scottish influence is still apparent. Indeed, this has governed the philosophy of the great architects who followed Ross at Pinehurst, where short game expertise is paramount and the game is played mainly along the ground.

The early courses tend to be shorter, with smaller greens and distinctive bunkering but with nuances aplenty. Imagination and sound course management are imperatives and more important than length of shot. Indeed, as on many British links, it's easy here to run out of fairway into the pines. Courses **No.1** and **No.3** are classical examples of the genre and both are perfect for an unspoiled afternoon.

Donald Ross would recognise Course **No.4** but he'd be scratching his head. His original routing aside, it's virtually a new course, designed by Tom Fazio as a tribute to Ross. It was the venue for the 2008 US Amateur Championship so if you're feeling frisky you might want to open your campaign here. But beware: 140 pot bunkers dot the landscape and there's water at the 13th and 14th holes, part of some of the most picturesque scenery at Pinehurst.

Opened in 1961, Course **No.5** holds true to the Ross philosophy that Mother Nature is the best guide in golf architecture. Hence, there's lots of variety in the layout: uphill and downhill shots, left-to-right and right-to-left fairways, long and short par fours. The course has more water hazards than any other at Pinehurst and it is very playable and an enjoyable exercise if you are still a little rusty.

Course **No.6** reopened in 2005 as a championship course after renovations by Tom Fazio that included new putting greens and re-bunkering of the entire course. The terrain here is more undulating and so a test from the tee, in fact the homeward loop is one the most difficult anywhere. It's a classical Fazio design.

Set on rugged land, **No.7** is one of the more dramatic of Pinehurst courses. This Rees Jones gem uses the topography to both assist and challenge the golfer—shots down off many tees into the fairway, back up on a number of holes into the large, undulating greens. Add the wetlands that dot the landscape, along with vast expanses of the sand, and this one will leave you visually stimulated. You'll need to keep your wits about you here.

Designed by Tom Fazio and opened in 1996 to celebrate the Pinehurst centenary, Course **No.8** replicates old-style Ross features such as dips and swales around the sloping greens. Like the old time links, the greens and tees are close together, making it a pleasure to walk. The venue for the PGA Club Pro Championship in 1997 and 1998, it is a proven championship course that daunts and delights all who play it. Located some two miles from the main clubhouse, it is a worthy celebration of a century of great golf.

What of Course **No.2**? The most famous and challenging of them all is fittingly left until last and deserves its own special treatment. For my review of Pinehurst No.2, compiled as *Golf Monthly*'s preview of the 1999 US Open, go to page 26.

Location:
   Pinehurst is in the Sand hills area of North Carolina some 75 miles from Raleigh Durham, the nearest airport and major conurbation. The city of Charlotte, NC, which also has an airport, is 120 miles away.

Facilities and activities:
   Health and beauty spa; fitness centre, croquet, scenic walks; tennis; cooking courses; helicopter rides; horse riding; carriage tours, quad biking; scuba diving and fishing and sailing on Lake Pinehurst. which has a man-made beach. There is a kids' club, where youngsters from ages 3-12 have supervised activities. In addition, there are bicycles, horse riding, hay rides, tennis, swimming pools and various activities on and around Lake Pinehurst.

Where to stay:

Pinehurst has 427 guest rooms throughout its 2,000-acre property, located within three hotels (The Carolina, The Holly Inn and The Manor), 44 villa rooms and 30 condominiums. A 1,600 square feet Presidential Suite was added to the property in 2008. Guests seeking a more relaxed atmosphere would appreciate The Manor, a sportsman-style lodge.. Families and larger groups would enjoy the spaciousness and comfort of the luxurious villas and condos.

Dining options:

Various, but The Carolina Room in the hotel is an imperative for at least one evening.

Alternatively, there are options in the village, which is a stroll from the hotel. They include the romantic 1895 Grille at The Holly Inn and the informal Tavern, also at The Holly, which is open for lunch and dinner each day. In addition, there are other informal options for casual meals, plus a pub, in the village of Pinehurst and the surrounding area of Sandhills..

When to go:

Unless there is snow, which happens occasionally, golf is playable year-round at Pinehurst. Mid-summer temperatures are as you'd expect in a southern state (July's average high is 89F; the average low is 69F) but spring and autumn are perfect for golf and most sporting activities.

Getting there:

The nearest international airport is at Raleigh Durham, 74 miles away. A limousine transfer is available upon request.

Getting around:

A complimentary limousine service is available for getting around the resort. Limos are also available for daytime trips beyond the resort.

Packing tips & dress code:

Gentlemen are required to wear collar and tie for formal dining at the resort. Smart casual is required for golf but other than that the dress code is "resort casual" as it is known here. Shorts and tops should be worn over swim suits in the hotel areas.

New England: a place of old fashioned values

The line of golf bags racked on the street in front of the celebrated Equinox Hotel endorsed my initial impression that here was a resort like no other I'd seen. Finding my bag among them, I expressed some concern for their security: they were, after all, antiques.

"Don't worry, sir," said the front desk clerk. "Someone from the pro shop will collect them shortly. Until then they're quite safe. We have no crime here."

I was in Manchester, Vermont, a community of 3,000 souls that luxuriates in a wooded valley overlooked by Mount Equinox. It is the epitome of small town America, squeaky clean and picture book pretty, with traditional New England architecture of white clap-board, all home-spun but with an air of modestly stated affluence.

The tree-lined main street, its fashionable shops, restaurants and small hotels clustered around the steepled church, is the focal point of a well-ordered township. Compulsory off-street parking leaves the roads uncluttered; advertising hoardings, like the police, are conspicuous by their absence. The traffic is minimal, the pace of life an amiable stroll.

Discovering it was an enriching experience. Unlike its UK counterpart, this Manchester was serene and safe as a bank, recalling a by-gone era for a Briton accustomed to a daily diet of mugging, rape and robbery.

I was worried about a set of clapped out old golf clubs? The people here leave their homes unlocked when they go on holiday and park their cars with the keys in while at work! This Utopian situation is, I discovered, common throughout Vermont. With a population of 560,000 it is one of America's least populated States, a collection of small rural communities where the terrain and climate make honesty inherent.

It's a mountain State so Vermont is subject to harsh winter weather: 20 feet snowfalls are common and then a flat battery or a bad fall can be life-threatening. So survival is a common cause. Everyone "looks out" for his neighbour, particularly the elderly; hence those unlocked doors...

As my host explained. "If a friend doesn't make the office, or show for a lunch date, or a neighbour hasn't been seen, then someone will investigate. It's part of mountain philosophy."

Which explains the paucity of crime and, for visitors, a serenity that is absolute, enhancing a peerless setting. Those seeking an exclusive holiday with style should investigate Vermont. For golfers it's difficult to imagine anywhere more agreeable..

The Green Mountain State, part of the region known as New England, is a winter ski destination so there's ample good value accommodation; small inns, ski lodges, de luxe motels and swish hotels, plus swathes of fine restaurants.

Come mid-April, though, and the snow has usually gone, leaving golf courses pristine and verdant. Go in May or June, when they've dried out, and you'll experience nothing quite like it. Better still, make that late September or early October when a million trees are changing hue and you'll be doubly smitten.

A minor problem then is that what's known as the Foliage Season is a high point of the year for the domestic tourist market. But there's a bonus for golfers: if you book your flight and accommodation now you'll find the courses uncrowded simply because everyone is away ogling the mountain scenery!

There are some 60 courses in Vermont, which geographically is an upright oblong in shape and slightly wider at the top. It is bordered by New Hampshire, Massachusetts, New York State and, to the north, Quebec, Canada. Two major highways run from the northern to the southern borders and one could complete the drive in about four hours. Travelling east to west on secondary roads takes about three hours at the widest point, although sight-seeing could double that.

Where you stay is dependant largely upon the duration of your holiday and your airport of arrival. The latter could be Boston, about 150 miles from both Manchester and Woodstock in the south, or Newark, New Jersey, from where there are connecting flights to Burlington, the State's largest city with a population of about 35,000, near the north western border.

From here there's a trio of appealing resorts within comfortable driving range: the Basin Harbor Club on the shores of Lake Champlain, and the mountain resorts of Stowe and Sugarbush each have a variety of accommodations and equally variable golf courses with one common attribute: a peerless setting.

Basin Harbor is a 750 acre sports resort complex near the town of Vergennes and close to Burlington. Its 18 hole parkland course, set mainly alongside the vast Lake Champlain, is an ideal holiday course whose major hazards are the short but cloying rough and the three inch deep collars of fescue that guard the superb bent grass greens.

The latter is a common hazard in Vermont and can be frustrating initially. But you'll soon get the hang of things and have the first of several unforgettable days. Carts are available but here most choose to walk and smell the flowers along the way...

Likewise at Stowe, a typical mountain town that's a winter mecca and whose course is only one of many summer attractions. I haven't seen many courses more appealing or in finer condition.

It's a wooded parkland and hilly in places so elevated tees and greens proliferate. Like all Vermont courses, it's lush and plays longer than the 6,200 yards on the card. Better your handicap and you'll have had a grand day.

Your next stop is Sugarbush and I defy you to walk this one! It's is a true mountain course where even the worms crawl downhill. There are 4,500 acres of resort out there and at the high point you'll be at 2,000 feet where the views impoverish adjectives and the ball flies a country mile.

Nestling in the Mad River Valley in the heart of the Green Mountain National Forest, the course was designed by Robert Trent Jones Sr. You wouldn't guess, though. Because of the terrain the layout is uncomplicated, its bunkering uncluttered; the pedigree is evident mainly in the configuration of the large greens.

Spectacular is a common adjective here and it's an ideal holiday course with every apres golf facility: a three star hotel, many restaurants and all sorts of night life.

You could spend a glorious week on this triangular tour, with no drive longer than about 90 minutes, and there's another of similar dimensions that covers the central and southern section of the State.

It starts at Woodstock (pop 2,500) and everyone visiting Vermont must see this enchanting village. It's as peaceful as a church at dawn and some visitors fall so in love with the place that they never leave.

Frequently described as "the most beautiful village in New England," Woodstock was founded in 1765, there's been an inn overlooking the village green since 1793 and golf was first played here in 1895.

Covered bridges, quaint shops, a warming ambience and gentle people, the attractions are legion; but our priorities centre upon the Woodstock Inn and its country club golf course.

I'll temper my admiration and say simply that, like the aforementioned Equinox, the 140 roomed inn has the highest US rating available and frequently wins international awards for cuisine, accommodation and facilities. And yet it's not stuffy or even formal: cosy and luxurious sums it up, with service to match and nothing overlooked. Most of its business is repeat; guests can't wait to return.

The same is true of the golf course half a mile away. There are other courses nearby but golfing guests seldom stray from Woodstock. Surrounded by wooded mountains, it's visually breathtaking, with hundreds of specimen trees, several lakes and a brook that's frequently in play.

It's only a spit over 6,000 yards from the back tees and an easily walked but challenging par-69 from the forward tees, with six par threes, three par fives and a clutch of holes that will have you reaching for the camera. Like the inn, it's impossible to tire of Woodstock's gem of a course. Readers familiar with Royal Worlington, or Woodenbridge near Dublin, will know what I mean.

For those wishing to see other areas, though, a scenic drive will take in a mountain course, similar in style to Sugarbush, at nearby Killington, and adjacent is a new pay-and-play, the Green Mountain National course, which will become a major attraction. Closer to Woodstock is the Quechee Country Club but an even greater attraction awaits for Woodstock guests.

It entails returning to my starting point, the equally disarming village of Manchester. The bonus is a five day, four night golf package offering two nights each at the Woodstock Inn and the Equinox Hotel, part of the Guinness chain and a sister resort to Gleneagles, after which its course is named. It's a prospect to sate a dedicated hedonist; two of the finest hotels in the United States and unlimited golf on their acclaimed courses.

There's more: en route between them and a short drive from Manchester is another jewel that should not be missed, the 27 holes at the famous resort of Stratton Mountain.

Despite all that's gone before, this will be a highlight of your trip; it's a scenically dazzling, technically demanding golf experience. Stratton's three loops have some heroic holes, including the longest three shotter in Vermont, where carding a five will be a prodigious feat, and some unforgettable par threes. Golf is rarely better than this; a day will not be long enough.

And then there's the Equinox and its Gleneagles course, the equal of Woodstock in quality and ambience.

The gracious hotel, steeped in history which in this case has its origins in the American Revolution, overlooks the course from across the main street, part of an estate that covers 1,000 acres.

Originally designed by Walter Travis and revamped by Robert Trent Jones Sr., the course lies in an undulating valley at an altitude of 1,800 feet and with the Taconic and Green Mountains as a backdrop.

More expansive than Woodstock's, it's a bigger test, a rolling parkland of 6,400 yards, par-71, with generous fairways and tightly-defended bent grass greens. It's walkable but you'd best take a cart, which is included in the package. You'll want to play 36 holes here on both days, in fact the likelihood is that you'll change your plans and linger longer.

That will be a common thought as your holiday progresses. And if you don't linger you'll certainly return....

For details of accommodations, maps and brochures contact the Department of Travel & Tourism, 134 State Street, Montpelier, Vermont.

Cape Cod: the names ring a bell...

You've only to study a map of Cape Cod to imbibe a sense of its history from the names that dot this peninsular off the Massachusetts coast. There's Falmouth, Yarmouth, Harwich, Sandwich, Chatham and Dartmouth, to scratch the surface. Slightly further afield, en route to Boston 70 miles away, is Plymouth where the whole box of tricks was unpacked by the Pilgrim Fathers in 1620. They named the place New England.

So a visiting Briton would feel at home here and if he were of a certain vintage he could become quite nostalgic. All those names are small towns and, walking around them, he'd be reminded of the Britain of another era, of clean, safe streets and a gentler, unhurried pace of life.

This is Small Town America at its beguiling best, close to nature and the sea, with sound values and a welcoming and simple philosophy. It's a grand place to visit and if you're a golfer you'll have a treat in store.

It's something of an unknown destination for Britons, mainly because no golf tour operator has discovered it and folks generally think of tropical sunshine when they plan their annual jaunt to far-flung fairways.

But, as I'll explain, you could make your own travel plans with confidence. Or for peace of mind there are a couple of local companies waiting to oblige.

As for the weather, well their winters are mild, and the year-round climate is temperate and ideal for investigating the 35 or so golf courses strung out along the peninsular. Summer's a delight, weighing in at close to 80F most days, but Cape Cod then is a major attraction for domestic holiday makers. It all becomes a bit hectic when school's out.

Go there in spring or autumn, though, when the beach crowds are absent and air fares are in decline. You'll find a warm welcome at the golf clubs and hotels that range from de luxe resorts to cosy inns or even an old sea captain's mansion. Like the green fees, hotel tariffs are good value, dining out is inexpensive and there are attractions enough to satisfy the most dedicated explorer.

The 300 mile-long coastline boasts pristine beaches and rocky coves, serene little harbours and fishing ports and scenic salt marshes. Sightseeing apart, there's a whale watching cruise, every imaginable water sport and ferry trips to the islands of Nantucket and Martha's Vineyard.

History, ancient and modern, awaits around every corner. At the Woods Hole Oceanographic Institute, for instance, you can see how the wreck of the Titanic was found. So non-golfers have a long leash, leaving their mates with a clear conscience in pursuit of the Royal and Ancient pastime.

To devise a schedule it's necessary to explain the local geography. Cape Cod sticks out into the Atlantic much like a flexed arm, the elbow level with the shoulder and with clenched fist up-raised. Provincetown is on the northern-most point, the fist; Chatham is on the elbow, to the north of the port of Harwich, and Falmouth, 70 miles from Provincetown, is just above what could be the armpit. From there, Martha's Vineyard is visible on the southern horizon with Nantucket Island a little further east, across the sound.

Falmouth would be an ideal starting point to your visit: it's a typical Cape Cod community with a population of 29,000 spread over eight villages and 44 square miles with the port as its fulcrum. It has miles of beaches, salt water marshes and woodland and is highly geared for visitors with a host of attractions — Woods Hole and its aquarium is one — and dozens of small hotels, guest houses, inns and restaurants. It is utterly bewitching and totally addictive, a place for strolling and pottering and finding your feet after the flight.

I stayed at the Falmouth Inn; it is up-market and motel-style, unpretentious, clean and comfortable and with a pleasant dining room and bar. It's central and a bonus for golfers is that the hosts also own the Falmouth Country Club and offer great value golf packages.

The course is similar to an English parkland, generally flat and accommodating, invariably lush and in sound condition. It's an honest and pretty lay-out (6,500 yards, par-72, from the back) that's receptive to golfers of all abilities, kind to the hackers and more demanding of the tigers stalking birdies. The clubhouse is more practical than elegant and here's the clue to golf on Cape Cod.

With only a few exceptions most of the 35 clubs are pay-and-play and several are municipal, owned and run by the local authorities but several cuts above the British version.

All have memberships and weekly competitions but visitors are welcome. Several were the equal of most private courses I've played, with a blue-blooded architectural pedigree and in pristine condition. As such, the value was astonishing.

An example was Ballymeade Country Club, a commercial operation, privately funded with expense no object. The palatial clubhouse is stone-built, covering 35,000 square feet on two floors and overlooking a tennis club with indoor and outdoor facilities, a swimming pool and a spectacular course set in undulating, heavily wooded country.

The changes in elevation make the latter a huge challenge from the back (6,928 yards, par-72) where raised tees and greens call for target golf of the highest order. But there are four sets of tees, used according to handicap range, the most forward being 6,005 yards. From there it's a fun course for the high marker who stops to think and has anything resembling a short game.

Falmouth has two other full length courses of repute, Cape Cod CC and Quashnet Valley CC, plus two short courses, so the dedicated swinger could have a ball without wandering far. And at nearby East Sandwich is the Round Hill Club. If you're an aficionado of the unusual this is well worth a day out, too.

Round Hill could loosely be described as a mountain course, more rugged, heavily timbered and with rolling, isolated fairways. Set in an estate of 700 acres, it is so secluded that not a sound intrudes. They say you can hear the grass grow and the views will leave you goggle-eyed.

It's a course of great character and lots of up-slopes and long iron second shots make the par of 71 seem too low by far. This is best played in autumn. Then it's an experience not to be missed. But take a golf cart.

Those seeking an alternative base need look no further than my next stop. From Falmouth it involved a 20 mile drive to Chatham, more specifically Pleasant Bay and the Wequassett Inn. The latter is unashamedly sumptuous, a resort with a four diamond rating that puts it among America's finest.

For added appeal, several top class courses are nearby and guests will have access to a new one, due to open this summer on the adjoining estate.

Set in 22 acres of gardens on the edge of the bay, the inn has 93 rooms and 11 suites in clusters of Cape Cod cottages, many with decks reaching onto the beach. The central building is an old sea captain's house, built around 1812, now an acclaimed dining room with views over the bay. It's idyllic. There's tennis, a swimming pool, a fitness centre, boating and fishing, and soon the golf course, which will be exclusive to hotel guests and members.

It will be known as the Cape Cod National GC and if you detect a hint of Augusta there you're spot on. The site is similar to Augusta National in its configuration, with elevation changes of up to 100 feet and great stands of oaks and pine trees in a sandy sub soil, with a five inch loam root zone and a high water table. One suspects that tradition will be similarly observed, too.

It was designed by Geoffrey Cornish and Brian Silva who found a natural site requiring minimal excavation: "a golf course waiting to be discovered." It was a long wait, but well worth it. The site is 150 acres but the final 80 acres in six lots took 22 years to acquire and ecological hurdles brought another long delay that ended in 1994.

Cornish is a renowned US architect of the old school, Silva is one much influenced by Donald Ross so the character of their creation will doubtless lean to the traditional. The course opening promises to be one of the major events of the year in US golf and it will add lustre and appeal to this delightful inn.

It's a touch more expensive than the norm but worth every cent and it also gives entrée to some outstanding golf. Only a short drive away are the Cranberry Valley and Captain's golf clubs and if you played no others on your visit you'd return home a happy camper.

See them and you'll be incredulous to learn that they are both municipal courses. Peerless is the only adjective for the presentation and design. I was green with envy when I heard that town residents pay $375 a year for unlimited golf. It must be the greatest value in the American game.

Captain's GC (6,794 yards, par-72) is owned and run by the town council of Brewster. It opened in May 1985 and was designed by the aforementioned Brian Silva, in fact it was his first commission in the area. It's obviously why he's in such demand.

The course was voted Best New Public Course of 1986 by Golf Digest and has been in the top 75 ever since. They have a ten year plan which guarantees constant upgrading and with close on 60,000 rounds a year it is a major business. Visitors and members share the tee times, one for one, and not surprisingly reservations are imperative and worth every effort.

I could virtually replicate these comments for Cranberry Valley from where my notes end with the comments: "Captivating; one of the great days I've known in golf." Impeccable conditioning and superb design (by Geoffrey Cornish) in a glorious woodland setting, it was easy to see why Golf Digest ranks this in the top 50 in the nation.

Cranberry Valley (6,745 yards, par-72) is owned by the town of Chatham and managed along similar lines to Captain's. They're only a couple of miles apart and I left pondering the luck of some golfers with such a combination on their doorstep. Then I discovered the golf courses at the nearby town of Dennis.

There are two, the Pines and the Highlands, and while I didn't play the latter it is comparable to the Pines in challenge, quality and condition and both compared favourably to Captain's and Cranberry Valley.

The Pines (6,525 yards, par-72) is a totally natural course, undulating, thickly wooded and tight off the tee. Rather more rugged than its neighbours at Brewster and Chatham, it has an old fashioned look, particularly around the greens which are much smaller, angled and generally flat with old-style bunkering. It could be a venerable parkland course in Northumbria, perhaps, or the Scottish Lowlands.

There are other courses in the locality but a visiting Briton could happily play these four jewels for a week. I'm hard pressed to recall a finer combination of courses, hotel, setting and welcome.

Those readers seeking somewhere unusual for their fly-away spring or autumn holiday should look no further than the map of Cape Cod. Tell the good folk there we sent you...

Where to stay:

The Falmouth Inn: for brochures and reservations: Falmouth Inn, 824 Main Street, Falmouth, Cape Cod MA 02540.

The Wequassett Inn,

(Member, Preferred Hotels & Resorts Worldwide) For brochures, reservations: Wequassett Inn, Pleasant Bay Road, Chatham, Cape Cod, MA 02633;

Further information:

For general brochures, maps and hotel listings/contacts write The Falmouth Tourism Council, Academy Lane, Box 582, Falmouth, Cape Cod MA 02541.

Charleston: simply fly in, tune in and drop out...

Travel broadens the mind, they say, and if you want to see how the other half really lives you should high-tail it for South Carolina. There they've elevated the good life into an art form that stops just short of mass hedonism. Lord knows where the locals go for their holidays!

The setting helps, of course, plus an idyllic climate and a relaxed pace that's a by-product of those lazy summer days when ceiling fans were *de rigeur*, before air conditioning came along.

So if you're desperate to unwind here's the place to do it. Simply fly in, tune in and drop out: the old batteries will be re-charged in no time. Mix golf into the equation and you'll have a holiday to remember and repeat.

Where you drop anchor is a matter of preference because the choice is endless; but those seeking serenity will find it in abundance in the south of the State, most notably at Charleston, perhaps the loveliest city in America. It is venerable, elegant and oozing old world courtesies and charm and with countless attractions, largely architectural and historical.

When you've exhausted the sight-seeing there's some outstanding golf, too, with three major resorts no more than 30 minutes away, at Wild Dunes, Seabrook Island and Kiawah Island. All are five star, have at least two golf courses and a plethora of attractions and accommodations and each is set in upwards of a thousand acres of scenic marsh and duneland.

In holiday terms the standards are peerless; I'd find it difficult to recommend one in preference to the others. They all want for nothing. The disparity of golf aside, the accommodations will knock your eyeballs back.

Consider Wild Dunes first. It covers 1,400 acres, with a long stretch of beach, two courses and every facility. There's self-catering accommodation in one to three bedroomed villas, there are various dining options and a 150 roomed hotel was due to open last autumn. Total luxury is the keynote and it needn't be expensive.

The two courses, both designed by Tom Fazio, are the Links and the Harbour, the old and the relatively new. Those who admire Fazio's work acclaim the Links as one of his finest but, good as it is, Fazio himself says the Harbour lay-out is among his favourites.

Consider that since its opening in 1980 the Links has been ranked among the nation's leading 100 courses and in the top 25 resort courses. It has been described as a cross between Scotland and the Caribbean, its 18th, a par five along the ocean, as the best finishing hole east of Pebble Beach.

Huge sand dunes, salt water marshes, rolling fairways and pot bunkers equate to a white knuckle challenge from the tiger tees (6,722 yards, par-72) and yet Fazio, the master of illusion, presents options that leave the average handicapper itching to play it again.

It looks fearsome but what is a difficult par for the scratch man is frequently an easy bogey for the rabbit who stops to think. Putt well and you could surprise yourself.

The Harbour course (6,446 yards from the back) has larger greens than its neighbour, but with more severe hazards. The par of 70 hints at the degree of challenge and with water lurking on 17 holes it's target golf personified, a stern test with three par fives and six par threes. Play it cool is sound advice; if in doubt lay-up and bring a solid short game and a hot putter.

Non-golfers will have a ball here because, Charleston aside, the apres golf action brings a bonus that will win you lots of Brownie points.

This applies to Kiawah and Seabrook Island, too. There is simply no excuse for not having a good time around here.

At Seabrook Island, for instance, they don't simply accept youngsters, they have a department that caters for them. So if you want to travel *en famile* this is the place for you. To this end, there are lavishly equipped villas, many fronting the three mile long beach, reached via quiet, tree-lined avenues. There are loads of places to eat informally and activities enough to keep the kids occupied from morn 'til dusk, whether they're tots or teenagers. You'll be voted Dad of The Year.

The golf is a bit special, too. There are two courses, Crooked Oaks by Trent Jones Sr., and Ocean Winds by Willard Byrd. The first is a forest course and great fun; the second, akin to a links that runs by the ocean, is tougher because of the breezes and higher shot values.

Both are par-72 and a whisker over 6,800 yards from the tiger tees, with multiple options further forward. You'll have more fun from the front: both courses have fairways of Bermuda grass, a heat loving species common to the south which reacts to the strongest tee shot like a well-soaked mattress.

So it stretches every hole, as you'll discover when you continually come up short before the penny drops. This is where you'll find out how far you really hit your favourite club. It's all in impeccable condition, reflecting a recent $2 million upgrade. Seabrook offers tremendous value and there's a bonus. Where many resort courses rack up 50,000 rounds per year the Seabrook duo barely reach that total in aggregate.

The reason: no public; the courses are exclusive to members and resort guests. It's millionaires' golf, uncrowded, unhurried and with ample time for a second round. There's more: at certain times of the year the second 18 costs only the $15 cart fee. How's that for value?

Just down the road lies Kiawah Island and if all you know about it connects with the 1991 Ryder Cup match then a few statistics will give you a fuller picture.

Kiawah covers 10,000 acres surrounded by a 10 mile long beach; it has two resort villages, two tennis clubs, 18 miles of bike trails, a 21 acre pool complex and a marina village. There are 350 rental villas of varying capacity, all de luxe and with views to kill for.

And four golf courses. If you had only a week to live and could still swing a club I'd say this would be the place. You'd go with a smile on your face. The golf alone would make the journey worth while.

There's a course by Gary Player named Cougar Point that runs along an expanse of tidal marshes. Those who know Kiawah will recall the original Marsh Point course, also by Player. Cougar Point is on the same site, but is a new design that opened in 1996. Friendlier than the original, it measures 6,808 yards, par-72, from the back tips but most would feel more comfortable from the blue tees (6,431 yards). Or there are three sets of tees further forward. So the very young or the very old could have fun here.

The oldest course is Turtle Point, by Jack Nicklaus. It opened in 1981 and was the venue for the 1990 PGA Cup matches, the club pro version of the Ryder Cup.

Those familiar with Nicklaus designs wouldn't recognise this one. It's low profile, almost totally natural in appearance, with the highlight being three spectacular holes set in a stretch of duneland by the ocean. Gorgeous, and very playable. Four sets of tees here, with cards reading from 6,925 yards down to 5,283, all par-72.

Tom Fazio has worked his usual magic on the Osprey Point course but he had a marvellous canvas to start with: four large lakes, a spider's web of salt water marsh and thick forests of oaks, pines and magnolias.

So there's plenty of water and some muscular carries, off-set by wide fairways with only light rough and large greens. It looked a picture. I met four Britons playing this one and they were having a ball.

If Kiawah had only these three courses it would be worth any detour. But there's also Pete Dye's Ocean course, the site of the War on the Shore and acclaimed as arguably the finest links on the East Coast. It's been described as awesome.

I'll drink to that. Indifferent form had made me dubious about tackling this one, until I considered the probable response in the office had I reneged!

In the event, the course inspired me. I reined in whenever I was in doubt, played the percentages and relied on my short game. My form improved progressively as the round unfolded and in a two club wind from the blue tees (6,861 yards, par-72, SS74) I returned a gross 81, which was about 20 fewer than I anticipated when I set out. It was an enforced refresher in course management and brought one of my more memorable golfing days.

The Ocean course is totally natural, all duneland and marshland. Nothing intrudes. It's a spectacular nature walk. We saw golden eagles, alligators, giant blue herons and thousands of sea birds.

Ten holes run along the beach, all 18 holes are exposed to sea winds and the final four invariably play into a head wind. Many tee shots are over water or marsh but often there's a safe line if the carry seems too formidable — and some of the latter are illusory when you look back from the fairway.

In fact there's plenty of scope for the competent driver: it's the second shot that counts here to angled greens that leave little margin for error.

Dye tempts you to bite off more than you should and distance here is difficult to gauge, particularly over water or scrubby marsh. The trick is to take the safe route and don't be bashful about laying-up to keep the big numbers down.

If you've a short game worth the name you'll get your share of pars and have a round to live in the memory, a fitting climax to your holiday in glorious, laid-back South Carolina.

When to go: Spring (late February until Easter) is the domestic high season so prices rise; summer (late June to late August) may be too hot for most and in any event trans-Atlantic air fares reach their peak then, although most other costs fall and the courses are uncrowded. Europeans will find the best all-round value comes in the months September to early December and then January. The winter weather can be good to agreeable but fine for golf.

My love-hate relationship with Hilton Head

This may sound odd, but bear with me when I say that it wouldn't be difficult to develop a love-hate relationship with Hilton Head Island. Adored the resort, you'd say, and hated to leave; but after this where on earth do we go next? It's a tough one. Ask me a music question...

Think of it: 24 golf courses, great facilities, fine restaurants and accommodations, miles of beaches, boats, babes and bars. And all this in laid-back South Carolina, where courtesy is second nature, and close to Charleston, that jewel among cities. A fellow could be spoiled something rotten....

Nine years had passed since my previous visit and it was good to see that little had changed. Predictably, there was a touch more traffic at peak hours as the workers streamed in and out on the only main road that leads to the bridge and the mainland.

But once you have sussed the rush hour timings and you've got your bearings (grab a map from the tourist information office as you arrive: it's on the right, near the bridge) you'll find navigation is a piece of cake.

The island, of 40 square miles, is foot-like in shape, joined to the mainland high on the instep where Highway 278 crosses the bridge, then sweeps down to the heel before turning sharp right, towards the toe. There's one main road and a ten or so subsidiary roads off the 278 and they give direct access to everything on the island.

It's all laid out in a dozen huge estates that were cotton plantations before the Civil War left the island destitute, populated only by descendants of the emancipated slaves who lived off land and sea..

It stayed that way for almost a century. Then in 1956 the authorities built the bridge, some far-sighted whiz kid spotted the potential for tourism and the old place has never looked back. All those plantations are now self-contained resorts, with hotels, shops, restaurants, multitudinous rental accommodations and country clubs with tennis, sailing, beaches, fishing, pools, golf, the works... Just thinking about it sets me drooling.

Golf came along in 1961 when the first course was built at Sea Pines Plantation, the home of the MCI Heritage Classic at Harbour Town, held each year in the week following the US Masters. Now there are 24 courses, many open to the public, and they represent the blue book of American golf course architecture.

Every designer worthy of the name has made a contribution over the years and a man could go potty scurrying around to play them all in the time available.

Most have associated hotels or country club accommodation on-site and they offer attractive packages, particularly in the low seasons. Space precludes my previewing all 24 courses but let me give a taster of nine or so that allow public access and are reckoned to be the pick of the bunch.

Harbour Town at Sea Pines Plantation, always ranked among the nation's leading courses, is the obvious starting point. It is wooded parkland and is tight, tight, tight. Narrow fairways, small, keenly bunkered and crowned greens with collars of Bermuda rough make this a challenge like no other I've known. Just miss the fairway, or even the prescribed line, and your troubles begin. Just miss a green and you'll think you're playing a US Open course.

The pros seem to like it and while it's no doubt a great course it's not one for the average player from even the most forward tees.

There are three courses at Sea Pines and of them the Ocean course, the original on the island, is much more appealing, a beauty of a holiday course. In 1995 it was redesigned by Mark McCumber who is obviously an architectural traditionalist and a minimalist who hates to see grown men cry.

His greens are generally flat with subtle breaks, his fairway targets are relatively generous, most of the bunkers are the saucer-type and there's under-stated mounding. A series of lagoons are the major hazard, the views the principal distraction. Think before you leap is the golden rule here; plot your way around and you'll have a ball. And wait until you see the par three 15th!

Arthur Hills is a major player in US golf course design and he has several notable creations around the island. Two of them fall into our selection, those at the twin resorts of Palmetto Hall and Palmetto Dunes. The first has been described as "a graceful masterpiece with a touch of genius.". It's all undulations and gentle curves, enough to make your mouth water. Not to be missed. Most people I surveyed, mainly club pros, had it on their list.

His course at the Dunes is just as the name suggests: a lay-out that rambles through duneland with dramatic but natural changes in elevation. It's spectacular in places. Oddly, there's little rough and no fairway bunkers. Awkward stances and the ocean breeze join forces with a chain of lagoons to keep you honest. Riveting. And the newly revamped greens set local standards.

Pete Dye is big around here, too (he laid out Harbour Town) and his latest project is the reworked Robber's Row at Port Royal Plantation. It's scenic and with generous landing areas but tightly defended greens and if you're feeling bushy tailed you might want to tackle this one from the back tees. The card reads a mere 6,642 yards, par-72. Sounds easy peasy? Don't believe it.....

You'll have heard of George Fazio, of course? He laid out a beauty at Palmetto Dunes, one that has a regular place in America's leading 100. This is for those who like their golf with mustard, a par-70 with a string of long par fours and only two three shotters. Birdies here are as rare as hen's teeth.

It starts benevolently and becomes progressively tighter, as it should. Neck hair has been known to rise on the run-in and some say this is the toughest test hereabouts.

And then there's Oyster Reef, on the Hilton Head Plantation: it was rated one of the top 25 new courses in America in 1983 and, being semi-private, it gets lots of tender loving care and is not over-played.

Make every effort to play this gem designed by Rees Jones but be happy off the forward tees (6,071 yards, par-72). Lots of elevated tees and dog-legs make this sufficiently demanding for anyone who doesn't breakfast on raw meat. It has everything a well-designed course should have and its signature hole, the 192 yards 6th, is as good as they come.

Some say that the Rees Jones' lay-out at the Country Club of Hilton Head is at least the equal of his Oyster Reef. It, too, has dog-legs galore, freshwater ponds, marshland and constant changes of elevation. Boring it's not. With pulpit tees stretching the card and and raised, often tiered, greens surrounded by pot bunkers it's every bit as demanding as it sounds.

Oh, yes; and a couple of par fives go to 575 yards or more. The tiger tees run to 6,919 yards, par-72, but don't even think about it! The front tees of 6,162 yards will do nicely, believe me.

We've come this far without a mention of the name Nicklaus but you must have been expecting it! So here goes.

For my money his work at Indigo Run ranks with his Reynolds Plantation course in Georgia as among his finest. And that, as the man said, is some statement.

Actually there are two Nicklaus courses at Indigo Run: one, The Golf Club, is private (although not inaccessible); the other is public. I played the private: it is breathtaking. Then I walked the public. The quality is comparable.

Big Jack's design philosophy has mellowed since he cut his teeth as sidekick to Pete Dye on Harbour Town all those years ago. His newer designs are a joy to behold, and for the average joe to play.

He adheres to tried and trusted principles and traditions, with options there for those with the nous to recognise them. A natural elegance is the style for the most part, simply giving Mother Nature a helping hand where necessary, all in a setting that defies description. A chap could wax lyrical...

So play your cards right; call or drop a note to the golf director when you arrive and you could be invited to play The Golf Club as a prelude to lunch and a round over the Golden Bear. It will be the high point of your stay.

There's much, much more. I've barely scratched the surface. You'll doubtless compile your own list of favourite courses because nothing you find on Hilton Head will disappoint: the golf is simply outstanding.

When to go: The summer months are the peak period for family holidays so accommodation and airline prices rise and the island can be crowded. The shoulder seasons of Spring and Autumn are best for golf, in terms of weather and course condition, but the best value period is the winter, from late November to March. The weather is invariably agreeable then and temperatures are frequently in the 60s, although a sweater will be needed after sun-down. Long-stay winter packages are generally available and prices are at a year-long low, with many green fees between $35 and $50 including a cart.

Myrtle Beach is big, bountiful and bulging with delights....

Myrtle Beach is a "come up and see me sometime" sort of town; expansive, bountiful and bulging with delights. A bit like Mae West, for those of a certain vintage. "If you don't have a good time here, boys," she could be saying, "then you ain't really tryin'...."

Consider the evidence. The bustling main street, an explosion of neon at night, is the temple of southern cuisine, eclectic entertainment and good times that last until the pre-dawn hours. Here is the Hard Rock Cafe and Planet Hollywood; there is the Grand Old Opry, the mecca for Country & Western fans; nearby is a sporty night-club or three, a clutch of theatres with live shows to suit every taste and more restaurants than you could count.

If it all sounds at odds with the genteel image of South Carolina, where gentlemen still stand for a lady and courtesy is second nature, the brashness is only skin deep. The old southern traditions are just below the surface: smiles are legion and the welcome is genuine.

And what golf! America's golf magazines have strewn so many awards around here you suspect they have a vested interest in the place. But see them and you'll know that the accolades are not misplaced, that the locals are not being immodest when they call their patch the Golf Capital of the World.

The game here is part of the fabric of life with more courses per square mile than anywhere on earth; the numbers increase annually and if there's a dud one they're keeping it secret.

Stay at any one of the 400 or so hotels and you'll be within easy reach of 105 courses of disparate quality and challenge, in fact by the time you read this the number could be 110, such is the pace of development.

This plethora of delights is scattered along the Grand Strand, 60 miles of coastline that touches the border of North Carolina. Drive down Highway 17, the main artery, and the word golf will hit your eye at every turn.

There are high street golf shops in profusion; there are putting greens and mini golf lay-outs by the dozen; restaurants and bars with a golfing theme stand shoulder to shoulder, and virtually every inter-section bears a sign enticing visitors to a golf resort or country club.

The area's hotels have their own 24 hour televised golf channel and its courses were the first to equip with satellite connected golf carts giving yardages and detailed course information on miniature computer screens. Reach the tee and the screen will advise the length of the hole, the distances to the nearest bunker or water hazard and suggest the prescribed line.

On one par three the screen requested me to repair my pitch mark "and one other," before asking: "Isn't this a beautiful hole?" I tell you, computers are taking over....

Reputation and emphasis aside, golf is not the only attraction at Myrtle Beach (permanent population 35,000). It's also a sea-side resort of renown, in fact it was a family resort long before the golf boom began in the 1960s.

These days it attracts some 12 million family holidaymakers a year. They're drawn by the sparkling, 30 mile long beach and a theme park that's second only to Disney World. There are gardens in profusion, an aquarium and a zoo; there's fishing and boating of all kinds on the Intra-Coastal Waterway that passes through on its way from Florida to Maine.

There are 1,500 restaurants, a dozen major theatres; there are expansive shopping malls and the aforementioned night life would exhaust an avid hedonist in peak condition.

Golf here began slowly. In 1961 there were only three golf clubs in town and by 1967 there were only eight. But when an enterprising businessman devised a holiday promotion for them, in conjunction with a small association of hotels, the fuse was lit. The golf boom had begun and was about to explode.

Soon they hired the biggest acts in golf architecture: George Fazio, Willard Byrd, Trent Jones Sr., P.B.Dye, Arthur Hills and the modern triumvirate of Palmer, Nicklaus and Player. All left their indelible marks on terrain made for golf; rolling, heavily timbered land, with a high water table and basking in year-round sunshine.By 1988, when that once loose-knit association had grown to include 51 clubs and 69 hotels, the number of rounds played topped the two million mark for the first time as golfers helped contribute some $98.5 million to the local economy. In 1995 the number of rounds played was 3.9 million and it topped 4.3 million in 1998, a 100 per cent increase in eight years.

You can guess its value to the local economy and it explains why Myrtle Beach is the world's leading golf holiday destination. The man who started it all is still the figurehead, now with a vast advertising budget, honours galore and a reputation for walking on water before turning it into wine.

That's the background, so where do you start? Good question. A man could expire from exhaustion before he'd played all 110 courses and even regular British visitors tend to stick with their favourite dozen or so. After five visits I doubt I've seen half of them, largely because each time I return there's another 20 or so to investigate!

If there is a criticism to be made it is that there's no guidance, no course ranking system. Even allowing for the multiple tees that abound, there are some courses that are beyond the less proficient golfer, the type of player who would relish some of the more laid-back lay-outs. That's experience talking.

My selection is in two sections, the first based on good value, the second on degree of challenge, which generally means the premier and thus more expensive courses.

The question of green fees is a convoluted one. They'll generally be included in your package (you pre-pay at reduced rates for the courses of your choice) and most hotels have access to specific courses at special rates.

Each year the course owners' association members agree a common base rate and add their own surcharge. So no two green fees are similar and all vary according to seasonal demand and quality of the course.

Most clubs have a replay policy that allows a second round, subject to availability, for only the cart fee. No bookings possible; check the starter before you order lunch. You'll seldom be disappointed, particularly if the club has two or more courses. Try not to burn the candle at both ends and you'll be happy you accepted the invitation to "come up and see us sometime."

Where to play: Taking it as read that most courses are in a spectacular setting, with water and trees in abundance and with multiple tees and sound facilities a common factor, my Good Value selection is as follows :

* Azalea Sands GC: par-72, 6,902 yards from the back tees, but forgiving for lesser players. A strategic course of traditional design with no gimmicks. Great sport.

* Bay Tree Plantation GC has three disparate courses, Gold, Green and Silver and the latter, recently up-graded, is the most friendly. All are good fun from the forward tees.

* Deer Track GC has two courses, both newly remodelled. The Links is an old-style design with large greens and huge sculpted bunkers. The South course offers a good test for players of every ability. Outstanding clubhouse facilities.

* Indigo Creek GC, designed by Willard Byrd, was nominated "Best Public Course for 1991" by *Golf Digest* magazine and it's even better now. Oodles of water with many dog-legs and at 6,744 yards, par-72, they say this one is addictive.

* Island Green GC has 27 holes and no combination is longer than 6,176 yards. Island greens add spice to the subtle challenge of this perennial favourite whose condition is renowned.

* River Hills GC was voted best new course in the region when it opened in 1989 and has lost nothing since. Not long (6,196 yards, par-72) but stretched by elevated tees and greens.

* River Oaks GC has 27 holes to leave you drooling. The longest combination

is 6,877 yards but try the forward tees for a sporty test that will tempt you back.

The hot shots wanting something meaty to chew on could play a different course every day for two weeks. Try these for size:

* Aracadian Shores GC. A Rees Jones design of great beauty and challenge; a tight 6,938 yards, par-72, with nothing hidden.

* Arrowhead GC. Ray Floyd has laid out three acclaimed loops in an idyllic setting. Only 6,666 yards at full stretch but the terrain and hazards mock the card. A tough par-72.

* Belle Terre GC. Arguably the finest creation of Rees Jones, this classic design is winning rave reviews. No gimmicks, no tricks; simply 7,013 yards of golf in its purest form. Don't miss it.

* Caledonia GC. Ranked the 5th best public course in America by *Golf Digest*, here's one for the memory bank. Only 6,503 yards but par-70 so have your game on-song here.

* Legends GC. Three award-winning courses, named Heathland, Moorland and Parkland, adjudged as "the equal of any 54 hole complex anywhere," offer contrasting challenges and options. Superb clubhouse. Brits love this one.

* Litchfield Country Club: a painted landscape of lakes and giant oaks, this jewel of a course by Willard Byrd is exclusive to residents and guests of specific hotels and British Airways. Litchfield's beach-side resort has two other fine courses, the River Club and Willbrook Plantation. A purist's delight.

* Myrtlewood GC. Two venerable courses, newly renovated. Pinehills (6,640 yards) is a testing design of elegant style and visual appeal; the Palmetto (6,957 yards) has traditional shot values and is among the area's finest, with superb greens.

* National GC. Three Arnold Palmer courses offer a variety of options from the gentle West course to the white knuckle 7,000 yard King's North, a memorable experience since being up-graded. All is enhanced by impeccable conditioning, good facilities and genuine welcome.

* Pawley's Plantation GC. A spectacular lay-out by Jack Nicklaus that is ranked in the State's top 10, as challenging as it is beautiful. A memorable experience.

* Prestwick GC. Designed by Pete and PB Dye to reflect the nuances of its

famous namesake, this is a massive challenge from the back tees (7,156 yards), a course destined for big things. Limited public access but worth any effort.

* Tidewater GC. Awesome sums it up. Options, nuances and drama aplenty colour this totally natural course in an unequalled peninsula setting. Tough but rewarding, with no detail overlooked; this is the finished article. Expensive but exhilarating. Don't miss it.

When to go: Peak golf season is March to May; low season is June-early September; the shoulder season is mid September-November; good value comes in December-early February. Summer is boom time for family holidays (average temperature then is about 85F) but good value on-course. Best value golf comes in October-November (average temperature range 61 to 71F) and December-January (average temperature 55F).

Lee Island Coast: Florida's hidden heaven

If you live in a climate where winter has your course shut tighter than a snowman's smile, no doubt you'll eventually get around to discussing your annual golfing junket with the usual gang of bandits.

So take a tip: suggest a holiday on an island in the Gulf of Mexico. Just the thought of it should bring raucous laughs, talk of 15 hours' flying time and Montezuma's Revenge.

String them along and then confess that the place in mind is part of the Lee Island Coast of South Western Florida, just north of Naples and about 150 miles from Orlando and Miami. It's an area of a dozen small cities and towns with upwards of 60 miles of pristine beaches, most of them on the 100 or so islands that dot the Gulf of Mexico thereabouts.

Part of it is known as Lee County, a fairly sizeable chunk of real estate that at last count had 34 golf courses, and the spot I'm recommending is Sanibel and Captiva, two islands linked by a bridge and reached via a causeway from the Interstate 75, the motorway that runs from Tampa to Naples.

Sanibel is an island roughly 20 square miles in size, of which a large portion is wooded and devoted to wild life sanctuaries. Hence, the serenity is tangible. There are no buildings higher than four storeys, the speed limit on single lane roads ranges from 20 to 35 mph and there's not a traffic light to be found.

There are miles of dazzling white beaches, maybe 100 hotels or various forms of beach-side accommodations, and a multitude of attractions, indoors and out. Such as tennis, sailing, cruising and fishing of all types.

There are 45 miles of bicycle track (most hotels offer complimentary cycles) and to fill in any idle moments between sporting engagements the lure of countless inns and a succession of restaurants will delight the inner man.

Golf? There are three clubs on the two islands, two are central and the furthest about 35 minutes away, with several others about 45 minutes away on the mainland. Among the latter is Pelican's Nest, one of America's finest, of which more anon.

All are top class resort courses, some with a considerable pedigree, most are in the impeccable condition that appears standard in the region, and many are as pretty as can be.

Indeed Sanibel-Captiva, which are usually considered as one, may be the most beautiful corner of Florida and the scenic splendour — seascapes, beaches, marshes, woodlands and old-style architecture — is enhanced by a laid-back ambience that is unique to island life, in this case conducted at a saunter. It could become addictive, in fact many visitors return as permanent residents.

As to the golf; there are two eighteen holes courses and one nine holer, and at the furthest point on Captiva this is the more distant. The others, The Dunes and The Beachview, are in central Sanibel and no more than a few minutes from most hotels.

All three are some way from championship standard but all offer a delightful day's sport and a keen challenge for the average golfer. Better your handicap on any of them and the gang should buy you drinks for the evening.

The Dunes, rebuilt by Mark McCumber five years ago at a cost of $2.5 million, spreads over 170 acres, 70 of which are water. But it's not penal; the fairways are generous and there are no huge water carries, nothing greater than about 120 yards, although where they lap the green approaches they appear longer.

It's a scenic course, with a wooded backdrop hiding some palatial homes on the perimeter, and a lovely clubhouse with first rate facilities, including tennis and a swimming pool. You'll love it.

The Beachview GC, only minutes away, is another little-known gem. Owned by a major construction company, it opened in 1975 and although lacking a high profile pedigree it has many pleasing architectural features.

It's not long but major trees have been cleverly enlisted in the design so although the fairways are wide you'll need to be in the prescribed spot to open up the greens, most of which are angled with off-set saucer bunkers creating a tight opening. A hint of James Braid there; it's lovely stuff.

There's some mounding, to enhance perspective, but it's subtle, as are the rolling greens. Lots of lagoons, avenues of huge Royal palms and a variety of trees and flowering shrubbery make this a joy to see and to play. Good value, too, and the clubhouse facilities are first rate.

A man could happily play these two for a week but for a change of scenery the nine holer on Captiva island will fill the bill, although access is limited to guests of South Sea Resorts which owns the huge plantation, its course and several hotels on Sanibel island.

Jerry Heard, the former Tour player, is director of golf here and although only a short course (2,800 yards) it enjoys great prestige. It's also one of some challenge and exalted standards. The scenery, too, will have your eyes popping so play like a man with no arms you'll still have a great day.

Those on an extended stay might care to wander further afield but there's no need to wander far. About 45 minutes will do the trick and by heading south down Highway 41 you'll bump into Bonita Springs, a beach-side community renowned for its resort facilities.

Among them are several good public access golf courses but the pick is Pelican's Nest, where Tom Fazio has designed 27 award-winning holes in a sumptuous setting, part of the 2,500 acre residential estate known as Pelican Landing.

America's pre-eminent golf architect has worked his special brand of magic on a site of rare beauty. It's bordered to the south by the wildlife reserve of Spring Creek and to the north by Estero Bay, an aquatic preserve which gives onto the Gulf of Mexico. In between are expanses of marsh and woodland and three loops of golf that have been ranked among the top 25 in America.

Fazio's penchant for illusion has been well exercised here with shadows, hummocks and water playing havoc with the imagination of first time visitors. Several tee shots play through an avenue of trees, perhaps, or over a menacing marshy area. It's intimidating, until you reach safety and look back. Then you realise what Fazio was up to because a gentle three wood did the trick and the half-hidden landing are a proved to be generous.

There's a collection of searching par fives but generally speaking the holes on all three loops are relatively short, although the only straight ones are the par threes. They tell me that better players get around quite nicely with the three wood or a long iron off the tee. That was my choice, too, but I did it through fear.

The loops are named the Seminole, the Gator and the Hurricane, all par-36 but with variable characteristics. The Seminole is regarded as the most user friendly, although its 7th hole, a par four dog-leg around a lake, may be the most demanding of all 27.

A partial solution to the riddles posed comes on the carts, which are equipped with an electronic yardage system giving an on-screen diagram of each hole as it's played, the distances to the various hazards and the pin and tells how far you've hit it and what's remaining.

It didn't help my game one bit but, being a Fazio fan, I was simply happy to be out there, losing balls and gasping with delight as the round unfolded. If you are within 100 miles of Pelican's Nest you must detour to play it. If you can persuade the gang to holiday at Sanibel island so much the better. You'll be doubly blessed.

Getting there: Sanibel is 170 miles from Orlando which equates to three hours easy driving, first down the Interstate 4 to Tampa, then south on the Interstate 75, turning west on the outskirts of Fort Myers.

Alabama is America's golfing secret so don't tell a soul

If you're contemplating a dream golf holiday that won't require you to hock the family jewels or take out a second mortgage I know just the place and I'll wager you wouldn't have thought of it.

It's a destination that's sub tropical, inexpensive and warmly hospitable but so exclusive that even our German friends have yet to discover it in their colonisation of the known golfing world.

We're talking of one of the southern United States and though it's not a well known golf destination that's about to change and not simply because the golf doesn't come much better.

The subject is Alabama, whose southern coastline is caressed by the azure waters of the Gulf of Mexico and whose mountainous northern boundary nudges Tennessee. To the east lies Georgia, to the west is Mississippi, and Florida has bitten a chunk out of the south east coastal corner of a state that otherwise is a vertical oblong some 350 miles deep and 250 wide.

If you're a regular visitor to the US you'll be aware of it and probably will know of its major cities, Birmingham and Montgomery being the biggest and Mobile the most appealing.

The latter is down near the Gulf, in fact it dominates Mobile Bay, the focal point of a scalloped coastline that includes the twin resort towns of Gulf Shores and Orange Beach, part of a collection of barrier islands that have barely changed in a century. It's a region I commend to those seeking all that's agreeable in golfing or family holidays. You'll have a ball.

My journey called for five nights in an ocean- front hotel at Orange Beach, convenient for first rate golf, before taking a ferry across the bay to Mobile. There I desecrated several other courses before seeing the sights of this gracious city and sampling some of its outstanding restaurants.

The highlights came thick and fast, and not all of them involved golf. To say the pace of life hereabouts is unhurried is to exaggerate: they know how to hang loose, down on the Gulf Coast. They reckon there's no point in rushing.

So the traffic is gentle, the drivers courteous. It's safe to ride a bicycle, which is a grand way to see the coastal sights, the 6,000 acre national park and the 32 miles of sugar sand beach and the dozens of coves, inlets and lagoons.

As you'd expect, water sports are big hereabouts, sailing and deep sea fishing being the favourites. Most folk seem to own a boat and come the weekend they're all out on the water, when they're not on the golf course. That, too, is big in Gulf Shores-Ocean Beach and getting bigger.

Several of the clubs are private but, along with a collection of first rate hotels, six of them are members of the Gulf Shores Golf Association, formed to market the game as a tourist attraction. You can buy an all-in package of golf with a choice of accommodations and it's all sound value for such quality.

They call the golf courses the Signature Series: the list of architects explains why. There are designs by Arnold Palmer, Larry Nelson, Jerry Pate, Robert von Hagge and Bruce Devlin and a local man by the name of Earl Stone, who's not out of place in such hot company. Standards of presentation are first class and without exception the courses are a delight to behold with clubhouse facilities to match.

All six clubs are conveniently situated — a couple have self catering apartments or villas — and are uncrowded and good value. Carts are generally included and they have what's known as a replay policy which allows a second round at reduced rates when demand permits.

All of which represents one of the most appealing destinations I've seen in a long time: it's the total package and well worth the additional travelling that's necessary (see information box).

There's little to choose between the courses which, generally speaking, are undulating wooded parkland with water or marsh at strategic points and vast areas of dazzling sand.

The playing options and course characteristics are predictably varied and if you're capable of strutting the back tees you'll need to be on your toes. There's not much change from 7,000 yards which ever course you play, but all offer forward options for the ordinary golfer. You'll want to play all six, I'll wager, but there is one you shouldn't miss. An exhilarating experience awaits.

The course in question is Kiva Dunes, designed by Jerry Pate and ranked as the second best public course in America when it opened in 1994. It's even better now, with the kinks ironed out and maturity enhancing an outstanding site.

As the name suggests Kiva is set in dune-land, on a slim peninsula between the Gulf of Mexico and Mobile Bay, and it carries most of the hallmarks of a traditional links.

An architectural minimalist, Pate treated the site sympathetically, retaining the natural features so that in places it looks a century old with found greens and tees hidden in the dunes. It's a joy to see.

The rippling fairways are wide, but don't miss 'em: likewise the greens; slick, elevated and undulating, often placed in spines of dune-land with trouble on all sides. There's a hint of the Ocean Course at Kiawah Island, than which there is no greater compliment.

There are multiple island tees but don't contemplate the gold tips unless you're a scratch man or better. The blues measure 6,500 yards and they are quite meaty enough for most, while the whites will give ordinary players a muscular work-out in a near-constant sea breeze. Here's one for the memory bank. In a region where superlative standards are the norm this will be the golfing highlight of your stay.

There's much more to see, if you have the time and inclination to visit Mobile and a tour of what has been described as the finest collection of public courses in the world. It's part of a story without parallel in golf, of one man's vision that was so outrageous in its scope that it almost defied rationale.

Dr David Bronner is the Chief Executive Officer of Alabama's State Retirement Fund and his dream was to invest the pension funds in such a way that the State would benefit and grow stronger in consequence, thus enhancing the investment.

Sounds logical until you learn that his dream was a chain of public golf courses with a pedigree from the top echelon. There must have been some who opined that taking the cash to a casino offered a better investment option but the good doctor got his way, the project was completed and became an instant success.

It's known as the Robert Trent Jones Trail, after the designer responsible, and it comprises 18 public courses at seven sites spread over 100 miles of Alabama. That's correct: 18 courses — and they were built simultaneously! They say there was enough tracked equipment involved to stage a second version of D-Day!

The trail runs north to south, each facility is accessible from an inter-state highway and each is within a two hour drive of the next. These are not your every day public courses, what's more: several are of true championship status when played from the back tips. Be too ambitious and you'll be eaten alive.

In some instances, though, there are up to a dozen sets of tees on each hole. Here the card reads from 7,000 yards-plus down to 4,700. You pays your money, you takes your choice; and don't be bashful about using the forward blocks. These courses are not for the limp-wristed but nor are they penal, providing you discover the tees to suit your game.

For instance, at Magnolia Grove, just outside Mobile, there are two courses, the Falls and the Crossings. I played the Falls and ill-advisedly opted for the gold tees, from where the card read 6,600 yards. That doesn't read excessively long but it proved to be beyond my scope, with up-slopes at driving length and every green elevated and defended by deep bunkers, with no gate to encourage a lay-up.

Heavy overnight rain had compounded the challenge and it was simply too muscular for me, a fact exacerbated by undulating greens where the bottom of the flag stick was seldom visible. It made pitch shots something of a lottery and the consequence, as the starter had warned, was that my first putt had me nicely placed to hole out in two more! I barely bettered 100.

But it was a spine-tingling experience in a stunning setting as, I gather, are all the Trail courses, with timber, water and marshland in profusion and clubhouse facilities of the first order.

The good doctor's project has attracted accolades by the score: some of the courses have been ranked with the best; all are affordable, all are in pristine condition. Fans of Trent Jones Sr would be in seventh heaven: playing them all would be a heck of a week's holiday, but there's more to see and play in Mobile, with a half dozen or so courses out of the top drawer.

Like the Gulf Coast it's a golfer's paradise. Combined they offer an memorable holiday prospect you'll want to repeat.

When to go: For climate and course condition Spring and Autumn are ideal. April and May are good, with low humidity and temperatures between 80 and 85F. October and November are somewhat cooler, between 70 and 80F. September is superb, although some courses are over-seeded in the final week of the month.

Courses you should play: In Gulf Shores: The Cotton Creek Club has 27 holes by Arnold Palmer, as has Lost Key GC at Perdido Bay. The Woodlands was designed by Larry Nelson, the Glenlakes by Bruce Devlin and Robert von Hagge. Peninsula was created by Earl Stone; Kiva Dunes is by Jerry Pate.

In Mobile: Magnolia Grove GC has two courses on the Trent Jones Trail; Timber Creek has three loops by Earl Stone who also designed Rock Creek. There are several other top ranked courses within a 45 minute drive.

How to get there: From the UK, Delta Airlines operates daily flights to Atlanta from Manchester and twice daily from Gatwick. Reduced fares are available for long-term bookings which may be made up to 11 months in advance. From Atlanta there are regular shuttle flights to Mobile, Alabama, and Pensacola, Florida, which is 45 minutes from Gulf Shores-Orange Beach. Telephone Delta on 0800.414.767.

New Hampshire: the jewel of Mother Nature's Wonderland

To paraphrase the philosophical Dr. Johnson: "If you're tired of London you should try New Hampshire." For those weary of grid-locked commuting and in desperate need of a pick-me-up this is the place to be. The butterflies are noisy and the bird song could drive you crazy after a while but generally they say it's so peaceful you can hear a leaf fall.

As holiday destinations go this mountain state is the ultimate battery charger: serene, rejuvenating, welcoming and full of good things to see and do. Add the historical aspect, scenery to diminish adjectives and it all equates to a holiday to remember, one that caters for every proclivity. It's all most affordable, too.

You can pick and choose where to bed down, from country inns to plush resorts, opting for a two centre stay, perhaps, or a longer, more relaxing tour. This is a holiday to be savoured.

New Hampshire, one of the six states that form New England, is home to 100-plus golf clubs, among them a clutch of resorts with first rate hotels. They don't come any finer than the Mount Washington Hotel, one of America's most gracious resorts. It's de luxe and then some and it has 27 holes, 18 of them laid out by Donald Ross.

The setting is the White Mountains National Forest in the state's north east corner: the focal point is Mount Washington, at 6,200 feet the highest peak in the region. It's a fitting backdrop to a spectacular hotel, a masterpiece of Renaissance architecture built by Italian craftsmen in 1902. It has been legendary ever since.

The six storey hotel, a bastion of luxury, colonnaded, red-roofed and white-walled, overlooks the golf course in a valley with the mountain beyond. Few hotels are blessed with such scenery, which accounts for its 900 foot long verandah, a popular spot for sunset cocktails.

The course shows few signs of the Ross signature. He doubtless had few options on such terrain in 1915. But it's of sufficient pedigree to be a regular venue for the New Hampshire Open and it's a fun course, with sufficient challenge to keep you on your toes, in first rate order and as handsome as can be.

The hotel golf packages allow unlimited golf and if you stay for four nights the fifth will be complimentary. Good value doesn't come any better and if you've a two centre stay in mind this could be an ideal stop-over in combination with our next halt.

As a guide, Mount Washington is two and a half hours by road from Boston Airport. The Balsams, an equally venerable resort, is a further 90 minutes away. That's allowing you can resist the temptation to stop for sight-seeing en route. Best add 30 minutes to both journeys....

The 232 roomed Balsams Hotel is dreamlike: serene in the splendid isolation of its mountain setting but with night life aplenty and with equally unforgettable cuisine and golf. Recognised as one of America's greatest resorts, it has been a favoured retreat for the discerning for the best part of a century. It shows in every nook and cranny.

Dress rules in the dining room apart, it is refreshingly informal and takes pride in its warmth of welcome, its level of service and variety of facilities. It's way off the beaten track but that's part of the charm: once there you switch off totally and luxuriate in whatever pastime takes your fancy.

As with most of New England, the altitude dictates only a five month golfing season, from June to October, and the course is usually in pristine order by early July. From then on simply choose your own superlatives. This is one out of the top drawer, a Donald Ross gem that is unchanged since the master laid it out in 1912.

It has all of his hallmarks: generous fairways but with a prescribed line of shot to small, crowned and deceptively contoured greens often guarded by a single bunker. A sound short game here is vital, just as at Pinehurst. It's a gorgeous course that's evocative of the Scottish highlands.

Non-golfing guests of the hotel come to see the elegant clubhouse and the breathtaking views that stretch across the course, fittingly known as Panorama, to Vermont on one flank and Canada, only 15 miles away, on the other. 'Tis indeed a site for tired eyes, a course that perfectly compliments a superb hotel.

From here we're going to slip across the state line, into Maine, the largest of the New England states. It is 320 miles deep by 210 wide with a population of 1.2 million, more than half a million acres of state and national forest and 32,000 miles of rivers.

It's obvious that Mother Nature is a big wheel around here and if you're one of her admirers you'll love the next stop. Golf with a mountain backdrop aside, it's a resort that offers every imaginable outdoor pursuit for all the family. Winter here is the model for Christmas cards but summer time is celebrated, too, and autumn, when the trees change hue, brings an ambience like no other. Golf in such a setting is the stuff of dreams.

You're in the little community of Bethel, an historic settlement founded in 1796 and now with a population of 2,300. It's the very essence of small town America and at the centre of it, overlooking the village green on the main street, stands the Bethel Inn & Country Club.

Founded in 1913, it has a style evocative of that era, at once genteel, cosy and welcoming. It couldn't be more different to our previous stops but it is equally first rate, with cuisine, facilities and service to match.

Surrounded by the White Mountains, with covered bridges over crystal streams and with waterfalls nearby, you can imagine the setting of the golf course. It's a good one, too, frequently the stage for the New England Open. Its bent grass greens are among the finest I've played, holding but hard and true with lots of subtle contours.

Those who know the work of Geoffrey Cornish and Brian Silva will recognise their design signature here. They extended the course from nine to eighteen holes in 1989 and, in the modern trend for resort courses, built five sets of tees, the most forward leading to a par three course. Thus, it is ideal for youngsters or those of a certain age out for a gentle spin and a little fun.

They say it plays differently every day and that it's one you'll never tire of: I can endorse that. Go there in September or October, when the leaves are turning, and you'll discover the course uncrowded and at its most beautiful.

Bethel is 170 miles north of Boston and easy to find. I'm tempted to suggest that you consider the inn as a first stop on a two centre break. One problem: you may not want to leave!

But leave you must, because having come so far it would be a crime not to go the extra distance, to play one of the most spectacular courses I have seen. That it is ranked in America's Top 20 should be sufficient motivation but your lasting impression will be the improbably beautiful scenery. It may be unique in golf.

The course is known as Sugarloaf/USA and it lies in the wilderness of the Carrabassett River valley, two hours north of Bethel. See it and you'll wonder how on earth a golf course could be built there, let alone one of such quality. It is awesome.

Designed by Robert Trent Jones Jr., for beauty and challenge it has several holes to rank with any in world golf, in fact the second loop starts with what the architect calls his "String of Pearls," six of the finest holes he has ever laid out.

The course is part of the famous ski complex and was added 15 years ago to extend the resort's summer attractions. It has been collecting accolades ever since. Now they're building a second course, such has been the demand. It will be a tough act to follow.

The terrain demands that each hole has either an elevated tee or pulpit green and several are dog-legged. There are ravines and the river to cross, and there is some serious bunkering, most of it strategic. The fairways, edged by wilderness, could be described as on the thin side of narrow, the bent grass greens magnanimous and undulating. In their pomp, late in the season, they get to Augusta speed, 12 on the stimp meter. Imagine! Here's a mental challenge you wouldn't want to face with a hangover!

As club professional Scott Hoisington advised when we set out: "Any mistake will cost at least two strokes and probably at least one ball. You're going to have several bad holes but forget your score; simply enjoy your good holes and the natural splendour." He was correct: it's the only way to play a course that will leave you breathless.

You simply must play this one twice, or more if time permits. You'll be in a fog of indecision at your first attempt. But it gets better. Or so Scott assured me!

Being a ski resort there's oodles of sound accommodation with all the usual facilities and a choice of good dining that won't break the bank. This one merits a detour from anywhere...

There's another treat in store as we turn towards the coast and our final destination, the Samoset Resort at Rockport. Halfway there, as you head south on Highway 27, you'll spot another golf course nine miles north of the town of Augusta. It's obvious from the road that it's a course of some quality so wheel in. A surprise awaits.

The club is known as Belgrade Lakes and you'll quickly confirm first impressions. It's a beauty with a hint of something traditional and British, particularly in the cross bunkering that's redolent of the great Harry Colt.

It was designed by Britain's Clive Clark, late of the Walker Cup, the Ryder Cup and BBCTV. Now living in Palm Springs, California, Clive is making a big name for himself in the world of US golf architecture— he won the Belgrade contact in the face of stiff opposition that included the Nicklaus organisation.

Belgrade Lakes is Clive's 20th course over here. It opened in September 1998 and it's that raris avis in US golf, a walking course that is open to the public.

It was a tough design job, Clive says. The heavily wooded site was riddled with about thirty acres of sacrosanct wet land, huge boulders and a string of lakes. But he created features with the cleared rocks, worked around the wet lands and incorporated the lakes into a design that encompasses many of the old fashioned virtues.

Several holes, for instance, involve strategies evocative of the Old Course at St Andrews in that some fairways have landing areas 80 yards wide but with a prescribed line of approach that frequently predicates a tee shot flirting with danger, a mark of Donald Ross design. The cross bunkering is another old-style trait, one that creates dead ground and hides distance in the green approaches.

The end result, with a multiplicity of tee options, is a sound and pleasurable test for golfers of all abilities, a course out of the top drawer. It looks a picture, the owners are delighted and so are the locals. Pop in and say hello.

Our final stop has us within sight of the Atlantic, in fact a couple of holes flirt with it at the Samoset Resort, near the town of Rockport, 275 miles north of Boston. It is chalk as to cheese with what's gone before, ideal as a starter or as dessert for this gourmet golf tour of New England.

Set in 230 acres on the edge of Penobscot Bay, Samoset has been attracting holidaymakers since 1904, although they've added a few attractions since those early times. These days it's a year-round resort with sporting facilities to suit every proclivity, indoors and out.

There are 150 de luxe rooms and suites, most with sea views, all wrapped in a gracious and yet casual ambience. The dining options are varied and appealing, there's nightly entertainment and a golf course that's been voted one of America's most beautiful.

Seven holes nudge the bay — the 4th is a dog-leg that dares you to take on the ocean — and the homeward loop winds through pond-studded woodland. You'll suspect that Maine has cornered the market in scenery.

It's all in tip top order, too, and the course is open from April to early November with golf at its best in the autumn when the temperature hovers in the 70s F. It's easy walking, which is permitted even though carts are available and included in the green fee.

You can fly from Boston to nearby Rockport, or vice versa if Samoset is your final stop. Go on, push the boat out: this may be your golf holiday of a lifetime....

Getting there: Various airlines connect with Boston from the major UK airports and all the resorts reviewed are within easy reach by road. To locate a tour operator see the Discover New England website.

When to go: May and June and September and October are prime times for golf which also coincide with trans-Atlantic air fare shoulder seasons.

Further information: The region has a UK marketing arm, known as Discover New England, which offers a brochure and information service for all six states including these hotels:

* The Mount Washington Resort has various standards of accommodation in its Bretton Country Inn, or the main hotel. Of interest to family groups are villas known as The Townhomes, which range in size from one to five bedrooms.

* The Balsams has seasonal rates for golf packages priced according to season.

* The Bethel Inn packages offer unlimited golf with cart, include dinner and breakfast and vary in cost according to season. For family groups there are two bedroomed Fairway Townhouses.

* Sugarloaf /USA has package rates to include 18 hole green fee, cart and bed and breakfast at the Sugarloaf Inn, sharing a twin/double, with use of all facilities.

* The Samoset Resort has various golf packages available from early May to mid-October. They all include shared double/twin room, two rounds of golf with cart, plus bag storage and extras.

Texas a Big Gun in Golf? You'd better believe it!

With competition hotter than a tin roof in a heat wave it seems incongruous that Texas should challenge the more well-publicised States as a golf holiday destination *par excellence*. Think of Florida, the Carolinas, Georgia and California, to list a few, and you'd reckon there's no comparison, no competition worth talking about.

Not so. The Lone Star State's slice of the tourism cake is big and increasing each year as visitors help employ 450,000 Texans and pour in excess of $40 billion into the economy and more than $2 billion in tax into the State's coffers.

And a handsome percentage of those visitors are golfers, drawn by a plethora of courses of every style, including a number that are world class and which stage PGA Tour and other prestigious tournaments on a regular basis.

A plethora? How about 900 courses and growing? Not quite Florida scale but more than most States and, whisper it around St Andrews and Dublin, almost twice the number in either Scotland or Ireland!

Of course the Texans have rather more real estate to play with than most. Would you believe 276,000 square miles, including 600 miles of coast line hemming the Gulf of Mexico? You could hide a heap of golf courses in there alone.

Which brings us to the problem similar to that faced by a first time golfing visitor to Myrtle Beach: where the heck do you tee up first? Such problems we should all have!

The State is comprised of seven geographical regions, each distinctive in its topography and climate. So rather than pick the leading resorts, which being scattered State-wide would offer no guidance to the first timer, here's a resume of those seven regions and highlights of what they have to offer. Choose one and go for it!

*Big Bend Country: This far west region is so named because it is marked by the conjunction of the huge bend in the Rio Grande River and the border with Mexico. It's a land of desert and mountains with golf courses and resorts set in dramatic and picturesque surroundings the equal of any. El Paso is not only the State's fourth largest city. Set in the Franklin Mountains, it is becoming a golf destination *par excellence*.

East of El Paso is the mile high course of Marfa, and challenging courses have sprung up in many small towns nearby. Typical is that of Lajitas at the southern edge of the Big Bend. Here a lush golf resort in a mountainous setting has just opened a new course, known as Ambush because of its escalating degree of difficulty. A unique feature: the 11th hole is actually in Mexico! The

Ultimate Hideout, as Lajitas is called, has been described as an oasis in the desert.

*The Gulf Coast & Hill Country: A strip of a region in the south eastern corner that is home to three major cities, all tourist attractions in their own right: Houston, otherwise known as Space City, is a place of parks, towering pines and tree-lined boulevards – and more than 100 accessible golf courses.

Galveston, known as the Queen City of the South in its heyday, has palm-lined boulevards overlooked by restored Victorian mansions and an ambience rivalling that of Charleston, South Carolina., with golf to match. Corpus Christi, named the Crystal City by the Sea, overlooks Corpus Christi Bay and is home to a multitude of sailing clubs and other nautical hedonism. The city has several courses and resorts in tropical settings, with a climate to match.

*The hill country: The name signals the topography of the geographical heart of Texas and is the home of Austin, the State capitol. Limestone hills abound, and rivers linked by spring-fed creeks and lakes. Spectacularly situated courses dot the region and the jewel in the golfing crown is the Barton Creek Resort & Spa, considered the premier golf destination in the State, with two courses designed by Tom Fazio that are ranked among the finest in the US.

Between Austin and San Antonio, 80 minutes to the south, lie more than 80 other courses and resorts, among them the Austin Country Club, home of the late Harvey Peninck, author of *The Little Red Book* that is considered the Bible of the game.

*   The Panhandle Plains: The northern end of this region is the rectangular bit that adjoins New Mexico to the west and Oklahoma to the east. This is wheat and cotton country, a place where cowboys still ride herd and break wild horses, a place of vast plains and punched, wind-cheating 3-irons. This is where Lee Trevino honed the distinctive style that brought him two Open Championships and a host of Tour victories. Links lovers would be at home here and there's oodles of golfing choice.

*Piney Woods: First time visitors to this East Texas region are stunned by the forests of soaring pines, oak trees and olive magnolias that decorate the rolling terrain. It reminds them of the Deep South, they say; indeed one of the region's golf resorts has been labelled "the Augusta National of Texas."

The Dogwood course at the Garden Valley Golf Resort just off the I-20 is ranked among the top public access courses in the State and others of similar quality are nearby. Equally beautiful and the ultimate in technical challenge is the Pete Dye creation at the Waterwood National Resort & Country Club, three times the stage for the USPGA Tour qualifying school and ranked among the finest courses in the country.

*   Prairies and Lakes: This region adjoins Piney Woods (above) and offers a multitude of attractions, cultural and sporting, in and around its major cities, Forth Worth and Dallas. Golf features strongly with major resorts and long-standing Tour events.

The fabled Four Seasons at Las Colinas is the only Five Diamond resort in Texas and is the home of Byron Nelson Classic. The nearby White Bluff Resort has 3,450 acres including four miles of shoreline along Lake Whitney. It lists 36 holes of top flight golf, the venue for the Texas Open, among its all-inclusive recreational facilities. To complete the trio, the renowned Bank of America Invitational is staged annually at the Colonial Country Club of Forth Worth.

*   South Texas Plains: This is a region marked by the historic Spanish and Mexican influences in its music, cuisine, art and numerous festivals. In the deep south of the State, its principal city is San Antonio, the eighth largest in the nation. Austin, the State capitol, is little more than 80 minutes' drive to the north.

The golfing highlight of the region is without doubt the Westin La Cantera resort near San Antonio. Its Resort course, designed by Tom Weiskopf, is the venue for PGA Tour's Valero Texas Open each September. Its Palmer course, opened in 2001, is laid out over similar terrain with stunning views at every turn.

And then there's San Antonio.....

A renowned historian once wrote that "every Texan has two homes: his own and San Antonio." See this enchanting place and you'll quickly grasp what he meant. In terms of its riverbank setting. its facilities, the quality of life and ambience there may be nowhere quite like what has been called "an urban masterpiece."

A blend of history and cosmopolitan progress permeates every nook and cranny of the fastest growing city in the US and which attracts 20 million visitors a year. It's a tourist attraction second to none.

It's difficult to pick a focal point: the mission that became The Alamo and is still a shrine; any one of a dozen venerated buildings whose names are etched in history that dates to 1691; the beautifully maintained parks and gardens; the museums, ancient and modern; the two major theme parks that are a magnet for family holidays; the board walks and the theatres that regularly stage Broadway productions and symphony concerts.

Nor is it difficult to get into serious mischief when the sun goes down, particularly in the district known as the River Walk.

Set 20 feet below street level, this is another one of San Antonio's jewels— the Paseo del Rio. These flagstone paths border both sides of the San Antonio River as it winds its way through the middle of the business district.

Quiet and park-like in some stretches, in other areas the Walk is brimming with activity: European-style side walk cafes,speciality boutiques, nightclubs and gleaming high-rise hotels.

It stretches for approximately two-and-a-half miles and Rio San Antonio Cruises, the river's floating transportation system, provide a tranquil method of sightseeing. Groups also dine aboard open-air cruisers and river taxis ply their trade, to the Rivercenter, a dazzling three-level glass shopping, dining and entertainment complex, and to the newly expanded Henry B. Gonzalez Convention Center.

And then there's golf. With more than 300 days of sunshine annually and an average temperature of 68.8 degrees Fahrenheit, visitors to San Antonio enjoy oodles of outdoor sports and recreation, not least some 80 or so golf courses within reach of the city.

The first public golf course in Texas was built in San Antonio in 1916, and the city has been busy hosting golfers ever since. A flurry of new course building began in 1993 and the city has become a magnet for visiting players with top-flight public courses opening every year. The jewel is La Cantera Golf Club, named by Golf Digest as the best new public course in the U.S. in 1995.

Rivers in the Texas Hill Country, which forms an arc around the northern edge of San Antonio, provide venues for canoeing and white-water rafting. Myriad lakes attract fishermen, as well as water skiing and sailing enthusiasts. Working ranches throughout Central and South Texas are available as hunting leases for wild game, while dude ranches offer a taste of the Old West, complete with horseback riding. Numerous state parks offer opportunities for hiking in the rugged terrain of the Hill Country. There truly is something for everyone in Sweet San Antonio.

SOME EXOTIC DESTINATIONS FOR YOUR DELECTATION

Magical, Mystical Marrakesh + Golf = Holiday Delights

There are few cities more ancient than Marrakesh, and none more fascinating. It's the place where Africa rubs shoulders with Europe, a city where the taxis are Mercedes but where camel trains from the Sahara send the traffic into chaos. It is enchanting, a mixture of ancient and modern, the rustic and the elegant, the languid and the frenetic. You would need a week to see its myriad attractions, and that's discounting the golf, of which more anon.

The original, ancient section of the city is contained within high walls of ochre coloured stone with narrow gates at strategic points giving on to a maze of cobbled streets. Outside of this lies the modern section, with wide roads embroidered by well-tended median strips and broad, palm-lined pavements giving access to contemporary buildings, including many new hotels out of the top flight and with every facility and luxury.

You could happily walk around the old city and spend half a day touring the labyrinthine souk where a thousand stalls sell everything, from silk to salt to silver, just as they have for hundreds of years. But take a licensed guide (your hotel will arrange one) or you'll not find your way out!

Equally imperative for a visit is Djemaa el Fna, the city's market square, a teeming, 24 hour panoply of non-stop commerce and activity that borders on the theatrical.

You'll see fortune tellers, snake charmers, belly dancers, tooth pullers and acrobats, all earning a living alongside make-shift cafes and a hundred stalls selling trinkets of brass and silver, carpets, fish and fruit. Here Bedouin traders in from the desert park their camels on the perimeter and make their deals over endless glasses of mint tea. It's a magical place at night, seen in the glow of a thousand flickering oil lamps, when most of the city, it seems, is there doing business.

Then there's the Medina to be toured, and the magical gardens laid out by the French artist Jacques Majorelle, a mecca for the green fingered. There's Fantasia, the ultimate in Bedouin cuisine and entertainment, where dinner is served to music in huge tents before guests repair to the nearby stadium for a nightly tableaux of theatre on horseback.

The Golf: Thanks to a golfing Royal Family, Morocco is one of the boom countries in golf tourism with 28 courses, most new, and with others in planning. Each Moroccan city has two golf courses but Marrakesh has five. It might well be called The Golf Capital of Africa and for a golfing holiday there are few places more enticing.

It all began at The Marrakesh Royal Golf Club, built in the 1920s by the Pasha, the local governor, a gentle, picturesque course with stately palms and flowering shrubbery hemming wide fairways dotted with old-fashioned bunkers.

Recently up-graded, the gently bending fairways are flat, the greens large, true and receptive. It's a pick pocket of a course, one that pilfers length. Even for those playing badly it's a delight, visually and technically.

A touch further away, only three miles from the centre of Marrakesh, is the de luxe Le Palmeraie Golf Palace, a 200 acre hotel-resort with a course designed by Robert Trent Jones Senior. Overlooked by a splendid clubhouse and a hotel of the top rank, the course is set in a valley, lined by hundreds of ancient palm trees and with seven man-made lakes. It's demanding, picturesque and great fun, although the grainy Bermuda greens are not to everyone's liking.

Then there's Amelkis. Many have it that the venue for the 2001 Moroccan Open is the finest course in the land and one of the most visually appealing. Designed by America's Cabell Robinson, it was created at a cost of US$5.5 million, including the finest irrigation system in Africa.

It's a big course, seductively mounded, with huge greens, voluptuously undulating fairways and a series of lakes with fountains. Instead of rough it has acres of waste bunkers, created from crushed rock. The consensus of a group of UK golf writers on a recent trip was "one of the finest courses we've played, an absolute joy." The clubhouse, a crenelated replica of a Foreign Legion fortress, isn't too shabby, either.

Samanah is one of two new courses in Marrakech, this one a Nicklaus lay out set in an expansive site and, predictably, with everything on a large scale. The meandering fairways are magnanimous, but you'll need to find the correct line; the bunkers are commodious and judiciously placed; the greens, some elevated, are equally large with movement that is not always subtle. There is little rough *per se* and what there is is of the old-style Bermuda strain that is the very devil to play out of, particularly short shots from near the greens. A distinctive addition are the many waste bunkers that line some of the fairways and bring perspective to a course demanding strategic contemplation. A handsome clubhouse completes a picture of a grand resort course of the highest quality.

The Al Maaden Golf Club, now five years old and a creation of Kyle Phillips of Kingsbarns fame, is a course of distinctive design but also one of some eccentricity. Water is a constant feature although it comes in the form of reservoirs, some requiring a considerable carry or a lay-up in the bail-out area. An added oddity is that the rough has been ploughed and declared a lateral hazard, but without the red stakes! So miss the fairway by a foot and you're obliged to take a penalty drop!

That said, the fairways are magnanimous; overlook the eccentricities and simply appreciate the architectural nuances and you'll come to no harm. Beacon bunkers will identify the target area from the tee, but miss it by not much and the second shot will generally require a lay-up or a flight over expansive bunkers to subtly undulating greens that are frequently slightly elevated or off-set. Keep your wits about you and if you have a short game worthy of the name you'll win the bets and have an enjoyable day.

The Hotels: The hotels cover every range and price bracket. The cuisine is eclectic, the service good if a touch relaxed, and the natives friendly. Morocco generally is a safe place to visit. The locals not only reject the anti-western philosophy that has permeated most of the Moslem world, they are furious at those whose actions have jeopardised tourism, their major industry and a source of some 600,000 vital jobs. Here, they couldn't be more welcoming

Marrakesh has long been renowned as the home of **La Mamounia**, one of the world's great hotels, a favourite of film stars and of Winston Churchill, who painted in its gardens. (If you're lucky you could stay in Churchill's suite, unchanged since he last saw it.)

This is for those who can resist anything but temptation, because here they lay on temptation with a golden trowel. Even the standard rooms will have your eyeballs spinning and the suites are incomparably opulent.

The hotel is ringed by the walls of the old city and has every facility you'd anticipate. There's a casino and a nightclub; there's tennis, a golf driving range with its own clubhouse, and there are swimming pools and a spa in the gardens, where you'll also find villas for those seeking a little extra privacy. Royal guests and film stars usually bunk down here. La Mamounia is not inexpensive, as you'd imagine, but it is romantic *in extremis* and thus ideal for couples.

La Palmeraie, on the other hand, is ideal for families and groups. A short distance from the city, it has every facility for a holiday of some style. It is a total resort. The hotel, designated a palace which is five star plus, encircles an ingeniously designed swimming pool complex, with lots of quiet corners and an open air restaurant area for lunches and drinks. A stroll from the front doors is a self-contained village of shops and restaurants; there's a water theme park near the main gate. The golf clubhouse is a stroll away; en route you'll pass the tennis courts. Taxis await in the driveway, to whisk you into town, or on a day trip to the Atlas mountains an hour or so away.

On this score: don't contemplate car rental. The airport is about 20 minutes away, taxis are inexpensive and all the local attractions, including the golf, are but a short drive. The hotel uses taxis with known and reliable drivers. Find one you like and he'll also be your daily guide, for shopping, day trips and dining out.

Mauritius: the place for romance and all things sporty

Superlatives and euphemisms apropos Mauritius are rather like umbrellas and wet weather gear in a desert: they're surplus to requirements. If you read that the average hotel on the island is "de luxe" the claim is not the euphemism it might be elsewhere. If you read that a resort or a golf course is beautiful you'd better believe that it's not an adjectival aberration. Take it as read. Mauritius, quite simply, is a place to diminish superlatives.

But all beauty is in the eye of the beholder, our more esoteric readers might say. Quite so. In which case they would be advised to visit this island in the Indian Ocean as quick as maybe and do a spot of beholding, first hand, up close and personal. They won't believe their eyes.

Perhaps the most striking aspect of Mauritius is the intensity of the colours. From the air the island imitates an emerald set on an unending sheet of gently rippling turquoise velvet. At ground level, under a cloudless sky, the colours are such as to make the eyes wobble.

The second most noticeable aspect is the people. Mauritius is a melting pot of races and religions but they offer a model for peaceful co-existence in all aspects of daily life. Each community makes a contribution in terms of cuisine and culture, which forms a major attraction of the island. And like island folk the world over they're seldom without a smile. They're so laid back they could hide under a beach mat!

It wouldn't take long, either, to become aware of the sheer opulence of the island's facilities. This is five star territory in every sense of the term. Hence the prices; they are high, although not exorbitant, but such is the quality that they represent remarkably good value. Aside from which, the costs and the remote location give the island a certain exclusivity: the clientèle tends to be as sophisticated as it is cosmopolitan.

They say about Mauritius that "once is not enough." Some people will consider no alternative for their holidays. It becomes quite addictive. You'll be spoiled something rotten. You have been warned!

Regular guests will tell you that Belle Mare Plage in Mauritius is their favourite golf resort. Comparisons are odious on this subject but one thing is certain: if there were a leader board for such a competition this jewel in Mauritius would be up there with the best of them.

The term leader board, indeed, has specific connotations here because golf is the central theme at BMP, as the regulars call the resort. The game is huge on this island but BMP started it all and still leads the way. It has two courses, the Legends and the Links, and they're out of the top echelon, the venue each December for the Mauritius Open Championship which attracts some of Britain's best known professionals.

The facilities: Set in fifteen hectares of tropical gardens, it is a family hotel-resort par excellence but it is also romantic *in extremis*. A pristine, mile long beach is only one of its facilities, and the stylish accommodations, quality of cuisine and choice of dining options are matchless.

There's a wellness centre and a spa, plus various retail shops near the main entrance. All this and golf aside, the major attraction may be the impeccable service provided by friendly staff. Add a climate that for much of the year is idyllic and it is obvious why many guests return each year.

Location:

Mauritius reclines elegantly off the East coast of Africa, in the Indian Ocean, and BMP is part of the Constance Hotels group which kick-started tourism on the island 20 or so years ago. BMP has a sister resort, known as Le Prince Maurice, a couple of miles away. Both are located on the east coast, a 50 minute drive from the island's airport and St Louis, the capital. There's a small town nearby (the bustling market is worth a visit) but other than that the resort lies in splendid isolation, as peaceful as a church at sunrise.

Pull into the hotel forecourt after your 11 hour journey from Europe and your shoulders will drop as your spirits rise at the smiling welcome. Take a leisurely lunch at the open-air, beach-side Indigo bistro after checking in and your holiday will be off to the perfect start.

Dining:

For beach lovers and other non-golfers the Indigo, sandwiched between one of the free form swimming pools and the beach, is the favourite spot for lunch, a late breakfast or mid-morning coffee. Golfers will find similar facilities at the two clubs and for more intimate dining there's a choice of five restaurants in romantic settings offering diverse menus but in comparable ambience.

The exception is the Citronnelle, which is open from early morning to late evening and caters, carvery-style, for families and other groups. It has several kitchens offering ethnic cuisine from around the world, reflecting a cross-section of the island's population.

The accommodations:

The accommodations are mainly apartment-style suites set in small blocks nestling among the acres of gardens or overlooking the beach. There are 235 Prestige rooms, Junior suites and Luxury suites and 20 villas, the latter with private pools and butlers. All are sumptuous and with a terrace or balcony for al fresco relaxation. This is the key word for Belle Mare Plage: relaxation is the raison d'etre here

Activities:

There's a range of sports associated with the ocean, from deep-sea fishing to catamaran cruising, water ski-ing and snorkelling. There's also tennis, archery, a health spa, yoga, you name it. Just lie back and enjoy it!

The golf:

And then there are the golf courses, the venue each December for the Mauritius Open. The oldest, named The Legend, measures some 6,600 yards to par 72, a muscular challenge from the back tees for those feeling their oats. The use of this course is complimentary to guests of the hotel but green fees are payable for the new Links course, designed by Rodney Wright and Peter Alliss and a tad shorter to par 71, which opened in November 2002 to coincide with the re-launch of the hotel after a major renovation. Golf carts are mandatory on the Links and caddies are available at both courses, as are rental clubs.

Awards:

Belle Mare has been awarded the crown of "Best Golf Resort of the Year " by the International Association of Golf Tour Operators. The criteria was the quality of golf and the degree of service and facilities and when you learn that 165 operators from 32 countries chose from a list of 2,000 golf resorts world wide you'll gauge the significance of their decision.

When to go:

The island is in the southern hemisphere so the seasons are in reverse of those in Europe. Winter is May-October when the temperature varies between 20-26C during the day and between 16-20C after dusk. Summer is November-April when the relative temperatures are 26-32C and 20-23C. The water temperature of the Indian Ocean can reach 28°C. Most rainfall comes in January-February but it is usually sporadic and short-lived.

Tips to enhance your holiday:

With the exception of the Citronelle, which is casual in every sense, the ladies will have an opportunity to wear something fashionable at the other restaurants. All are romantic and merit a visit. Daytime dress is casual *in extremis*, although smart casual is required for golf and a hat is imperative, as is bottled water and sun cream.

The currency:

The currency in Mauritius is the rupee, which is best acquired at hotel reception upon arrival. You'll need some for tips and small purchases but everything else, including bills for dining, golf and the spa, may be added to your room account.

For true golfing exotica Egypt must be the place!

The itinerary had us salivating, even a little breathless: "Visit the Pyramids and the Sphinx; see the Valley of the Kings at Luxor; have lunch aboard a yacht on the Red Sea and dinner at a Bedouin desert camp; take a cocktail cruise down the Nile; see Cairo by night."

For once, the realisation was equal to the anticipation, I'm glad to report. Add outstanding hotels and daily golf, including a round on a memorable desert course designed by Gary Player, and you'll see why a bunch of wizened old golf-travel writers gave the trip top marks all round. It had every ingredient for the holiday of a lifetime.

You didn't know Egypt had golf? That's not surprising. They caught the bug only in recent times but now they're building courses at a rate of knots and no expense is being spared. Like many tourist destinations, they've discovered the value of the Royal & Ancient game and the type of people who play it. They like the cut of our jib, it seems.

In fact Egypt has something of a history in golf, albeit a chequered one. In the old Colonial days, when Cairo was a major diplomatic nerve centre, there were half a dozen courses scattered about, some dating to the 19th Century.

They were all nationalised in the catharsis of the traumatic 1950s. With the exception of nine holes here and there, they either disappeared under building construction or fell into disuse.

But the wheel turned full circle in the 1990s when eight new courses were opened, most property-driven and with resort hotels in situ. The fuse had been lit.

There are now ten courses under construction around the country, with plans for others, some the focal points of de luxe resorts with top flight hotels and convenient for airports only four hours' flying time from most European capitals.

A major point in Egypt's favour is that at the coastal resorts, those near the Red Sea for instance, it is possible to play year-round. And holidays here are not expensive, considering the standards of presentation and the quality of the hotel infrastructure.

Then, of course, there are the apre golf attractions: the culture, the gentle people, the desert and the incredible residue of 7,000 years of recorded history bringing sights to die for. It's a unique destination for a holiday.

Egypt is an expansive country and its golfing centres are linked only by long journeys. Unless you have a couple of weeks to saunter I would suggest that you restrict yourself to two centres at most. Make one of those Cairo, where we began our tour, and you'll start on the right foot.

An aside here: While the Valley of the Kings at Luxor is an hour away by air, Cairo is not lacking in historical attractions. The Sphinx and some of the nation's 85 pyramids are only a few minutes' drive from the city centre. Initially they were in splendid isolation in the desert: the spread of the metropolis has brought them to the doorstep of the city.

There are five courses scattered around the city suburbs and we played two of them, the Dreamland Golf & Tennis Resort and Katameya Heights. The former is a 2,000 acre resort, complete with theme park, hotels and every facility. It's quite a sight, a big, sprawling emerald oasis.

The course, designed by Karl Litten of Dubai renown, is one of the highest quality in design and presentation, with some of the finest greens I've seen in Africa; they're large, gently undulating and slick as a knife edge. They're of bent grass, with fairways of fescue and light rough of Bermuda. It's an unusual combination for Africa but it works well. It's eminently playable, with a pleasing tempo and movement, and it looks as good as it sounds.

There are five sets of tees stretching from 5,530 yards (for the belly dancers) to 7,205 yards (for the head sheiks), a big driving, par-72 course with water in abundance, some big two shotters, four par fives in excess of 550 yards and a quartet of solid par threes. Resort courses don't come a whole lot better than this.

There are good facilities, too: a grand clubhouse with outstanding catering, an expansive practice area and there are knowledgeable caddies to be had for about £45 Egyptian, which equates to £9 sterling.

The Katameya Heights club is what westerners would recognise as a country club. It has a tennis centre, swimming pools, a health and fitness centre, a crèche, a medical clinic, in fact everything that opens and shuts.

In golfing terms there's a par-72, a nine hole par 35, a double ended practice range with target greens, a golf academy and all the usual in-house facilities, including seven restaurants and bars, plus caddies, carts and pull trolleys. The opulent clubhouse would win awards anywhere and visitors are made most welcome.

The course is set on undulating country in one of Cairo's more desirable suburbs and there are 250 or so swish villas on the high points. Living here wouldn't be too onerous. It's a most unusual course on two counts: the first is that it resembles a British moorland course, heavily undulating and with sparse foliage; the second is that it was designed by a Frenchman, Yves Bureau. He obviously knows his onions. It's another cracker.

The elevation changes are quite marked and because of this lots of shots are "up" although several are in the reverse. Rising ground in the tee shot landing areas helps stretch the course, too, but the greens are superb. If you can putt and know something of course management you'll have great fun. The views from the high ground are a bonus. Don't forget your camera.

A hectic schedule precluded our seeing the other city courses but they came highly recommended by the American editor of Egypt's national golf magazine, to whom I am indebted for the potted history.

There is only one golf course at Luxor but it is well worth the journey and in any event you'll want to see the ancient relics that attract millions of visitors every year. Those with an appreciation of history will find The Valley of The Kings an awesome experience.

The valley is a series of tombs, cut into the sand stone hills, that house the remains of those whose dynasties ruled Egypt centuries before Christ was born. Each tomb is individual in design, a series of highly decorated rooms off a long tunnel-like corridor that leads to the last resting place. They're virtually apartments, somewhere for the departed monarch to rest while awaiting his call to the other side.

You'll gather how large they are from a fascinating tale I heard on the tour. It concerns BMW, the German auto company, who wanted to stage a launch function with a difference. So they hired one of the tombs for the night, entertained 200 guests to dinner while a string ensemble and a trio of vocalists performed excerpts from the opera *"Aida"*. I can't say that dinner in a tomb would hold much appeal for me but it's impossible not to admire such elan!

My admiration was extended to the nearby Royal Valley Golf Club course, another jewel and the focal point of a US-style country club where elegance and style are as all-important as the service. The latter was impeccable: the on-course beverage cart found us every 15 minutes or so (it was March but unseasonably hot because of desert winds) and a second cart dispensed ice cold towels with similar frequency! And this was not because we were VIP's: it's part of the daily service.

Lunch in the Nubian-style clubhouse was a bonus. These people know how to look after a fellow. One could become quite spoiled.

The course is by Arthur Davis and in keeping with the philosophy of most American architects it was designed to be played on wheels. Don't even think about walking. This is white knuckle country with lots of muscular holes, although we were unfortunate to have played it in a four club desert wind in reverse of prevailing. Doubtless it would be somewhat less physically demanding under normal conditions.

Even so, your knowledge of course management will be tested to the full: you'll be laying up more than once, particularly on the outward loop where water awaits. Take a tip: don't be bashful about using the forward tees. There are four sets: one named Nerfertiti, for your harem, comes in at 5,215 yards, and the high priests use those named after King Tut, which stretch the card to 6,735 yards.

This is not over-long for a par-72 but the fairways are of Bermuda grass, so there's no run or bounce.

The outward loop is more open, with wide fairway targets and large, tightly defended greens of Bermuda 419. The homeward half is tighter, with lots of sandy waste areas. Both loops have cloying Bermuda rough, often in collars in the green approaches: hence my tip about laying up with the approach shot and taking enough club for the one to the green.

It's all part of the rich tapestry of golfing life and great fun in a fascinating country. End the day, as we did, with a cocktail cruise on the Nile, and your cup will runneth over...

Luxor, just to the north of the great Aswan dam, was as far south as our journey took us. From Luxor we turned north again and east, to the shores of the Red Sea. It was a short drive to our next stop, only 40 miles or so, but it was a world away from what had gone before. This is the modern face of Egypt, created for the tourist industry, a place of plush resorts, grand hotels and wall-to-wall luxury. The Pharaohs would have loved it.

We were at the El Gouna resort, near Hurghada, the capital city of the Red Sea region that is an hour by air from Cairo. The city is ancient, the resort as modern as can be, only five years old and still growing apace. It is the ultimate beach side resort in a stunning setting with every pleasure on tap. There's a collection of four and five star hotels, villas and apartments for sale and rental; there's tennis, squash, horse and camel riding, in fact every sport you can imagine from hang gliding to scuba diving. And the night life is guaranteed to stop a devout hedonist in his tracks.

Gourmets, too, should take up the challenge. The choice of restaurants is bewildering and there's a "Dine Around" programme that allows hotel guests to take their pick of places to eat.

Almost forgot the golf! Not really. Just saving the best bit until last. There's currently only one course at El Gouna, but it's of some pedigree and others are in the pipeline. A bonus: the aforementioned Gary Player course is not far away.

The El Gouna course winds around a series of lagoons (one of which acts as the driving range) that double as nature reserves. So there are lots of water carries and a high water table brings lush growth and tip top presentation. It looks a picture.

It was designed by Gene Bates and Fred Couples, a partnership I have long admired. This one doesn't disappoint, either, and as you might expect from its provenance it's a big driving course with greens of comparable size and configuration. A chap could open his shoulders here, and if he were using the back tees he'd need to! There are five decks of them and they stretch from 4,600 yards for the hand maidens to 6,800 for the hot shots who breakfast on red meat. Take your pick but be warned: virtually every hole has water lurking, so don't be too ambitious.

They tell me that it's possible to play here year-round. The temperature reaches 40C in summer time but it's a dry heat and there's always a sea breeze. Sounds good to me, but then I'm always seeking new ways to work up a thirst! I gather, though, that it's idyllic in the winter.

The major attraction, the Gary Player course, is about 45 minutes away: be assured it will be worth the trip. It may be one of Gary's finest, which is saying something.

The Cascades resort is close to 2,500 acres strung out along the shore line of the Red Sea. It is an awesome concept, the realisation of one man's dream to create a something of extravagant beauty. I'd give my address book and the family jewels to see it in five years' time.

By then it will have a marina, a diving school, a swathe of five star hotels, another golf course, an academy course and a caddie school. A three storey club house is about to open, as is the golf academy; the second course is taking shape as I write and a five star hotel is rising alongside the new clubhouse.

All is presented with flair and élan: hand laid cart paths and dry stone retaining walls; course surrounds that are vast and pristine waste bunkers hemmed by kikuyu rough, greens as true as a bride's kiss. Nothing intrudes, no detail is over-looked.

It has all the appearance of a desert setting but in fact the sand was trucked in from the desert, as cover for the shale that permeates the landscape, as was the top soil. There's a desalination plant producing three million litres of irrigation water every day. It must all have cost a pretty piastre. Think of a figure and double it.

The fairways, of kikuyu grass, cut emerald swathes through the dazzling sand. The greens, of Bermuda Tifdwarf, are jade islands set in parchment. Six holes are hard by the Red Sea, including the signature hole, the 5th, a par three. It's a sight for tired eyes. From the tiger tees it measures 207 yards, although the secondary tee of 170 is meaty enough for most. The green pokes into the sea like a fat finger, side on, and from all but the most forward tee the shot is all water carry, although there's a bail-out area to the left for the faint of heart. There's a narrow strategic bunker running around three sides of the green that, just to make things really interesting, is laid out in steps! It's a hole to lift the spirits and it is almost matched by the 14th, another par three, calling for a shot over a desert ravine with the sea as a backdrop. It's worth a painting.

A mark of Player design is his use of illusion in green configurations. They're all different in shape and movement and never quite as they appear from second shot distance. At Cascades this is complimented by a melodic tempo and a routing that brings oodles of variety. Most fairways bend a tad but there are only four true dog-legs – one, the par four 12th, has a split fairway – which in my view is a mark of superior design, in this case matched by flawless presentation – would you believe there are 70 greens staff?!

This would be an out-standing course in any location. Set as it is, where the desert meets the sea, it deserves every accolade. Go see it and marvel at man's artistry and ingenuity.

Our final day on safari involved a dawn ferry boat ride across the Red Sea, from Hurghada to Sharm El Sheikh, a remarkable resort on the southern tip of the Sinai Peninsular. To the north lie the mountain and the desert of Biblical renown. It's an incongruous juxtaposition for a de luxe resort.

It's remarkable because less than a decade ago the place was simply a fishing village. Now it's a full blown resort city, its palm-lined avenues hemmed by dozens of high class hotels and every attraction required by the tourist industry. It's a great venue for a family holiday. The kids would adore it. Even teenagers would find boredom difficult to accomplish!

There's one golf course. It's known as the Jolie Ville GC and it has common ownership with Movenpick, the renowned European tourism group which has an hotel nearby.

Opened in 1998, the course is a Florida-style lay-out with 16 lakes, thousands of specimen trees and luxurious villas on the perimeter. The backdrop, though, is one you won't find in Florida: mountains fill the skyline; at their feet lies the desert.

The course was designed by America's John Sandford and it has all a golf resort requires: good practice facilities (they're big on golf schools), a luxurious club house and an easy walking course with variable tee boxes according to handicap. They have a marshalling system that seems to work (they say a touch over four hours is about right...) and the whole package brings a most pleasurable experience. Which nicely sums up golf in the Land of the Pharaohs.

Egypt is about to climb the leader board in golf tourism. If you're searching for somewhere exotic for your next golfing holiday I commend it to you.

The weather:

Average daily maximum temperature (Centigrade) is Oct 34; Nov 31; Dec 25; Jan 23; Feb 26; Mar 30; April 34. Summer temperatures frequently touch 40C but with very low humidity and, near the coast, a sea breeze. The months of January and February are the rainy season but it is intermittent.

Health:

Tetanus and polio vaccinations are recommended as are a hat and sun block. Although malaria is not endemic to Egypt an insect repellent is advisable when golfing. The normal precautions will suffice apropos eating and drinking, Standards of hygiene are high in the hotels and bottled water is readily available everywhere.

Visas:

A visa is required but this is usually available via your your operator/travel agent.

The Cape and Sun City:
South Africa offers a plethora of delights

It wasn't the first time I'd had an offer I couldn't refuse but this one had rather more appealing overtones. It provided a fitting climax to my tour of South Africa's Cape and its golfing delights.

"I don't know where you've played so far but you must see Erinvale," said Larry Gould, my Cape Town host. "I've arranged a tee time and a spot of lunch."

I knew Larry by reputation only, as the author of South Africa's leading golf guide. But, as I discovered to my cost, he plays off single figures, has seen most of the 300 or so courses in his country and plainly is a man who knows his stuff.

His summation was spot on. Erinvale is one of those courses I could roll up and take home. It would go down a treat on the Lancashire coast and the Irish Sea breezes would give it added piquancy. Not that it needs any more muscle. It is one of Gary Player's finest creations, one of his many jewels that are scattered over that incredible land like so much confetti.

My tour began at Johannesburg but like most tourists these days I gave the city a wide berth, opting instead for the security and the delights of Sandton, an exclusive suburb 20 minutes from the airport and 30 minutes north of the city. Here, the focal point is a collection of exclusive homes, de luxe hotels and air conditioned malls that, for sheer style would leave even a Milanese gasping.

From Sandton it was a 120 mile drive north west, through Pretoria, to my first stop, the resort of Sun City, one of the modern wonders of Africa. A cross between Las Vegas and Xanadu with a hint of Disney, it covers several thousand acres adjoining the Pilanesberg National Park, a 150,000 acre game reserve.

Founded in the 1970s, Sun City is difficult to describe in a few words. It has a monorail sky train, a man-made rain forest, a massive water theme park and a 6,000 seater super bowl but all this is only a small part of a resort encompassing theatres, cinemas, casinos, shops and every imaginable facility, sport and service.

There are upwards of 20 restaurants and four hotels, offering accommodation from economy to the luxurious. Of the latter the Sun City Palace is the ultimate, in scale and style.

Imitation palm trees in huge pots, flaming torches, acres of muralled ceilings and mirrors, cascading fountains and waterfalls, life-sized statues of elephants — this in the hotel dining room! — with neo-savage artefacts scattered around the public areas.

Restrained it is not; the presentation borders on the theatrical but the attention to detail is absolute and by heck they know how to run a hotel!

194

In all, there are about half a squillion bedrooms and what seems to be a comparable number of staff and at no point do they prevent you from having a good time! A simple philosophy prevails: if you don't see it, ask and ye shall receive; but you wont need to ask.

There are two courses at Sun City, the Gary Player Country Club and Lost City Golf Club. Either will knock you out, visually and technically.

You'll know of the Country Club course, no doubt: it's the venue for the annual extravaganza known as the Million Dollar Challenge and is the nation's top ranking lay-out. It's also one of the most exacting, largely because of the wall-to-wall kikuyu grass, a species similar to Bermuda in its appearance and response.

You'll soon become aware of the rough. It's only about three inches deep but it plays like loosely packed steel wool that's been soaked in treacle. Hack out and smile.

When mown, it's great grass for the fairways where the ball sits up and begs to be smacked but it gives minimal bounce and plays long, long, long, no matter which tees are used.

As a pointer: from the green tees, which are some way forward of the pro tees, the card is par 72 but SS 75. It's a big driving course but one where illusion reigns, with large landing areas half-hidden by foliage or undulations. There's water on seven holes, but variable tees offer options and if you have anything like a short game you'll reclaim strokes on the immaculate bent grass greens.

It's a joyful experience, a visual delight and walking is encouraged. A bonus: the fee is the equivalent of £23 and that will include a trained caddie. You'll never find better value...

That the neighbouring Lost City course is not rated in the nation's top ten was due solely to problems, since alleviated, associated with its playing surface.

They centre upon the heat-loving Bermuda grass used for the fairways. This has proved less than successful in the lower temperatures of the peak season of June to August when crystal clear skies have night temperatures falling below 15F. But it's all been replaced by the kikuyu strain that works like a year-round charm next door.

Lost City is totally different in character. The terrain is much hillier and carts are mandatory because of this. Consequently, everything is in view from most tees and, a couple of holes excepted, driving is somewhat easier here.

The approach shots, though, are much more demanding: large contoured greens have multiple defences and the emphasis is on imaginative course management. If in doubt lay-up is sound advice. The opening loop is desert-like, with lots of sand and waste bunkers; the inward loop can only be African. It's akin to a walk in the bush, in fact only a wire fence separates it from the game reserve.

The green at the short 13th emulates the map of Africa and the tee shot must carry a huge pit that's home to 40 or so crocodiles. As local colour goes it takes some beating....Legend has it that a local pro once played a recovery shot from down there, but it's not recommended practice! Gary Player rates this course, which opened in 1992, as one of his finest and says it can only improve. You may see nothing like it.

My next call involved a one hour flight north east to Hoedspruit on the edge of the Kruger National Park. There, near the township of Phalaborwa, came two more memorable discoveries.

Think of a game lodge and, as I did, you'll probably conjure up visions of a hut or two with basic necessities, questionable plumbing and meals cooked on a camp fire under the stars. Wrong again! The Kapama Lodge, set in 12,000 acres of private game reserve, is a five star inn overlooking a lake where luxury is a by-word and the standards are incomparable. A bit like the Ritz but with a thatched roof and lions at the bottom of the garden!

There are 20 twin bedded cottages and a central lodge with lounges and dining room and an open air bar alongside a small swimming pool. The staff ratio seems to be one for one and the service was as outstanding as the cuisine.

The serenity was tangible. Some guests call in for two nights on tour; others, seeking the ultimate stress removal, luxuriate here for two weeks and return frequently. It's not cheap but it's worth every penny.

There's a game drive each morning and evening, three hours in a Land Cruiser or one hour on foot, the ultimate spine tingler, with an armed safari guide. We saw every species, close up. It was exhilarating.

I pondered a holiday combination of game lodge and golf club and discovered that it's possible. About an hour away by road is the Hans Merensky Country Club, equally unique and uplifting. The focal point of a mining town, it has a clubhouse with every facility, first class accommodation and a golf course ranked 12th in South Africa.

The architect, relatively unknown, deserves wider recognition. The course is a beauty, carved out of the bush but still a part of it, to judge by the frequent sighting of game: a cheetah has been photographed making a kill near a green; a lion is a frequent visitor, and I heard a hippo snort, presumably after watching my tee shot.

It's a course that has won many hearts, including mine. The scenery is spectacular, the condition flawless, the design player-friendly. You can open the shoulders off the tee but you'll need your thinking cap thereafter because the principal features are the greens and their defences.

They're slower than appearances suggest because of the grass. It's Bayview which looks similar to Bermuda but is in fact napless. Intriguingly, the grain has little effect on putts so they're true as can be. They say they can be quick in winter when lower temperatures allow keener cuts. It's course with no tricks or gimmicks, simply a succession of glorious holes, some of which would grace any course.

To tempt you further: there are twenty or so self-catering chalets on the course; there's an airport ten minutes away with three flights daily to Johannesburg and the Kapama Lodge is a one hour drive. Dream on!

All of this is simply a taste of golf in the northern region of the country and we haven't touched upon Johannesburg, where a ring of superb courses can be reached without venturing into the city.

But after five days my schedule called for me to head south, to the Cape and the coastline they call the Garden Route. I had three ports of call, the first being the Fancourt Hotel resort a few minutes from the airport at George and four hours east of Cape Town.

A de luxe hotel in a garden that's big enough for three golf courses sums it up nicely, but there's much more to savour.

The main house, now a national monument, dates to 1847 and is the centre of a 230 hectare estate nestling between the Indian Ocean and the foot of the Outeniqua mountains.

Oozing style, it's been a resort for many years, a retreat for the seriously wealthy seeking a multitude of diversions, but golf was introduced only in 1991.

Enter the ubiquitous Gary Player, peripatetic architect, with plans for 18 holes. He added a third loop the following year and a fourth in 1997. You'd wonder how he finds time for all that travelling...

The original 18 is known as the Montagu; the new course as the Outeniqua, after the mountain range which overlooks it.

They're dissimilar in all but presentation: Striped fairways, shining bent grass greens, pristine bunkers, all reflected in the lakes that dot the rolling, wooded estate.

The Montagu is somewhat easier off the tee, although the kikuyu grass stretches the fairways and the second shots require your best attentions to ingeniously contoured greens. With the flags in position A you'll have your work cut out but it's a joy to play at any time.

The Outeniqua is trickier, with more water, and it makes all the demands associated with the great courses. Still maturing, consensus says it will become a major course within five years but be assured it's not so dusty now!

A week here would be unforgettable. It's all at prices to surprise and a relaxed ambience, rare in a hotel of such elevated standards, will entice you back — British visitors increased by 30 per cent last year; the word is spreading.

Too soon I was heading west again, to Cape Town. First, though, a call at Steenberg, the hotel with a golf course in a vineyard.

It lies in the tranquil Constantia Valley, hard against the lower slopes of Steenberg Mountain with False Bay on the other flank.

Originally a farm dating to 1682, Steenberg is the oldest vineyard in the Western Cape. It's still going strong, in fact it's been modernised, as have the manor house and out-buildings which form the delightful hotel around a courtyard green.

Another national monument, it is five star de luxe and has 19 rooms, each of individual style and furnished with antiques. Sublime cuisine and welcome aside, it's an uncommonly rewarding hotel, not least because guests have access to the ultra-private members' course designed by Peter Matkovich, architect of the fabled Leopard Rock.

It's an agreeable course that requires a modicum of precision and though the greens are large they don't appear so because, in most cases, they're level with the fairway. There's water here and there and some large bunkers — one par-three is virtually all bunker — and it's one to reward players of all abilities.

For those tempted to linger, there's another course nearby, to add variety. It's called West Lake and it's an English-style parkland. In fact if it were not for the mountain backdrop it might be in Surrey, perhaps, or Bucks. It's a joy to see and to play, with several outstanding holes and, like Steenberg, offers easy walking and a welcoming clubhouse.

To Cape Town, finally, and the realisation of a life-long dream. I'd heard that it is arguably the loveliest city on earth and having now seen it I concur. It is visually exquisite, elegant and hospitable, well-endowed culturally and gastronomically, and with an ambience to soothe the spirit. Its golf is a bit special, too.

The Royal Cape club is an imperative. Venerable, traditional, picturesque, challenging; it's all you'd expect of a Royal club. It has impeccable greens and its kikuyu fairways give crisp lies that invite the fairway woods you'll be using frequently when the sea breeze is whipping in from South America!

The South African Open has been played here, so it's a course requiring contemplation, but it's not a monster. Any competent golfer will have a ball, although he'll probably lose one or two in the ponds that await the cut tee shot. The clubhouse ambience is a bonus and Craig Ross, the club pro, will give a warm, Scottish-style welcome, too.

Which brings us full circle, back to Erinvale and a fitting finale to an unforgettable tour.

This is the wine region of the Cape and the most popular golfing area for visitors. It is scenic, safe, convenient for Cape Town and close to the beaches.

It's known as the Monaco of South Africa, a privileged residential area. Erinvale sits comfortably in the centre.

The course is ranked 11th in South Africa and all I can presume that someone miscounted because this is the jewel in the crown of Cape golf. It's an awesome challenge from the back tees (heck, even from the members' tees!), a major driving course whose principal hazard is vast greens, the product of immense cunning, all zealously defended.

From knowledge of his other courses Gary Player usually favours greens flat to the fairway, presenting small, stoutly guarded targets. At Erinvale he has used the natural movement of the land to create elevated greens, some long and narrow, some side-on, most scalloped by mounded, gathering bunkers. Others are huge, perhaps angled to the line of shot, sharply sloping and defended by deep pits of sand, some with sleepers and steps. You'll get the picture.

Of the larger greens, some have concave sections, some convex. So from a distance a ridge or a swale will hide part of it, and often the base of the flag stick. The consequence is indecision and, like as not, a 40 foot putt across a slope, or worse, down it

So even on the short par fours — and there are a couple of beauties — you need to have your thinking cap on. On the longer holes it frequently pays to lay up. Pin position is all-important. Plus precision on your part, naturally. It's a course you'll want to play frequently, one of the most enjoyable I have played. Thinks: must ask Larry to book another tee time....

Getting there:

South African Airways offers daily non-stop flights from Heathrow to Johannesburg and thrice weekly flights to Capetown. Flight times are 10 hrs 30 mins and 11 hrs 50 mins respectively. A two hour time difference means no jet leg.

When to go:

South Africa is in the Southern Hemisphere so the seasons are reversed. Their winter is June-September; summer is December-March. But spring and autumn are best for golf when courses are in peak condition and day-time temperatures hover around 75 to 80F. In the north, day-time winter temperatures can reach 70F but early mornings and nights can be close to freezing, particular in Johannesburg which has an altitude of 5,000 feet. Cape Town can be wet in the winter, although there is no rainy season as such and long warm spells are common.

Health:

No vaccinations are required but a course of anti-malaria tablets is recommended for those intending to undertake game drives.

Amazing Thailand: the next Big Thing in golf

My caddie was about five feet tall and might have tipped the scales at 100 pounds while carrying a suitcase full of small change. But she had a smile that would melt a miser's heart, she knew the course like the back of her tiny hand and could read the greens like a book.

 Being a gentleman, I was reticent about taking up her offer, not least because my bag probably out-weighed her. But she twirled it around like a weightlifter on steroids and was ready for another 18 holes when my playing partner and I staggered into the bar for a reviving noggin and lunch.

Welcome to golf in Thailand.

All the caddies we saw there were female and employing one was obligatory at the clubs we visited, and justifiably so.

Their fee averages 180 baht, or about £3 sterling, an indication that some Thai people are not overly familiar with life's little luxuries. They're grateful for the employment and it shows in their demeanour and the ever-present smiles. In fact the Thai people are one of the major attractions of a golfing holiday in that hauntingly beautiful country. They simply can't do enough for the visitor, and that includes those who have no expectation of a gratuity for services rendered.

Golf is a relatively recent phenomenon in what was once Siam. The game has been played in some quarters there for the better part of a century but of the 240 or so clubs now extant most are associated with resorts that have emerged in the past two decades.

The highest concentration is in the greater Bangkok conurbation. Some are within the city limits and about 30 minutes or so from the central hotels; others are slightly further afield. A taxi would do the trick here: they're not expensive and the driver will know the ropes apropos the city traffic, which is never less than chaotic.

I decided to avoid the city and began my tour at Hua Hin (it's pronounced Warheen), a gently bustling beach resort town 120 miles from Bangkok airport. It has every ingredient for a memorable holiday, an amalgam of the ancient and modern that typifies Thailand. Crowded street markets selling every imaginable commodity stand in the shadow of splendid hotels, all luxury and glinting marble, overlooking the beach.

There are a dozen or more de luxe hotels of which the dominant is the Sofitel, the most venerable and one redolent of a by-gone age. Stylish, serene and elegant, it was built in 1923 as a stop-over on the Bangkok-Singapore railway. Some stop-over!

There are five clubs in the vicinity, none more than 20 minutes distant. They offer a disparate mix, from the gentle and picturesque Royal Hua Hin Club that is among the oldest in Thailand, to the more muscular versions devised by modern architects such as Jack Nicklaus.

Twenty minutes from the Hotel Sofitel, halfway to the city of Cha Am, lies the Imperial Lake View golf club, part of a resort set in 1,200 acres in a valley at the foot of a mountain range. You can imagine the views.

There are 27 holes designed by Australia's Roger Packard, and the initial 18 have a links-land look about them; they're ruggedly beautiful and you'll need to step up a couple of gears if you played Royal Hua Hin first.

Also about 20 minutes from the Sofitel you'll find the Majestic Creek Country Club, designed by a local man, Dr Sukkitti Klanvisal. Symphonic in its tempo and movement, it has a charmingly old-fashioned aura about it. Harry Colt and Alister Mackenzie would have approved of the good doctor's endeavours.

Equally eye-boggling, although for quite different reasons, is the Springfield Country Club and its course, designed by Jack Nicklaus. It's part of a self-contained beach resort that would be ideal for those with lively youngsters.

As you'd imagine with such a pedigree, the course is out of the top drawer. It's a regular stop on the Asian PGA Tour and the venue for the annual Tour School but it was designed primarily as a resort course. The average Joe Hacker won't be intimidated if he tempers his ambition and selects a suitable tee.

Add superb conditioning and an opulent clubhouse and you'll see why many rate Springfield one of the finest clubs in this golf-mad nation.

And so on to Chiang Mai: It didn't disappoint. The second city of Thailand is a major tourist attraction, a bustling place full of colour and character, enhanced at night when the main thoroughfare becomes a mile-long street market illuminated by lanterns.

You'll want to linger there, but not for too long: greener pastures await no more than 40 minutes away in what could be another world. There's a choice of four clubs, one of them the focal point of a resort par excellence. This is the Royal Chiang Mai Golf Club, a splendiferous establishment full of good things for the visitor.

The accommodation comes in a low profile hotel of elegant lines and sumptuous standards, all white marble and cool as a cucumber on ice. One side overlooks a swimming pool, the other a golf course that will leave you spellbound. When you learn that the architect is Peter Thomson you'll doubtless nod in approval, sight unseen.

The course offers a design of great subtlety, as you would expect of such a cerebral traditionalist. It's not over-long (6,900 yards from the back) although it plays rather longer than the card indicates and offers a challenge from every tee. Thomson believes that golf is a game played along the ground and that getting to the green is what it's all about. Amen to that. Once on the green you'll have fun deciphering the subtle breaks and rolls in greens of beguiling configuration.

If your fancy is a two centre stay with a night in the city of Chiang Mai then look no further than our next combination, the Westin Hotel and the Chiang Mai Lamphun Golf Club.

I'm not a great fan of international hotel chains but I was mightily impressed with the Chiang Mai Westin. It was first class in every respect: comfort, service, facilities and cuisine. They know how to take care of a chap. And it's only a few minutes from the airport and convenient for the golf.

You could fly into Chiang Mai en route to the aforementioned Royal Chiang Mai. So the Westin would be the ideal spot for your final night, before the flight back to Bangkok and home. Investigating the Lamphun course during the day and taking a city stroll in the evening would be a perfect finale to your adventure in Thailand.

The course is another jewel from the drawing board of the man who designed Majestic Creek. It's an equally impressive lay-out, oozing visual delight and technical challenge. It lies in a wooded valley at an elevation of about 1,000 feet with mountains on three sides. It's a blaze of colour, a photographer's dream and a delight to play, although don't expect to finish without losing a ball or three.

The clubhouse facilities are first class and like all Thai courses there are several "pit stops" for drinks, snacks and toilets, all invaluable in this climate. The course offers easy walking and enjoyment enhanced by highly competent female caddies for whom a 100 baht tip will bring even wider smiles.

Ask them nicely and they'll pose for a photograph, a warming memento of a land they justifiably call Amazing Thailand.

San Roque: here's a new course to Dye for....

The wheel has turned full circle for golf on the Costa del Sol. Forty years after Robert Trent Jones Senior built the first two courses at Sotogrande to kick-start European golf tourism, the scion of another US architectural dynasty has created a comparable masterpiece on the adjacent San Roque Club resort.

Comparable is an apposite adverb. While the architectural style and terrain are only vaguely similar, Perry Dye's creation has elevated the stylish San Roque into the exclusive echelons of European golf resorts of which neighbouring Valderrama is the flagship.

Known as the New Course, it perfectly compliments the David Thomas lay-out that transformed the site back in the 1980s and which put San Roque onto the world stage of golf.

Both Trent Jones and David Thomas had expansive sites on which to practice their arts. In this case, Perry Dye, son of the illustrious Pete, found a limited canvas at odds with the expansive acreage to which most US golf architects are accustomed.

The New Course is laid over a scant 45 hectares, a vaguely triangular-shaped oblong lying parallel to the ocean and with a sacrosanct nature reserve running along one boundary. To complicate matters, its centrepiece was a huge hill festooned with cork and oak trees. Plainly, "shifting dirt," as the Dye dynasty has it, was a priority, as was transplanting trees, hundreds of them.

Because of a wet winter, two years were to pass before the first ball was struck, in September 2003.

The consensus: it may be one of the finest new resort courses in Europe and certainly one of the most beautiful. Visually it is a joy; technically it is a masterpiece of the art, fun for beginners and a thorough test for those capable of strutting the back tees.

Because of the shape of the site most of the holes run east to west, or the reverse, so the prevailing winds, from the mountains or the sea, are generally across the line of shot. The exceptions are holes 4, 5, 6, and 13 that lie at right angles at one end of the site. There are sea views from 12 holes, often over a carpet of waving tree tops. You'll gather it is not displeasing to the eye.

Illusion, the architect's accomplice, is rampant. Stand on most tees and the knuckles will turn white. But a treat, not a trick, lies in wait: the course is much easier than at first it appears. The fairways look narrow but frequently they widen out beyond a mound, or a sand dune that gives a links appearance in places.

In the Dye tradition, all the bunkers are visible. Some are strategic, some are penal; some purely aesthetic, some are traditional pot bunkers and some are monstrous. The latter are US-style waste bunkers that, as at the short 8th, stretch the length of the fairway or, as at the 7th and the 9th, act as buffers on the edge of a lake that guards each green.

It's an all-round examination of ability and character where the major test invariably awaits with the approach shot.

This is because the greens, though large, present small targets in that they have a narrow opening or are angled, often side-on and partially hidden by subtle mounding. The lay-up will be a popular option here.

Horticulturally speaking, the New Course is unique in several aspects. In what he classifies as his wilderness areas, the architect has introduced a species the Americans know as love grass. Similar to marram grass but finer stemmed and lusher, it lays a knee-high carpet that gives a "Mexican wave" in a breeze. It forms a beautiful back-drop to many holes, along with another innovation: cascading wild flowers, acres of them, whose seeds were brought over from their native Colorado, where Dye is based.

The more practical grasses are unusual, too. Dye has used five varieties of hybrid Bermuda on each hole: tees, fairways, green surrounds and on the putting surfaces. On the greens it is Tifeagle, a species ideally suited to the climate of Southern Spain. It is one that doesn't hibernate in winter. It gives a good matt cover and has a finer grain, too, bringing a more consistent roll than the old fashioned Bermuda. Good putters will be licking their lips, although they'd better be sharp-eyed. The greens get a tad slick down-grain and consequently more than a hint slower against it. On cross-grain putts the ball will wander just a touch at the death so bring your reading glasses!

A compelling vista is enhanced by a series of rock retaining walls, built from material unearthed in the construction, and two large lakes. The latter provide irrigation and add spice to four holes: the 7th and 14th greens overlook one lake; the 9th and 18th are separated by the other.

In time, the New Course will have its own clubhouse and a 100 bed-roomed hotel. Other than this, there will be no construction on or around the site. The New Course is simply a celebration of golf in its purest form. We commend it to all who love the game.

Location:

Adjacent to Valderrama, San Roque is 20 minutes from Gibraltar Airport and 75 minutes from Malaga Airport.

The New Course card:

18 holes, par 72, with five sets of tees ranging from 7,136 yards to 5,052 yards. The accommodation: The centre piece is the former home of the

Domecq sherry dynasty, now converted into a de luxe hotel. Alternative accommodations are hacienda-style cottages, some 50 guest rooms and suites set in clusters among cobbled courtyards and gardens, only a stroll from the hotel reception in the clubhouse lobby.

San Roque has all the facilities expected of an international five star resort with two restaurants, a lagoon pool, tennis courts, private beach club and an equestrian centre. A recent addition is the golf academy with a two storey covered driving range, pitching areas with bunkers, two practice putting greens and short game area. Club, cart and trolley rental available as are preferential rates at Valderrama, Sotogrande and other courses.

Matchless golf on my island in the sun

Mark Twain summed up Bermuda beautifully: "You go to Heaven if you wish," he wrote. "I'll stay right here."

The great author wasn't thinking of golf when he expressed his sentiments — Bermuda had no courses in those by-gone days — but they'd be endorsed by any golfer visiting for the first time. Islands have a unique charm but, in my experience as one who once knew it well, Bermuda's is inimitable. On my previous visit as a foot-loose young reporter I had popped in intending to stay for a month or three. But a pretty lady golfer had other ideas. I stayed for five years.

Only recently, and many years later, I returned to confirm that memory hadn't dulled the sheen of Bermuda's beauty: the purity of its sapphire waters; its beaches of pink sand; its pastel-coloured, toy-like buildings; that dazzling harbour....

The youthful script was virtually unchanged, although memory had re-written a line or two. There is a touch more traffic these days, but the speed limit remains at 20 mph, a fair indication of the pace of life, and visitors even now are barred from driving anything with more than two wheels and pedals.

Building development remains stringently controlled in volume and height — Hamilton's towered cathedral is the capital's tallest structure, visible on virtually every skyline. Front Street, the main street where cruise liners hitch up each week, was just as memory dictated, except that some of its restaurants are a tad more exotic.

Crass commercialism is still anathema in the oldest self-governing British colony — my visit coincided with a two day Parliamentary debate on allowing a fast food chain onto the island: the move was rejected. Nothing is allowed to intrude on that gentle ambience still redolent of those heady pre-war days when Bermuda was the holiday venue for much of Western society, most of whom had summer homes there.

In those days it was known as the millionaire's playground and yachts were the preferred mode of arrival. One needed to be both well-keeled and well-heeled.

The boom in post-war aviation ended all that and what became known as the jet-set decamped south, to the Caribbean. But Bermuda is still a five star destination where quality is paramount in cuisine, service, facilities and accommodation.

The latter ranges from svelte hotels and exclusive lodges to beach-side cottages and small guest houses and apartments, all overlooking the harbour or the ocean beaches. Golf aside, the attractions are legion. There's something to suit every taste and most budgets. Ordinary folk with a sense of style will be as welcome as any millionaire.

That's another common factor: the welcome couldn't be warmer. The locals stop just short of hugging visitors and nothing is too much trouble.

"No problems," is the standard reply to any request, but there'll be no hurry, either. Bermudians are so laid back they're almost horizontal.

And, perhaps because their standard of living is among the highest in the world, they never stop smiling. They've long since twigged what Mark Twain was on about, all those years ago.

Bermuda had only five courses back in the 1950s: now there are eight and soon there'll be another. The steady increase is all part of the plan to keep the island's lifeblood surging, to stay in the forefront of up-market tourism. Thus it continues to attract thousands of golfing visitors each year, mainly from the United States but in increasing numbers from Britain and Europe.

It's not accidental that Bermuda has long been a major player in the international golfing holiday field. One of the factors is its accessibility. It's not in the Caribbean, as many people suppose, but some distance north. It is 600 miles east of the Carolina coast, 80 minutes by air from New York city and about seven hours from Gatwick. It's been called the Crossroads of the Atlantic.

Shaped like a fish hook, it is only three miles wide and 20 miles long and it sits on an atoll washed by the warm waters of the Gulf Stream. Hence the idyllic climate. Bermudians say they have only two seasons, summer and spring. The mean temperatures are about 60F from November to April and up to the high 80s in July, August and September.

So while gentle breezes make summer golf a heavenly prospect, winter brings one of the world's biggest golf festivals, a series of events for both sexes and all ages that takes place from November to March. Prices are lower then, too.

The island's love affair with the game began back in the 1950s with the foundation of the Bermuda Goodwill Tournament, a major pro-am played over four courses. This started in a small way with about a dozen teams of four: now it attracts upwards of 200 or so teams, mainly from the US but from as far afield as Argentina and Europe. The bottom line spin-off from this alone features a long row of noughts.

So over the years golf's fiscal value to the island has been inestimable, hence the new courses and the heavy emphasis on the game in the marketing programmes.

The climate and quality of the courses aside, the head-spinning scenery helps to sell it. Some of the golf views impoverish adjectives. What's more, golf in Bermuda needn't be expensive if you go about it sensibly.

Of the eight courses, three are part of hotel complexes, three are government-owned pay-and-play and two are private, although they accept visitors by arrangement. One of the latter is the Mid Ocean Club, still numbered among the world's great courses, of which more anon.

The hotel courses, Marriotts Castle Harbour, Belmont Manor and The Southampton Princess, are those which feature most strongly in the brochures of European golf tour operators. The latter two have associate hotels which share the golfing facilities, and all hotels will arrange access to other courses, including the exclusive Mid Ocean Club.

The courses vary markedly in style and character but they have a common attribute: impeccable conditioning. The strain of grass known as Bermuda is prevalent but as this hibernates in the winter over-seeding with rye is common, to give courses colour.

My brief stay at the Southampton Princess Hotel was memorable by any criteria: the golf brought double the delight. It's a par three course, but this is no pitch and putt layout. It's 18 holes of real golf laid over wooded, undulating terrain with the ocean as a constant backdrop. It's one of the loveliest I've seen and some of the holes would grace more renowned courses.

The card reads 2,684 yards, par 54, and the holes range from 110 to 211 yards, with water in abundance. This is the place to polish your irons and in the process you'll have more fun than is normally possible with your clothes on.

There's a bonus: you'll whiz around in very short order. Play after an early breakfast and you'll have the rest of the day for other activities, to explore the island or to play elsewhere. A blissful alternative: play a round at sunset, just before dinner. It's an incomparable experience. Cheaper, too.

Three other courses, plus a state of the art golf academy, are close to the Princess Hotel, so this is an ideal locality for golfers. The Belmont Hotel course and Riddell's Bay Country Club are but minutes away and either will repay a visit. They're both of modest length but tricky as a cart full of monkeys and they offer good sport and considerable challenge. Don't forget your camera.

Port Royal is the third nearby course and it's right out of the top drawer. What's more, it has one of the world's most scenic golf holes. The other 17 are not to be sniffed at, mind, but the short 16th will stop you in your cart tracks.

It's 176 yards from the back of the elevated tee and the shot must carry a fissure which falls about 100 feet down to the beach. From the tee, the green below appears to be reclining on a turquoise mirror. In fact it is on a tiny promontory, with jungle behind and left. The green is long and quite narrow in the front where bunkers guard the entrance, although it widens at the rear, the target area. There's a strategic, semi-circular bunker beyond that, designed to prevent the over-hit shot tumbling down the scrubby cliff-side.

The green has some subtle rolls and breaks which, as I discovered, can nullify a good tee shot. I three putted but my excuse was total distraction. The hole has a beauty that may be without peer in golf.

Perhaps the most surprising aspect of Port Royal is that it is a municipal course. Actually it's government-owned and operated, but it amounts to the same thing. It's pay-and-play and at US$60 it's good value, even better after 4pm when sunset rates apply.

Designed by Robert Trent Jones Sr. and measuring 6,561 yards, par-71, Port Royal is a regular venue for the Bermuda Amateur Championship and when the winner breaks par it's not by much.

The card indicates a modest length but the fairways have a thick blanket of Bermuda grass, the type that nullifies bounce and pilfers length. Hit the fairways, though, and you'll have an interesting second shot to greens that have good putters purring.

This is a course that's tough but fair, as challenging as it is beautiful. It won't over-awe the lesser player who stops to think and it will reward the scratch man who successfully accepts its challenges.

And that scenery.... To paraphrase Mark Twain: "You take Pebble Beach if you wish. I'll stay right here." It's one quarter the price, too. Don't miss it.

The three alternative courses on the tourist trail are at the other end of the island. The furthest is St George's, near the old capital of that name. Everything about Bermuda is scenic but the course here has an historical ambience, too, because legend has it this is where the ship-wrecked founding fathers staggered ashore in 1609.

At 4,043 yards, par-62, the course is of deceptive proportions and Trent Jones Sr. has shown what can be achieved with a limited canvas. Well worth a round if you're touring the town.

Castle Harbour, on the other hand, presents a major examination largely because of the rugged terrain. Golf carts are mandatory here and it's the only way to fully enjoy a panoramic course of some stature.

It has several memorable holes and the first is a classic: a gun platform tee is dominated by views of waving tree tops, the azure waterway that is Castle Harbour and, beyond, the darker-hued ocean.

Far below a valley turns gently left around a stand of trees as it rises to a tiered, well-bunkered green. It's only 330 yards but because of the elevations it plays more like 390. Par this one and with all those distractions you'll be off and running with a grin from ear to ear.

It should be said that several holes at Castle Harbour have blind tee shots, although that could change through a $67 million project, currently nearing completion, aimed at refurbishing both course and hotel.

But in any event this doesn't detract from the round. The fairways are not restrictive and if you temper ambition off the tee your good sense will be rewarded. You'll need patience on the greens, too. They're very grainy and hard and quick. Castle Harbour is typical of the rich tapestry of golf in Bermuda where the game is a way of life played against a backdrop without equal.

Like the 16th at Port Royal, Mid Ocean's 5th is unforgettable but of infinitely greater challenge. At 433 yards this is a classical par four, one always included in the world's finest composite courses by those who know their subject.

It's a dog-leg, right to left, and from the high pulpit tee the green is visible in the far distance. But the fairway lies on the other side of Mangrove Lake and the safe route for even the frail hearted demands a carry of close to 200 yards, half of that over the narrowest stretch of water.

Legend has it that a US baseball player once found the green with his tee shot and doubtless young Tiger Woods would savour the challenge but for mere mortals even a career-best drive would leave a strong mid-iron approach. Bite off as much as you dare, is the unspoken challenge, but distance is difficult to estimate over water and more so from a tee that's close to 100 feet above it. A hook is often partner to such ambition so even a middling-aggressive shot is not without risk

A fade over the narrowest crossing point is the sensible option, followed by a lay-up to the bunkered opening of a banana-shaped green that slopes sharply from right to left. A chip-up, one-putt par will win the bets most days on a marvellous hole that is the jewel of a glittering creation.

Mid Ocean was laid out in 1921 by Charles Blair Macdonald, the first great American architect, who was smitten by Scottish courses while at St Andrews University. Naturally, then, his philosophy was minimalist; he preferred to let nature dictate matters, typified at Mid Ocean which may be the equal of his finest design, the National Links in New York.

Surrounded by the ocean, it is a compelling site enhanced by soaring pines and flowering shrubbery. Much of the course is laid over gentle hills and vales, with lakes featuring on several holes and traditional-style bunkering prominent. Many greens are above head height, adding to the problems in judgment of distance induced by the terrain, and on the higher ground, around the course perimeter, the sea wind is a constant factor. Shot values are of the highest here, even on the gentle holes.

A round at Mid Ocean has a lovely tempo, a series of crescendos finding counterpoints in more subdued passages, the mark of exemplary design. There's not a weak hole and most are memorable.

At 6,512 yards from the back tees, Mid Ocean falls some way short of the modern trends in length but the wind, the light but cloying rough and the rolling fairways serve to disguise this.

To prove the point: although many great players have tackled it the course record is still 64, seven under. So better your handicap at Mid Ocean and you'll have holiday memories to savour.

Golf resorts Down Under will reward a trip

It's a question that might pop up on one of those televised quiz programmes. "In one word, what is the link between the north west coast of England and the south eastern coast of Queensland, Australia?"

Aside from the fact that both regions have a town called Southport, a well-versed golfer would quickly realise that golf is the subject, that the north west coast is the capital of English golf and might deduce, correctly, that Queensland is now its counterpart Down Under.

The great Lancashire courses are all more than a century old but those in Queensland have been in existence for little more than a couple of decades. The former, such venerable private clubs as Royal Birkdale, Royal Lytham, Royal Liverpool, Southport & Ainsdale, Wallasey and Formby, are all international attractions for the golfing tourist, largely because of the major events to which they regularly play host. The Open, the world's oldest championship, has been staged thereabouts 31 times in its 142 years, other important tournaments even more frequently.

The Lancashire courses are neighbours on the coastline that runs from Hoylake, south of Liverpool, to Lytham St Annes, just north of Southport. That's about 50 miles as the sea gull flies. All are dune land courses, known as links, laid in the sand hills that are a feature of the region's terrain. All are close to the Irish Sea, whose often-ferocious winds add stimulus and challenge to the form of golf and its architecture found in few other places. It is golf in its purest and traditional form, similar to that of the great Scottish seaside links where the game began in the 15th Century.

The Queensland coast, on the other hand, is just getting into its stride in terms of international tournaments but, because of the sheer volume of resort courses, has justifiably become the capital of Australian golf. And it's still growing. New resorts are emerging at a metronomic pace. All are first class, the equal of any in the United States where the *genre* originated. Here it is enhanced by an idyllic climate that enables golf to be played year-round.

Back in 1987 the region had only a handful of golf clubs, largely private with limited public access. The first golf resorts emerged in 1988, although these were built as magnets for real estate sales. The boom began in 1989 and soon there were a dozen or so major resorts strung along the coast, large estates with every attraction for golfers on holiday with their families.

Accommodation is in luxurious hotels, apartments or villas; each resort has multiple restaurants, bistros and bars, plus gymnasia, tennis courts, swimming pools, bicycles, often a beach and a supervised club offering entertainment for the youngsters. Most have a health spa, the latest resort accoutrement; all have at least one golf course, some have two.

Such investment is not cheap but the stakes were high, the potential rewards gilt edged. In the past four decades the number of golfers world-wide has increased to an estimated 55 million.

And as the market has grown so has the need for new destinations, preferably off the beaten track, hence the growth of the industry in Australia.

The Queensland State Tourist Board has a slogan that describes their home as "Beautiful one day, perfect the next." It refers to the climate but it could equally be applied to the coastal scenery. It is uncommonly beautiful.

Known as the Sunshine State, it has a coastline of some 2,000 miles. Brisbane, the capital city, is in the southern section, within easy reach of the coast and the two principal tourist regions that include many of the state's golf resorts.

They are the Gold Coast, to the south east of Brisbane, and the Sunshine Coast, to the north east of the city. Both are an hour by road from Brisbane airport and are regular retreats for city folk.

The Gold Coast adjoins the state of New South Wales from where it stretches northwards for about 45 miles, encompassing a succession of pristine beaches and small communities devoted to tourism.

The focal point of the region is Surfers Paradise, a vibrant, non-stop town where life revolves around the surf beach and a swathe of nocturnal attractions, from discos to casinos. Bathed in sunshine by day and by an explosion of neon at night, it never stops sizzling. It's a cross between Las Vegas and Myrtle Beach with a hint of Greenwich Village or Soho thrown in.

Only five miles away a plethora of plush resorts and clubs offer a more esoteric form of hedonism. It's another world, a golfing utopia.

There are 40 or so courses accessible to the public, several of them world class in design and presentation. Simply to read the names of the architects is verification of their pedigree: Jack Nicklaus, Peter Thomson, Arnold Palmer, Greg Norman and Graham Marsh, to name the most famous.

Such leading lights don't come cheaply and there's a further indication of quality. Golf course construction is governed by two factors: the size of the architectural budget and the quality of the site in terms of available water and soil conditions. The leading designers will refuse to compromise their reputations so, ergo; the finished articles here are all of the top echelon. The hot shots capable of playing the back tees will be thoroughly tested; the rabbits using the forward tees will walk off smiling after a fun round. "Capital golf," they would say. And they'd be correct.

Where to stay and play:

* The Nicklaus creation is **Lakelands GC,** voted the leading public access course in Australia when it opened in 1997. From the tiger tees it stretches to 7,100 yards, par-72, with water in play on 11 holes. This is a jewel in every respect. The design, routing and presentation are matchless and the playability meets every criteria. Accommodation is available at the neighbouring Radisson Hotel, which offers various golf packages to local courses.

* Arnold Palmer worked his magic at **Sanctuary Cove,** the Hyatt Regency resort that's as beautiful as the name suggests. Here is luxurious accommodation in plush, low profile apartments with balconies overlooking gardens and a lakeside beach; a village surrounding a marina with shops and 20 or so restaurants, fine dining in the hotel, all in a setting that's romantic *in extremis*. Simply strolling around the gardens and the beach will soothe the soul. The usual sporting facilities include two golf courses; one exclusively for members and hotel guests that Arnold says is among the finest he's built. Resorts don't come much better than this. It is sumptuous.

* A Peter Thomson course is the centre piece of the nearby **Hope Island** resort which, like the course itself, is distinctive, elegant and stylish, exhibiting all the traditional hallmarks of another, more gracious era. This is essentially a residential resort, gated and exclusive, but with holiday accommodation in spacious two and three bed-roomed apartments, all with two bathrooms and kitchens and serviced weekly, that are ideal for families and small groups.

  The five times Open Champion spent most of his playing career in Britain and, being a purist, his golf designs reflect his love of the great links where he was so successful. Here, the course, widely regarded as one of the finest in Australia, has lots of pot bunkers, undulating fairways and modestly sized, crowned greens redolent of those designed a century ago by Donald Ross. It looks a picture.

* **The Royal Pines** resort covers 500 acres and while its 22 storey, 330-roomed hotel is not externally prepossessing, internally it is exemplary in every respect. Among its attractions: a top floor restaurant – one of five — where dinner is a nightly celebration of the culinary arts.

Two golf courses are the focal point of the resort. They are known as the East and the West; a Japanese architect deserving of greater recognition created both. His designs are a combination of the subtle and the inventive with an emphasis on sound driving and good course management.

The West, with more undulating, tree-lined fairways and split-level greens, is slightly the shorter to a par of 71. This will test your short game and your imagination. The East, a par 72, and the venue each March of the Australian Ladies' Masters Tournament, has wide fairways but with water in play on 17 holes. You can open the shoulders here but best keep your wits about you. The girls love it.

*   Our next stop, on the Sunshine Coast, is about one hour north of Royal Pines. We're at the **Twin Waters** resort, a 1,000-acre estate set between a river and a lagoon hemmed by a necklace of man-made beaches, all on the edge of expansive gardens. Here, too, accommodation is in spacious and luxurious apartments in low profile clusters, all within walking distance of the amenities. It is ideal for families and conferences, with every sporting facility from sky diving to sailing.

The main attraction is a gorgeous golf course designed by Peter Thomson. Known as The Links, this is top drawer but player-friendly for the most part, requiring imagination, a deft touch on and around the greens and infinite patience. The fairways are generous, but don't always appear so, and the main defence is the configuration of the greens, which are surrounded by bunkers, swales and hummocks with rising ground in the approaches and frequently domed, *a la* Ross. An unusual touch: each hole is named, British-style, and here they replicate the hole names of the Old Course at St Andrews. Ignore the stunning backdrop and you could be in Scotland.

*   Our final stop in this brief selection is the Hyatt Regency at **Coolum Beach,** one of Australia's most bounteous resorts. It reclines elegantly alongside the Pacific near Noosa Heads some 90 minutes north of Brisbane airport. A central hotel houses all the usual amenities and the golf clubhouse but accommodation is principally in apartments and villas in the surrounding gardens. Most are within strolling distance of a small village where there are restaurants, bars, shops and the main swimming pool complex.

Coolum is renowned for its facilities – the claim is that there are 155 activities available! The *raison d'etre*, though, is the golf course, the venue in November for the Australian PGA Championship.

Designed by America's Robert Trent Jones Jr., it is a unique blend of contrasts, ranging from holes overlooking the ocean to others in wooded bush land. It's a big driving course over undulating fairways that twist and turn and with water and sand in profusion. The major challenge is the shot to beautifully configured greens, all tightly defended but mainly flat and very quick. Avid golfers love this place.

Without doubt one of Australia's most scenic courses with millions of trees, Coolum is virtually a bird life sanctuary and kangaroos are a common sight.

Like the resort, it is utterly serene and indescribably beautiful. Not to be missed. It would bring a fitting finale to an unforgettable holiday.

This new resort raises the bar in Africa — and beyond

It would be easy to become over-excited about the Sofitel Mogador resort in Morocco, so a few deep breaths are in order here, to get the pulse rate under control. Let's say simply that it may be the finest golf resort in Morocco and some way beyond. Yup, it's as good as that...

Opened in March 2011, it has raised the bar for its competitors. It is an astonishing creation in superior hospitality with incomparable facilities and service. Situated on an ocean-front estate of 1,500 acres near the charming resort town of Essaouira mid-way down Morocco's 2,000 mile Atlantic coastline, it is three hours by road north of Agadir and 40 minutes by air from Casablanca, the nation's main airport hub. Those seeking a romantic hide-away, with world-class golf and accommodations, need look no further. This is the place you've been searching for.

The region boasts 300 days of sunshine a year with average temperatures seldom lower than 25C and rarely higher than 30C. Atlantic breezes temper the hottest days and the under-populated beaches are a glittering bonus to the multifarious attractions that await the holiday-maker.

The town deserves their close attentions but our focus here is the new resort a short drive away. Lacking a golf course, it would still reward investigation: the one in situ completes an unforgettable combination. Go once and you'll be hooked.

The hotel is regal, the golf course a sublime example of the architect's art, in this case that of Gary Player. More on this anon.

The hotel first: it is a low profile — only three storeys — of 147 rooms overlooking the ocean and with 26 two bedroomed villas in the grounds for those seeking the ultimate privacy. This is one of the finest hotels I've known in many years of international travel. The ambience, like the level of service, beggars description.

The public areas are similarly appealing. There's a spa and a gym and swimming pools. The hotel's standard bedrooms are all minor suites where no detail has been overlooked. Each opens onto a spacious balcony giving views over the gardens that run down to the beach, no more than a seven iron away. At one end of the hotel is the spa; nearby is the golf clubhouse. Both are models.

The course is arguably one of the finest resort courses in the world. It is challenging, rewarding and demanding but fair. It is strategic rather than penal, as a resort course should be and as usual with Gary Player's creations.

Big targets abound: wide fairways, expansive greens but equally large bunkers for those who stray. There's ample lateral and vertical movement to provide variety and it is all in a wooded setting with the sea as a backdrop. From where the tigers prowl the card reads 7,213 yards (that's 6,558 metres) to a par of 72, but there are six sets of tees, three each for men and women, to cater for all levels of ability.

The condition and presentation is flawless. The tees resemble some greens we've seen recently; the bunkers are pristine, the greens true but slick and with just enough movement to demand your full attention. Imagination and sound course management will pay dividends and a sound short game and a hot putter will help, too. Patience is a virtue here: take your time with the shortest putt and, above all, be positive.

Stand on the first tee and it will be obvious that a treat is in store. True to Henry Cotton's philosophy that a sound opening hole calls for simplicity of design with everything in view, this par four is a classic and a preamble to a course of lilting tempo that brings fun and challenge in equal measure. It is the perfect resort course.

GOLF CLASSIC AND HISTORIC

The Wirral and Hoylake; the Heartland of English golf

For the thousands in the vast galleries who will watch the Open Championship in July their first-time trip to Royal Liverpool will be a pilgrimage the like of which they have seldom known. Because the venue is the hallowed heartland of English golf; this is where the Amateur Championship was founded in 1885, where the Open became a regular fixture from 1897 when it moved from Scotland, and where in 1902 England met Scotland in the first international match the game had known.

Nearby Southport may claim to be the capital of English golf but Hoylake, as the host club is affectionately called, is the spiritual homeland and has been for a century or more since Harold Hilton and John Ball, the great amateurs of the late 19th Century, set their beloved club on its path to glory.

But the region known as The Wirral on England's north west coastline has more than one great golf club to shout about. They may lack the venerable and historical significance of Hoylake but such clubs as Wallasey, Caldy and Heswall are attractions in their own right. Hoylake is simply the glittering icing on the cake of golf in The Wirral.

The duneland coastline of Lancashire and Cheshire is the anvil upon which English golf was forged and after more than a century of major championships and momentous events famous names have become common coinage in the twin counties.

None shines brighter than those associated with the Wallasey club, home to a links of impeccable pedigree. Sandy Herd, James Braid, Harold Hilton and Fred Hawtree have in turn made architectural contributions to the course that Old Tom Morris laid out in 1891.

All the modifications have been enforced, by nature and fate, for few clubs have known such a chequered history and lived to tell the tale. Originally 240 acres of wild duneland alongside the Mersey estuary, 100 acres and many original holes have been swallowed up by drifting sand. Only four of the Morris greens are extant and numerous replacement holes have been lost over the years. A succession of short term leases compounded the threat and twice the dread combination took the club to the brink of demise.

Happily, both problems are now distant nightmares: a coast road and marram grass have helped stabilise the sand, and a 100 year lease, signed in 1986, assures the future of one of England's premier links.

It is one which has been a final qualifying venue for the Open since 1930 when Bobby Jones waxed lyrical about it en route to winning the championship and his immortal grand slam. The original of the famous portrait of Jones, painted by a Wallasey member and signed by the great man in admiration, has pride of place in the clubhouse. Nearby is a portrait of Frank Stableford, originator of the scoring system used around the world and regarded as the club's greatest benefactor.

Dr. Stableford, a Wallasey member and later captain, devised the system in 1931, largely in frustration at his inability to reach some of the long two shotters when frequent westerlies made a mockery of the bogey competitions then common. The first Stableford competition was held there on 16 May 1932, an event commemorated by an annual open tournament for the Stableford Memorial Trophy, presented by the first winner.

History permeates the grand old clubhouse and it's impossible to be unaware of it on the links where it seems there's a story attached to every hole. It's easy to sense the ghosts of Old Tom, Bobby Jones, James Braid and a host of other great players striding the fairways that wriggle through sprawling sand hills on this austere, wind-haunted coastline. You'll quickly become aware, too, of the source of their captivation. This is a links to pose the ultimate test of technique and character.

Elevated tees or greens are numerous; few holes are straight and none fails to punish the wayward. Strategy is paramount here: your score is granted by a miser. You must drive well and to the correct line or you'll have no second shot worth the name.

Take the 17th: it's 464 yards and bends around huge sand hills, with the green in a dell at the end of a gully. The drive must be sufficiently left and long to open up the green, leaving a second shot of 230 yards or so. Be marginally right off the tee and you'll be blocked by the dunes, a lay-up the only recourse. Be wide with the approach and you'll struggle with the next. Fives are more common than fours here, and from personal experience sevens outnumber fives!

The greens, modestly-sized at best, are as hard and fast as you'd expect, and the running pitch or chip shot is the vogue — usually for the third shot! There are only 70 bunkers: others would be superfluous.

The 371 yard 11th, for instance, can be unreachable; stroke index 1 and 2 are both par fives and the four hole finish is the equal of any. The remainder are simply memorable.

It is a regal links and another glittering chapter in its history will be written in June when, in tandem with neighbouring Royal Liverpool, the club will host the 100th Amateur Championship. Players and spectators alike have a treat in store.

The fact that the Caldy club's links was laid out by James Braid would be reason enough for most golfing purists to beat a path there. Its pedigree is such that it has staged a swath of top class events.

It's not a man-eating links, as Hoylake can be when the wind gets its dander up, but it's not one to be sniffed at, either. Play this one in a three club breeze that's common hereabouts and you'll know you've been in a fight.

The course, of 6,651 yards, par 72, is in two sections: holes 3 to 10 are on an out-and-back strip of dune land overlooking the Dee estuary; the others are inland, although still influenced by the breeze which exacerbates the challenge of a constantly changing direction of play. Members say the links doesn't play the same way two days running.

The first nine holes were laid out in 1906 by Jack Morris, a nephew of Old Tom, who for some years was professional at nearby Conway. Braid came along in 1930, remodelled the existing loop and added a second nine. The original design is all largely extant although a considerable investment in recent times has seen the greens and tees up-graded to USGA specifications.

Thus, it's a tad more verdant that your average links and, the inland section being somewhat wooded, it looks a picture, not least because of views from the high ground across the estuary.

They'll be celebrating their centenary next year and doubtless running competitions to mark the occasion. If you're up for the Open pop into Caldy treat yourself to 18 holes and you might just be invited to participate.

Heswall GC is of comparable vintage and provenance to Caldy, having been laid out in 1902 by Jack Morris on a site overlooking the Dee estuary. Some regard it as one of the UK's most beautiful courses but it's rather more than simply a pretty site. Like Caldy, this one will bite your ankle if you transgress.

Heswall has been the venue for the English Seniors Amateur Championship and in July will host the R&A's Junior Open Championship. So its pedigree is plain, although rather more chequered.

It was designed as an 18 hole course but has been altered and extended several times as land became available. Thus, its length has increased from 5115 yards in 1909 to 5889 yards in 1957 and 6556 yards today.

Harry Vardon, Frank Pennink and Donald Steel effected improvements over the years, and Steel will oversee further changes later this year as yet more land has been purchased to provide capacity for five additional holes. The new lay-out will have a different routing and order of play and the end result will be a course of two distinct loops, each with two par 5s and two par 3s.

The present much-loved lay-out is similar to Caldy's in that it is in two distinct sections with six holes overlooking the Dee estuary and the remainder inland. The major difference between Caldy and Heswall is that the latter is best described as seaside parkland. It is set on a gently rolling site adjoining the Wirral Country Park and a salt marsh that in winter becomes a bird sanctuary.

A series of ponds equate to a high water table and encourage a first class presentation. If you've had your fill of links golf and are seeking a different challenge in a lovely setting then Heswall is the place for you.

On the other hand, if you can't get enough of links and golfing history a diversion to the West Lancashire course will satisfy the inner man. But a word of caution: check the weather forecast the day before. If a blow is predicted, transfer your attentions elsewhere and hope for better conditions on the morrow.

At 6,763 yards (SSS 72) from the medal tees, the course at Lancashire's oldest club is not over-long on the card but it is totally exposed and with the wind whipping in from the sea it becomes a test of character and stamina.

This is not to deter the lesser players: on a fine day and from the visitors' tees it offers a lovely prospect of typical sand belt golf on a course renowned for its condition.

West Lancashire, founded in 1873 and the oldest course in the county, is arguably the toughest of all venues for final qualifying at the Open Championship. A splendid clubhouse offers every amenity and completes an appealing scenario of English golf at its best.

Seaton Carew: a links that takes no prisoners

Tackle the awesome links of Seaton Carew and, like a hole in one or your first sub-par round, you'll be justified in carving a notch in your putter. Play it when the breeze has the flag sticks touching their toes and you can make that two notches! Because here's one to stir the red corpuscles into a frenzy, a grizzled links of the old school, one that takes no prisoners but leaves a warm glow for those equal to its challenge. It's not a pretty sight: you don't go to Seaton for the scenery because there isn't any. You go there to complete a golfing education over hard-bitten, wind-scarred duneland that's changed little in a century and not much before that.

The course falls off the end of the promenade in the town of Seaton Carew that's really a suburb of Hartlepool. Out there is the North Sea, a forbidding, heaving mass of grey: on the skyline at the southern reaches of the course the accoutrements of heavy industry stand in high profile. In between is an expanse of buckthorn and marram-covered dunes running down to a forlorn beach.

Monte Carlo it's not but Seaton is one of Britain's great seaside courses where barely a year passes without a national championship. To this end there are 22 holes, the original 18 plus four down near the beach, used as alternatives for the championship Brabazon course. This measures 6,920 yards, a par-73 with only three par threes and is some 300 yards longer than the Old course, which is par-71.

The fairways are generous enough, once you've cleared the matted rough that stretches from the end of most tees. Many fairways bend at driving length, are edged by marram-covered dunes and wander off at all angles. This exacerbates the problems of the major hazards, the wind and a scattering of voracious bunkers lurking below the huge, gathering hummocks, frequently just short of the greens.

These are the old fashioned monsters that formerly had railway sleepers and steps for access. You'll get the picture. Playing out side-ways is usually a good bet. Because of them, each of the long holes has a prescribed angle of approach. If in doubt a lay-up is a good bet, too, followed by a chip and run up the length of the green. But you'd better be accurate with your lay-up and that's not easy: a lack of perspective and the ubiquitous cross wind compound the problem.

The greens are all large but variable in shape and configuration: three of them are tiered, Mackenzie-style. Most are elevated to some degree, although two of the par threes are flat. All of which puts a premium on nerve and character. You can't be ambivalent about Seaton: you'll either love it or hate it. Take plenty of ammunition. Card: Old course, 6,613 yards, par-72. Location: off the A178, the coast road, at the end of the promenade.

Ireland's Causeway Coast, The Home of Champions

If ever you go across the sea to Ireland you should hold your hour, as they say thereabouts, and tarry a while on the Antrim Coast. They call it the Causeway Coast on account of the world heritage site they know as the Giants' Causeway, and it's as dramatic and beautiful a coastline as you'll find anywhere.

The region is a grand holiday destination for couples and active families and doubly so for golfers on account of three venerable and first-class links thereabouts being in close proximity to one of Ireland's finest small hotels.

You'll find all of this at the top end of the country, where Ireland tumbles into the sea, and here the northern coast has a rich golfing history that's been given added lustre by the recent exploits of its trio of native sons. Graeme McDowell, young Rory McIlroy and Darren Clarke all honed their skills in what has been justifiably re-named the Home of Champions and the three great links that await the visitor were their boyhood stamping grounds.

You'll know of **Royal Portrush**, of course: it's a former venue for the Open Championship and, thanks to its trio of major winners, may soon be once again. It's a mighty links and locals aver that **Portstewart**, its neighbour, is but a whisker behind in quality of setting and challenge. Then there's **Castlerock**, an unsung links of sublime character, no more than four or five miles away. The Home of Champions is as close to Golfing Heaven as most mortals will find.

Play them turn-about for a week and the most demanding links man would have a holiday to savour for a lifetime. And if he based himself at the historic Bushmills Inn he'd opine that all his birthdays had come at once! Exquisite is one fitting adjective for this small but perfectly formed hotel. Matchless is another....

A golden bonus and the only possible finale after such a week: he could break his return journey to Belfast airport and play **Royal County Down**, one of the world's greatest links and perhaps the ultimate golfing challenge. Now that would be an unforgettable holiday!

Where to stay: No contest here! A golf writer chum is on record as saying that "if I can't stay at the **Bushmills Inn** I postpone my visit until I can..."

Located in the ancient village of Bushmills mid-way between the Giant's Causeway and the Royal Portrush Golf Club, the now-renowned hostelry dates to the 17th century when it was a small coaching inn. A chequered history followed, but a series of extensions between 1987 and 2009 elevated it to the ultimate level of luxury while retaining the old world charm that plays such a role in its appeal.

Open log fires, gas lights, oak beams and stripped pine enhance the ambience of the various public rooms: the Gas Bar could become addictive; the Drawing Room is a hideaway, the dining room a delight for all the senses. And you'd want to hide away in one of the bedrooms....

I last saw the inn some 20 years ago and was smitten. Since then it has been extended but has lost nothing in the transformation. In the old days it had a mere handful of rooms; now it boasts 41 sumptuous bedrooms and suites of varying configuration and a string of awards from all corners of the travel industry. Progress invariably comes at a price but not at the Bushmills Inn. In more than 50 years of international travel I have seen no small hotel with higher standards of luxury and service. It may be incomparable.

An unusual aspect is that it hosts groups of disparate configuration. There are two or three family suites and most bedrooms can be adapted for either twin or double use. Thus, the summer and autumn seasons attracts mainly small golfing groups; the other seasons are ideal for couples seeking a romantic break. With or without golf it would be memorable.

About the golf: If you don't want to play **Royal Portrush** at least twice there's no hope for you. Best go lie down in a darkened room and curl up your toes.

Suffice to say that those who compile the annual ranking lists of Irish courses have reached a simple solution to the problem of separating the great triumvirate of Royal County Down, Portmarnock Old and the Dunluce links of Royal Portrush. They merely shuffle them around at the top of the pile so that each has a turn at number one spot. It's the epitome of Irish logic.

The great Bernard Darwin, the doyen of golf writers in the first half of the last century, described Portrush as "arguably Harry Colt's ultimate creation; a monument more enduring than brass." It has lost nothing with the passage of time, indeed the reverse may be true: the years have burnished Colt's legacy.

The setting helps. Portrush is at one with the sea, indeed its 5th green and 6th tee were once threatened by it until the golfing world answered the clarion call and subscribed to the cost of the sea defences that saved the day.

So a teasing breeze is standard and frequently it graduates into something more muscular. Then the narrow, meandering fairways shrink, the greens become even smaller and the hazards expand. You'll need your wits about you now, and a philosophical outlook, to say nothing of a good supply of ammunition.

It can be a fearsome test of driving, with tiger country awaiting anything off-line. Hack out, smile, forget par and hope for a chip and one putt, which is easier said than done.... You'll need a sound short game to effect salvage operations plus unlimited imagination and a hot putter on greens with lots of subtle movement.

Portrush is a links that gives little beyond red-blooded exhilaration. Good holes are legion: the 5th is a dream and wait until you reach the 14th and 15th, known as Calamity and Purgatory respectively. You won't believe your eyes. Don't forget your camera.

Royal County Down, overlooking Dundrum Bay at Newcastle, is the nation's most venerable links and its most regal. History has it that Old Tom Morris was responsible for the design but in truth this was a site waiting for golf to be invented. It merely required a little fine tuning, a placement of tees and greens and the introduction of bunkers.

With fairways swooping between majestic dunes, ablaze with gorse for much of the year, it may be the most natural links in the game. Heavily undulating for a links, it may also be the toughest! To the newcomer it can be penal in anything more than a breeze. Here even the ladies' card reads 6,249 yards and from the tiger tees it is in excess of 7,000, to par-72, (standard scratch 74). This is not one for the faint-hearted.

It has been written that "the Open Championship has been played on courses that are not as good" and while today's leading players would cavil at several blind tee shots they'd be forced to doff their collective cap at every other demand this great links imposes. Patience, judgment, imagination, power and finesse, all play their part and in a three or four club wind they'd need dollops of character, too. Seeing red here is not uncommon, with unkind bounces and fearsome rough.

The course has a peerless routing and a symphonic tempo but if there's an easy hole I haven't found it in half a dozen attempts. Even the short holes will test your mettle. Then there's the breathless scenery. The place is a photographer's dream, given just a hint of sunshine and shadow. From the high ground the lonely beach of Dundrum Bay counterpoints the smoky Mountains of Mourne that form the backdrop to a sea of golden gorse and emerald fairways. It has a grandeur that may be incomparable.

So a word to the wise: take a caddie and forget about your score, at least the first time around. Simply relax and enjoy the occasion. You'll play the better for it. Then after lunch, more aware of the wiles of one of the world's great links, you'll want to do it all again. You'll be hooked. Welcome to the club!

Visit the **Portstewart** Golf Club and you'll be looking green-eyed at the members: they have three links courses from which to choose, one of them of a championship standard, the other two offering a variety to delight those of a certain age and that also attracts visitors seeking something less than a red-blooded challenge.

The **Strand** course is the big one, at 6,895 yards, par 72; the **Riverside** is the secondary course at 5,725 yards, par 68, and at 4,730 yards, par 64, the **Old** course is popular with golfing couples and seniors out for a spin of a summer evening. It's a rare combination and one that must delight local families and lucky visitors, particularly couples on a romantic golfing holiday.

But for those who like to play where the tigers prowl the Strand course is the stuff of dreams. It is red in tooth and claw, particularly when the wind gets frisky, and there's not a huge gap in quality between this and the championship course of neighbouring Royal Portrush. Which is why the Strand has hosted various amateur and professional championships over the years, most recently the British Girls' Championship in 2006.

First laid out in 1894 and redesigned by Willie Park Junior in the 1920's, this great links was given a major up-date in 1981 with the purchase of additional land that enabled the construction of seven new holes through towering dunes and fabulous links land. Stunning is a suitable adjective.

As at Royal County Down, the dramatic changes in elevation to be found here add to the challenge: several elevated tees bring sea views as well as long carries and a test of nerve, while elevated greens magnify the demands upon course management and imagination. This is a jewel of a links that shouldn't be missed.

And then there's **Castlerock**, long a personal favourite and the source of happy golfing memories. The Irish PGA Championship was played here in 2001, the club's centenary year, and the pro's loved it, particularly the quality of the greens. But above all it is an idyllic members' course, a lovely combination of challenge and delightful scenery, dominated by rolling sand dunes and sea views, that never fails to delight.

There are five par fives, nine par fours and four outstanding one shotters but at 6,500 yards, par 73, from the members' tees it's not a man-eater, although as with all links the sea breeze plays a major role. Rather is it a links of strategic challenge where sound course management and a solid short game are as vital as accuracy and imagination.

To illustrate this: from the white tees only one par five, the 15th of 510 yards, is in excess of 500 yards, and most of the par fours are shorter than 400 yards, some appreciably so. You'll get the picture. Add an imaginative routing and impeccable greens with subtle movement and it becomes obvious why many rate this as one of Ireland's true hidden gems.

Have a golfing holiday along the Causeway Coast and Castlerock will be one of many highlights. But be warned: such a week could become addictive!

Druid's Glen: a modern masterpiece is revealed

It was a challenge to make an architect salivate; a brief to create the finest inland course in Ireland. Expense was no object, commercial considerations were irrelevant, quality was paramount.

Two years and several million pounds later the golfing world began beating a path to Druid's Glen on the outskirts of Dublin as Pat Ruddy and Tom Craddock revealed the fruits of their architectural labours.

Six months on, the finishing touches still being made, their newly-unveiled jewel received what promises to be its first major accolade: it was selected as the venue for the 1996 Irish Open. The challenge had been met, a dream realised.

"This wasn't designed for the beginner," Pat Ruddy said. "The better golfers these days are getting so hot that any new course worth the name must be testing. We think Druid's Glen is an amalgam of beauty, challenge and excitement."

The Irish, all fire and passion in matters sporting, are not given to understatement but Ruddy wasn't being immodest. He was merely echoing the consensus of the army of visitors who have been bewitched by the latest Irish masterpiece.

At 6,845 yards, par-73, from the back blocks, the course rolls over a sumptuously aesthetic site, a former family estate whose mansion is now a clubhouse of unalloyed luxury. There are 400 acres — a second course is planned — with wooded valleys, a river, several lakes and a string of waterfalls, all offering visual images the equal of any in world golf. Augusta is a frequent comparison. It's one not misplaced, particularly in the Spring when a profusion of flowering shrubs runs riot in the balmy Dublin climate.

The comparison doesn't end there. At least two holes are redolent of the Masters' course and another will ring bells at St Andrews: Ruddy is not averse to encompassing accepted design principles into his visual images.

"I've been to Augusta many times," he said, "and I've had fun watching them play the par three 16th. So you could say our 8th hole has developed along comparable lines, a broad green with a variety of interesting pin positions. Similarly the 14th, a short par four which demands a pitch over bunkers to an elevated green sloping sharply back to front and with a crescent of trees behind. It's the type of hole which works very well at Augusta, a big green demanding an accurate approach for par or better."

It's a principle common to Druid's Glen. The average-sized green covers 800 square yards so be too far from the pin and you'll be in three putt territory. And unless you have a devilish short game you'll need to place your drive precisely, not always a simple matter. This place has more dog-legs than a team of huskies.

On many holes, though, everything is in view from the tee. Which is how the round starts, with a hole of classical simplicity, slightly downhill and nothing hidden, as is the 18th, a par five with a tee shot over water and three lakes, cascading over weirs, guarding the green approaches.

In between is a series of other memorable holes: the 7th, Ruddy's favourite, a big sweeping dog-leg; the 13th, which demands accuracy, character and imagination in equal parts, and four outstanding par threes.

Three of these involve water carries and one, the 17th, has an island green that like the home hole is sure to become famous. It all awaits the golfer with soul, one eager to test himself to the limit in a sublime setting.

Druid's Glen GC, Woodstock House, Kilcoole, County Wicklow. Card: 6,845 yards, par-73.

Location:

Take N11 from Dublin (Wicklow road) then the Newtownmountkennedy by-pass. Watch for left slip road into village and go left for Kilcoole. Club is 1.5 miles on right.

The Wales Coast offers a golf tour to light your fire!

Most golfing holidays will be an anti-climax after this week-long golf tour. Imagine two rounds over each of five courses which collectively are the equal of any you'll find. The clubs are Conwy, Royal St David's, Aberdovey, Pwllheli and Holyhead. Each is within reasonable proximity of the next; all are in breathtaking seaside settings; each is renowned for its condition. Add a collection of fine hotels and this may be the ultimate British golfing holiday.

You'll know of Conwy and Royal St David's, no doubt. Both true links, they've staged countless major events over the past century. The first lies near the great castle, opposite Deganwy in the north. St David's, also overlooked by a castle, at Harlech, is an hour to the south. Aberdovey, an historic links of rare quality, reclines in regal splendour alongside Cardigan Bay, about an hour south of Harlech.

North west across Cardigan Bay, on the enchanting Lleyn Peninsular, lies the little-known golfing jewel of Pwllheli (pronounced Perfwelly); north west again as the sea gull flies stands Holyhead, a cliff-top moor land course in a spectacular setting on the south western tip of Anglesey.

If you're arriving from the North or the Midlands, head first for Conwy then to Holyhead and Pwllheli before going south, down the coast road, to Harlech and Aberdovey. If you're from the south, follow that route in reverse. There's about an hour's driving between each stop but the scenery alone will make your journey worthwhile. And after the first day you'll be so full of reminiscing the miles will fly by. The betting is you'll make this an annual tour.

Two of the three great links have a common bond, one that has a bearing on their style and character and which has influenced the third. It is this: St David's and Aberdovey had no recognised architect; they evolved in the course of play, just as did some of the great Scottish links. So like the Old Course they appear totally natural.

Conwy, or Caernarvonshire as it is officially named, was laid out by Jack Morris of Royal Liverpool whose members discovered the site in the 19th century. Jack, the Hoylake professional for 60 years, was a nephew of Old Tom and like his uncle was under the spell of the Old Course where he'd played as a young man. When invited to lay out Conwy he simply reverted to those early influences of a natural links.

In all three instances many of the greens are flat, simply extensions of the fairways, tightly defended by gorse and sand and subtle undulations. The consequence, as at the Old Course, is a marked lack of perspective with all but the minority of sculptured greens. Once reached the greens are generally expansive but even as close as mid-iron distance they present small targets, encouraging indecisive clubbing which invariably leaves the ball short. Then, too, the greens are perfectly placed, often slightly beyond a depression, "dead ground" that hides distance or a rise that creates it. Illusion was the stock-in-trade of even the earliest course builders worth their salt. They knew how to use the wind, too.

The knowledgeable say that because of this Conwy is a not a links for the less accomplished. As an indication of its stature, the British Ladies Open and the Home Internationals have been held there in recent years, as was the 1992 European Boys' Championship. Nobody left unscathed.

From the medal tees the card reads 6,901 yards, par 72, SSS 73. Suffice to say that the record for the present course is 71, established since 1985 when the A55 motorway carved through the perimeter necessitating minor changes that added 200 yards to the overall length.

Jack Morris was not famous as a player or an architect but no man could wish for a finer memorial. He'd be proud of it today. There's not a weak hole and many are outstanding, each different from the one before, bringing a lovely rhythm to the round.

The links is probably far in excess of 1,000 yards longer than when Morris laid it out in 1890 but 16 of his greens are still in play and most of his original layout is extant. You'll need length and accuracy off the tee, and a generous measure of imagination for the next shot!

After gentle beginnings the game is really on at the 4th, the first of a series of long par fours — there are six up to 459 yards, all with crooked fairways and fierce, lurking rough — interspersed with a couple of long iron par threes. The 9th, 10th and 12th holes are all in excess of 512 yards, and the closing three holes comprise a finish as demanding as any, particularly the par four 17th, a real card wrecker.

The club recently acquired the lease of the land and plans are afoot for further improvements to the course and its homely clubhouse. It merits a detour now; one can only relish the delights in store.

Conwy is a lion of a links, so what price Royal St David's? Many consider it the equal of Royal Porthcawl at the pinnacle of Welsh golf and in one respect it is superior: the setting is breathtaking.

On one flank the granite pile of Harlech castle broods over the course, its turrets the markers from several tees. In the middle distance Mount Snowdon stares down, completing a mystical backdrop. Around the great old links towering sand hills rise to blot out sight of the sea, creating a basin that funnels the wind cruising in from the bay. All around is gorse and heather and rough as thick as unmown hay in August. Golf here is of another dimension. As with the

Old Course, the ambience of Royal St David's is guaranteed to stir the emotions. It too is a mecca for the true believers.

Par 69, standard scratch 71; the bare statistics speak volumes but don't tell the whole story. Numerous holes would grace any links of world class and of those the 15th would win many votes as arguably the finest par four in Britain and some way beyond.

Like Portrush and Birkdale, its Royal counterparts, the fairways of St David's wander in all directions, following the gentle contours of the land to a succession of exquisitely placed greens. Thus, the constant breeze attacks from every angle. To exacerbate the problem, most of the fairways bend at driving length, some markedly so, where bunkers await to ambush the wayward.

The fairways generally are wide enough to stage a parade, but stray too far from the prescribed line and a stranger could require a compass bearing for his second shot. Miss the fairway and be prepared to hack out, if you can find the ball. The rough is uncompromising.

The inward loop, the shorter by almost 300 yards, is the more difficult with the general direction of play being into the prevailing breeze. The 10th is stroke index one and, the short 11th and 18th aside, expect no mercy from here. The four holes from the 14th to the 17th are, at first sight, quite awesome.

Sprinkled around a moonscape of dunes, they may well be the finest four consecutive holes in Britain. Consider the 15th: it's of 427 yards and dog-legs right, into the prevailing wind. The drive must carry a swathe of dunes and rough to find the sliver of fairway visible from the elevated tee; the second shot is at least a long iron to a hidden green. Few reach it. There's not one bunker but it's a hole to demand comparison with the greatest par four anywhere; and the 17th, also of 427 yards, is almost comparable in its challenge.

To complete a magnificent landscape the greens are superb; large and undulating and disarmingly true. This is a course one could play non-stop for a week. It's easy to rationalise the large number of country members.

The green fees aside, the outstanding aspect of the region's golf is the peerless condition of its courses. Some of the greens are the equal of any we know but good as they are at Royal St David's, John Barnett, the club's long serving professional, graciously acknowledged that those of Aberdovey were — just marginally! — superior.

There is no debating the point. The Aberdovey greens are velvet swards. Always firm and holding, they've been calibrated at 9.5 on the stimp meter, according to club professional Jo Davies. Indeed they're perhaps the outstanding feature of this delightful links made famous by the late Bernard Darwin, for long the prince of golf writers who learned his golf there as a boy and and enjoyed a life-long love affair with it.

It's a spectacular sight viewed from the terrace of the Trefiddian Hotel, perched on the hillside overlooking the links. With the old clubhouse to the left, the first three and final three holes are contained in a corridor of crumpled land, no more than 60 or so yards wide, between the railway line which forms the landward boundary and a stretch of sand hills which defends the course against the sea.

The wind holds the key here, too. On a calm day its generous fairways and minimal rough offer a subtle examination of technique, largely of the short game. But it's another tale when the weather flexes its muscles, particularly over the six holes down the corridor which channels the prevailing wind and makes a magnet of the railway line.

Then the home hole, with its huge green, can be a drive and a short iron, for instance, or be quite unreachable in two, when a ditch comes into play. Add a high water table which brings a rare lush growth to the sea-washed fairways and on windy days it plays far in excess of its 6,445 yards (par 71).

It's a forgiving links which the less accomplished can appreciate but one which will stretch the better players — the first three greens are partially hidden, for instance, and there's a handsome collection of one shotters. Bunkers litter the course and on most holes, as at Royal St David's, for the better player the second shot is the vital one to those indescribably beautiful greens.

Play the glorious course at Pwllheli and you'll want to roll it up and take it home, though you could never replicate the lovely setting.

One is in envy of the members on such a course, at once beautiful, challenging, varied and serene. The greens are of rare quality, some say the equal of Aberdovey; the fairways are emerald carpets, hemmed with matted rough, lateral water hazards and peppered with bunkers. Every hole is in contrast to the last, each green has a perfect setting.

At a whisper under 6,100 yards to a par of 69 but with a course record of 66, this is plainly one out of the top drawer. There are no par fives, although several par fours play that way in the prevailing sou' westerly breeze to compliment three memorable short holes. Uniquely, the first seven holes are lush parkland, the following nine are true links and the final two virtually heathland.

The original nine holes of links were laid out in 1890 by Jack Morris, the Hoylake professional responsible for Conwy. In 1908 James Braid re-designed the course into an 18 holer, in play until the 1920s. Then the club leased the parkland section and incorporated the new holes into the best of Braid's links.

The River Penhros meanders through the landward boundary, hence the high water table and the superb fairways, so lush that over the heavily wooded parkland section they'll shrink the best tee shot and stretch the second. The greens generally are large and receptive but deviously confusing. All are different: one may be an up-turned saucer, the next quite flat, though with subtle borrows, the following one a Mackenzie or an undulating Braid — his signature is everywhere.

The links section begins by running clockwise along the shore of Cardigan Bay. From the 11th tee above the beach there are views of Abersoch to the south, with the Pembrokeshire coast in the far distance and the Snowdonia range rising at your back. It's an incomparable setting enhanced by a links of lyrical proportions.

Every hole is memorable but our favourite was probably the short 10th. From an elevated beach-side tee, the shot is over dunes and a dry stone wall, North Berwick-style, to a large, sloping green half hidden by hummocks and defended by bunkers. Behind is a white-washed old cottage that doubles as an occasional half-way house. At 197 yards, with the beach to the left and a cavernous bunker short of the right front of the green, it's an heroic hole, typical of one of Britain's hidden jewels of golf.

Holyhead is similarly enchanting, although in a romantically remote moorland setting at Trearddur Bay, high on an Anglesey headland. Here the wind comes off the Irish Sea just looking for trouble!

From the medal tees the course is 6,058 yards, par 70, SSS 70. It's 400 yards shorter from the yellow tees, with the three par fives reduced to fours giving a par of 67. Take a tip: you'll be closer to your handicap off the back: this is white knuckle territory!

Much of the course is in a plateau-basin overlooked by high ground. At the lower level the fairways are wide, the rough minimal. Get up top, though, and tunnel vision will be a decided advantage. Some of the tee shots, several blind down corridors of gorse and heather, will curl your hair. You could use all your ammunition in anything more than a stiff breeze.

A number of tees and greens are placed high on rocky outcrops — the short 2nd is from an elevated tee to an elevated green, an awesome prospect with a head wind whipping in from the sea — and you'll play most shots either up, to an elevated target, or down.

It's a lovely design, by James Braid, the greens perfectly found, some in spectacular settings, each imposing different demands upon technique. Drive well here and you'll have a grand day. It's comfortably easy walking, frequently through stands of trees that afford some protection when the wind gets frisky.

The course condition is in keeping with the region's high standards: the greens are pampered and though the fairways have only a thin layer of top soil they were in pristine order and well defined.

Come to think of it, Holy Island is a fitting finale to a heavenly week.

The Dublin region: calling all heroes!

You'll need either an iron constitution or steely determination to undertake a golfing tour of Dublin and its precincts: the old place is fraught with more temptations than the devil himself could devise. Anyone who's tried it and lived to tell the tale will aver that getting into Dublin is easy enough; it's getting out that's the problem.

Silver tongued barmen aside, the alluring capital has distractions most places haven't invented yet. For most of the time, especially after dark, the old place is six feet off the ground and swinging like a candelabra at an orgy. It helps if you have a thirst you could hang your hat on and you're fond of twelve hour debates.

For golfers there's upwards of fifty courses no more than an hour's drive of the city centre and another thirty not much further away. But there's not much respite there, either. Most have clubhouses where the barmen take no prisoners. Your best bet is to tell him your morning tee time as you pull up a stool and sip your first Guinness. Don't bank on breakfast, though.

All that aside, Dublin may be the ultimate golfing city and so let us assume that, like us, you're all tee-total devotees, early-nighters impervious to most off-course blandishments and eager to play 36 holes a day for a week. If you fit that description, and have consummate self-discipline, then this is the place for you.

Dublin's city centre traffic would make a bishop blaspheme so it's best to bed down on the periphery where some first rate hotels allow easy access to golf and are within range of the the nocturnal attractions that aren't terminal.

About a dozen major courses lie on the northern outskirts, for instance, and the Grand Hotel at Malahide couldn't be more convenient. No more than a few minutes away will be found the pick of Ireland's great links and parkland courses, some new, most old.

You should begin next door, at The Island GC at Malahide, a gnarled but captivating links that is part of the history of Irish golf. It once required a boat to reach it but these days there's a new bridge from which a wriggling road leads to a warm welcome

Of similar vintage is County Louth at Baltray, a links of consummate charm designed by Tom Simpson and regarded by many as one of the world's unsung gems. You'll need a day here to fully appreciate the ambience and for those on a budget there's a cosy Dormy House which offers inclusive packages at bargain rates.

Close to Baltray, sharing a boundary where both courses touch the beach, is the Seapoint course. Designed by Des Smyth, this is part links, part parkland, a sparkling combination that has already staged the Irish Matchplay Championship.

Try a round, too, at Royal Dublin, a frequent venue for the Irish Open and one which has its own chapter in Irish golfing history. You might even bump into Himself, Christy O'Connor, reckoned to be the finest golfer never to win the Open, but there'll be a welcome who ever greets you at this grand old club.

Ireland is awash with new courses and one causing a considerable stir is the nearby Portmarnock Links, designed by Bernhard Langer and adjacent to the venerable club of that name.

It has had rave reviews and for those who enjoy being pampered there's a de luxe hotel, formerly the home of the Jameson family, that already has a considerable reputation.

In the opposite direction but convenient for your hotel is St Margaret's, twice the venue for the LPGA Irish Open, where a collection of classical holes adorn a landscape that's been transformed by Tom Craddock and Pat Ruddy, an architectural duo par excellence, responsible, too, for Druid's Glen.

There's another of similar quality nearby that's also new but also appears ancient, a mark of sound design. Luttrellstown Castle Golf Club is set in a deer park where the castle is not the only memorable edifice: the new two storey clubhouse is thought to be the largest timber structure in Europe. If, as is likely, you find yourself trapped in the bar, there are several most amenable bedroom suites in the courtyard. Don't miss this one.

Nor should you miss Headfort, at Kells, from your hotel about forty minutes to the north west. It is the longest drive you'll face on this itinerary, but the journey will bring rich rewards. The course is a touch less than 6,000 yards but one of the finest parkland lay-outs you'll play.

That lot should keep you occupied for a week and an indication of Dublin's riches is that we haven't mentioned Hermitage, Powerscourt, City West and the string of gems to the south of the city. Better stay for two weeks!

If you want to venture further into the enchanting countryside then here's a tour that will leave you wide eyed and with senses soothed.

We start by heading south of Dublin, en route to a base at the Royal Hotel at the coastal town of Bray. To save time check in later. First take the ring road 15 miles or so south again, to the mystically named Druid's Glen, the venue for the Irish Open when barely a year old. Tour players waxed lyrical upon first sight and compared it with Augusta National. Yes, it's that good, in beauty and challenge, with a clubhouse to match. It's not cheap but it shouldn't be missed.

Once bedded down at Bray go next to nearby Woodbrook, a famous old seaside parkland that's just re-opened following major renovation. Formerly one of Ireland's principal courses, it is once again challenging for the major professional events it staged in the 1960s.

Not far away, at Brittas Bay, is a monument to one man's improbable dream, of owning a links. Pat Ruddy has the advantage of being a first class architect and his creation, the European Club, was ranked sixth in Ireland within a year of opening. It improves with maturity and is remarkable value, too. A must on any tour.

Brittas Bay is perhaps thirty minutes down the coast from Bray and the Vale of Avoca, our next call, is about fifteen minutes further. Here is Woodenbridge golf club and if you find a prettier course in all of Ireland we'll thank you for letting us know.

It was a nine holer when I first saw it and such was its appeal that four of us went around five times without once calling into the bar! They struck a medal in our honour.

Four miles west of Arklow, it lies in a wooded valley with tree clad mountains forming a glorious backdrop and a tumbling river the major hazard (it once swept the little wooden clubhouse away in a storm). Now it has 18 holes and the consensus is that it's better than ever. Well worth the detour.

So too, on two counts, is Rathsallagh, your final stop. The one hour drive from Bray will take you through the Wicklow Mountains, perhaps the scenic highlight of your tour, and the visual delights don't end when you arrive.

The Rathsallagh course, designed by Peter McEvoy and Christy O'Connor Jr., is laid out in a wooded estate of 500 acres with a country house as its centre point. The latter dates to 1798 and is now a de luxe hotel with every amenity. The course is new but you'd never guess and if the greens aren't the finest you've played they'll come very close.

Have an evening round upon arrival, enjoy the many pleasures of the hotel and with another round before you depart for the Dublin ferry in the morning you'll have known a glorious finale to your week.

Here's a royal tour like no other, and you're invited!

From a personal and professional viewpoint a royal tour holds marginally less spectator appeal than formation knitting or underwater ballroom dancing. All have a certain journalistic novelty value, no doubt, but I'll leave others to report on the proceedings, thank you.

So upon reading that there was to be a royal tour of Ireland I was about to turn the page when my eye registered a couple of names guaranteed to quicken the pulse: Royal Portrush and Royal County Down.

That's when the penny dropped, when I realised that the Irish, sharp as a tack in all matters of tourism, had pulled another master stroke.

Because their royal tour is all about golf and, what's more, you're invited and you can bring your friends. As the Irish catch phrase has it, "you're very welcome..."

Taken sedately, the tour in question won't be too onerous. You'll simply be required to submit yourself for pampering at a couple of cracking hotels, one near Dublin, the other near Belfast, and spend four or more days besporting yourself over the glittering collection of Royal courses those two cities call their own.

There'll be the occasional glass of champers, naturally, and a Guinness or three to soothe the fevered brow at the end of successive days spent on some of the finest links you'll ever clap eyes on. What's more, you needn't worry about driving: for an extra groat or two each — for conviviality and competition this is a tour best undertaken by small parties — you'll be whisked around in a chauffeur driven vehicle. The red carpet will be laid out all the way.

On the other hand, you could take your own vehicle and catch a high speed ferry. Or if you can't wait to get at it you could fly in and take a rental car. You pays your money, you makes your choice.... There'll be no compromise in golfing terms, though. To the aforementioned Portrush and County Down add Royal Dublin and Royal Belfast. There may be a quartet of comparable quality in such proximity but I'd need an hour or so to identify them. We're talking the real McCoy here. In each case the architectural pedigree is blue blooded.

Consider Royal Belfast, for instance. Founded in 1881, it is the oldest golf club in Ireland. The course was laid out by Harry Colt in 1925, when the club moved to its present location, Craigavad House and its 100 acre estate on the shores of Belfast Lough

Unlike the other stops on the tour this is a parkland course, wooded in parts and lush as can be, as beguiling as it is testing. The site is on two levels with the first three holes rising to higher ground and several others nudging the beach that hems the loch, as the Scots would call it..

So the start calls for a gentle climb which also serves to stretch the opening holes, already lengthened by the lush grass. Thereafter the walking is gentle, the views sublime.

Several holes are as good as any you'll find and Colt's signature is much in evidence: cross bunkers hiding dead ground in the green approaches, large greens, gently tilted and with subtle breaks. Like all Colt courses, accuracy and sound judgment are at a premium, although the loam-based fairways are more than generous.

There's a choice of tees and the card reads from 6,306 yards down to 5,961, all par 70, the standard scratch reducing from 71 to 69. My guess is that they used an elastic tape measure.

This is strategic golf as it was meant to be played. No matter your handicap, it will be challenging, great fun and hugely rewarding, and the warmth of welcome matches the course presentation.

And wait until you see the clubhouse. Craigavad House, once a country mansion, is numbered among the finest in Ireland, with facilities to match. Ask for a tour, stay for a slap-up lunch and play 36 holes. You'll never know a finer day's sport. A bonus: The Culloden, one of our host hotels, is only two minutes away.

Although close to the city, Royal Belfast is in County Down and from The Culloden Hotel the royal club of that name is a 30 mile drive that imitates a journey back in time. For if Royal Belfast is the most senior of Irish clubs, Royal County Down, overlooking Dundrum Bay at Newcastle, is the nation's most venerable links and its most regal.

History has it that Old Tom Morris was responsible for the design but in truth this was a site waiting for golf to be invented. It merely required a little fine tuning, a levelling of tees and greens and the introduction of bunkers.

With fairways swooping between majestic dunes, ablaze with gorse for much of the year, it may be the most natural links in the game. To the newcomer, though, it can be penal in anything more than a breeze.

Here even the ladies' card reads 6,190 yards and from the tiger tees it is in excess of 7,000, to par-72, standard scratch 74. This is not one for the faint-hearted.

It has been written that "the Open Championship has been played on courses that are not as good" and while today's leading players would cavil at several blind tee shots they'd be forced to doff their collective cap at every other demand this great links imposes. Patience, judgment, imagination, power and finesse, all play their part and in a three or four club wind they'd need dollops of character, too. Seeing red here is not uncommon, with unkind bounces and fearsome rough.

The course has a beguiling routing and a symphonic tempo but if there's an easy hole I haven't found it in half a dozen attempts. Even the short holes will test your mettle.

Then there's the breathless scenery. The place is a photographer's dream, given just a hint of sunshine and shadow. From the high ground the lonely beach of Dundrum Bay counterpoints the smoky Mountains of Mourne that are the backdrop to a sea of golden gorse and emerald fairways. It has a grandeur that may be incomparable.

So a word to the wise: take a caddie and forget about your score, at least the first time around. Simply relax and enjoy the occasion. You'll play the better for it. Then after lunch, more aware of the wiles of one of the world's great links, you'll want to do it all again. You'll be hooked. Welcome to the club!

And if you don't want to play Royal Portrush, our next stop, at least twice there's no hope for you. Best go lie down in a darkened room and curl up your toes.

Suffice to say that those who compile the annual ranking lists of Irish courses have reached a simple solution to the problem of separating the great triumvirate of County Down, Portmarnock and the Dunluce links of Royal Portrush. They merely shuffle them around at the top of the pile so that each has a turn at number one spot. It's the epitome of Irish logic.

The great Bernard Darwin, the doyen of our profession in the first half of the last century, described Portrush as arguably Harry Colt's ultimate creation, "a monument more enduring than brass." It has lost nothing with the passage of time, indeed the reverse may be true: the years have burnished Colt's legacy.

The setting helps. Hard by the Giant's Causeway, one of the natural wonders of the world on the north coast of County Antrim, Portrush is at one with the sea, indeed it was once threatened by it until the golfing world answered the clarion call and subscribed to the sea defences that saved the day.

So a teasing breeze is standard and frequently it graduates into something more muscular. Then the narrow, meandering fairways shrink, the greens become even smaller and the hazards expand. You'll need your wits about you now, and a philosophical outlook, to say nothing of a good supply of ammunition.

It can be a fearsome test of driving, with tiger country awaiting anything only slightly off-line. Hack out, smile, forget par and hope for a chip and one putt, which is easier said than done.... You'll need a sound short game to effect salvage operations plus unlimited imagination and a hot putter on greens with lots of subtle movement.

Portrush is a links that gives little away beyond red-blooded exhilaration. Good holes are legion: the 5th is a dream and wait until you reach the 14th and 15th, known as Calamity Corner and Purgatory respectively. You won't believe your eyes. Don't forget your camera.

And so to our final port of call. Unless there's a howling gale on duty you'll find Royal Dublin less physically demanding than its northern counterparts, although you'll know you've been in a scrap, wind or no wind. This great links has frequently staged the Irish Open and has seen a host of international amateur events as well, so the pedigree is obvious.

The second oldest club in Ireland moved to its present site, on Bull Island in Dublin Bay, in 1889. Harry Colt redesigned the original links after the first world war and, without changing the essential qualities, Donald Steel effected modifications preparatory to the Irish Opens of the mid-1980s.

It is appreciably flatter than the two northern links although being on a somewhat compact site it is equally demanding in terms of precision, albeit with minimal blind shots.

It is an out and back links in the old style and wind-assisted to the turn. They say if you've ambitions about a good score you'd best set off smartly. The outward par is 34, with three one shotters, and it's 37 coming home with a quintet of card wreckers awaiting from the fearsome 11th.

The inward loop is the longer by some 500 yards and a series of ditches, plus an out of bounds on the teasing 18th, make life interesting after the turn. Better be safe than sorry could be the club motto.

This is one of those links you'll enjoy whatever your form and the welcome couldn't be warmer in the historic clubhouse. The members are immensely proud of their fine old club but they're not stuffy with it. You'll have a grand day here, a perfect finale to your personalised royal tour of Ireland.

Where to stay: The 5* Culloden Hotel, Bangor Road, Holywood, Belfast.

One of Ireland's most distinguished hotels, The Culloden is set in 12 acres of gardens close to the city airport. Once a bishop's palace, it has 79 rooms including 10 palatial suites, a health and beauty club with pools, a spa and steam rooms. The Mitre Room is an admired restaurant and informal dining is available at an inn in the grounds. Visiting international sporting teams make The Culloden their headquarters and the hotel offers tee reservations at the three royal clubs, along with practice facilities and a golf bag storage room. Squash and tennis are also available.

The Conyngham Arms, Slane.

An Irish jewel hidden in the tiny town of Slane about 45 minutes from Dublin, the Conyngham Arms has been in the same family since 1929. Evocative of a by-gone era in decor and ambience, it has 14 luxuriously furnished rooms and a renowned restaurant. Part real pub, part elegant inn, the Conyngham Arms is a highly recommended halt on the royal golf tour of Ireland.

Ireland: Here lies golf for the true believers

If you have the hand-eye co-ordination to hit a barn door with a bucket of water then I know how you can find the perfect golfing holiday destination with all the extras a chap needs: good food, friendly natives, oodles of après golf distractions and courses to make your eyes stick out like chapel hat pegs.

Here's how. Pin a map of Ireland to the wall and throw a dart at it, then make tracks for where ever it sticks. You're almost guaranteed to find a cluster of first class courses with agreeable accommodation nearby, plus all the other things required to soothe the inner man.

My view is that Scotland may be the historical home of golf but Ireland is the spiritual home of our game. The Emerald Isle has more first rate courses, pro rata, than just about anywhere on the planet, most of them oozing history. For many years the number was static at around 230: now the figure is 440-plus and rising.

Thanks to the exploits of the Irish contingent in the Ryder Cup of late, plus the recent successes of Rory McIlroy and Graham McDowell in the US majors and Darren Clarke's epic victory in the Open Championship the grand old game has overtaken horse racing, football and that other pastime enjoyed by two members of the opposite sex as the main topic of conversation in bars and clubs up and down the land. It's become the in-game. Everyone wants to play. The architects are beside themselves.

Much of the nation's coastline is now protected so few links are being built these days but parkland courses continue to spring up in all corners of this green and pleasant land, much to the delight of the tourist boards, regional and national, whose work in keeping them busy with overseas visitors has become a central plank of the economy.

You'll doubtless know of the golfing attractions of Dublin. Suffice to say that the there are 50 or so courses within easy reach of the city centre, and another 30 only half an hour further away. This may be the world's dominant golfing city. Numerically, only Myrtle Beach and Sydney are superior but neither has courses of comparable quality to Dublin's. Just think of Portmarnock (Old and New), Baltray, The Island, Malahide, Royal Dublin, The Hermitage, Powerscourt, City West, Palmerston, Druids Glen, and Druids Heath, its new neighbour, another gem designed by the ubiquitous Pat Ruddy, whose links at the European Club is winning rave reviews world-wide. But that's another story...

If your dart hits the south east corner of the country a quite different treat awaits. Bed down in the charming city of Waterford on the banks of the River

Suir (you'll be pampered to distraction at the Tower Hotel and the nearby après golf attractions would exhaust a hedonist in full fig) where a lustrous collection of parkland courses awaits your pleasure.

The region boasts of 30 courses and not for nothing is it known as the Sunshine Coast. I was there with the usual suspects in mid-October and on a couple of days we might well have been in Spain, although the club's house wine at Waterford Castle was superior.

The Tower Hotel is convenient for Waterford Castle, Faithlegg, Tramore and Mount Juliet and if you know of a finer collection of parkland courses you should drop me a line, post haste. There's a good value green fee passport available, too.

The south west is your target? Then take your prayer mat: your golfing holiday will become a pilgrimage as you drool over a collection of historic links in what's known as the Ring of Kerry. Ballybunion, Tralee, Dooks and Waterville are the main attractions but there are scads of others, not least the two glorious parkland courses of the Killarney Golf and Fishing Club, which gives a clue what awaits out there. It's a bit of a hike but you could fly into Shannon and the Great Southern Hotel at Killarney takes some topping, particularly since it was up-graded. And there are 20 or so cracking pubs within strolling distance on the main street. A word of caution: identifying the best pint of Guinness on offer is a local challenge not to be taken lightly.

If you've the time, you should wander up the west coast where the counties of Galway, Mayo and Sligo have links that impoverish adjectives. En route, though, you must pop into Lahinch, in County Clare, where Old Tom Morris laid out "the St Andrews of Ireland." I could tell a tale or two about this grand old links but I doubt you'd believe me.... OK. How about a blind par three and goats that forecast the weather? Told you.

The west coast is one of Ireland's premier golfing destinations and its list of courses will tell why: Connemara, Enniscrone, Donegal, Carne, Ballyliffin and Rosses Point, where dinner at Aunties is a traditional imperative if you effect an escape from the club bar.

Another word of caution, though: allow plenty of time for navigation. You'll frequently find yourself in the middle of nowhere, where the only sign of life is a solitary sheep which appears equally lost. Whatever you do don't make eye contact or she'll never leave you.

Great golf aside, there's not a lot of activity hereabouts where the next stop west is Boston, USA. So golf tourism is a vitally important facet of the economy and the appreciative locals do a grand job in making you feel welcome. It's a glorious bonus to outstanding golf. I once went to Connemara for two days and stayed in the region for two weeks. I blamed the sheep. My expense claim took a bit of explaining but fortunately my then editor was Irish and most sympathetic.

That's a quick Cook's tour of golf holidays in the republic and we haven't mentioned the K Club, venue for the 2006 Ryder Cup matches, or Mullingar, the Midland's gem by James Braid, or Tullamore, where they lock the clubhouse doors when you go in for a post-round Guinness, or Woodenbridge, now 18 holes but a delicious nine holer when the clubhouse floated away after a storm prompted the river to break its banks: they say no one noticed until the Guinness ran out.

Then there's the Mackenzie-designed Cork that's a combination of parkland, heathland and links; and nearby Fota Island, and Rathsallagh, with its exquisite hotel, and Adare Manor, one of Ireland premier golf resorts with a course by Trent Jones Sr. I really have had a mis-spent life....

And then there's Ulster, up north. An indication of the quality that awaits here is that the Irish Golf Union, which commendably governs national golf without recognition of borders, has little difficulty in identifying Ireland's top links: they simply alternate each year between Portmarnock, Ballybunion, Royal County Down and Royal Portrush. Easy peasy, although the European Club is coming up fast on the rails.

That said, you'll realise that County Down and Portrush are both in Ulster which has only 100 or so clubs. Most are parkland, and some beauties they have, too: Belvoir Park, Malone and Royal Belfast to scratch the surface. But I have fond memories of playing Royal Portrush, neighbouring Portstewart and nearby Castlerock over one glorious summer week on the Antrim coast. It's an incomparable combination of links.

Those who prefer tournament golf on holidays would enjoy the Tullamore Dew tournament, played each June over the links of Portrush, Portstewart, Castlerock and nearby Ballycastle. It's a 72 hole teams' event with individual prizes too and huge fun if you like cut-throat golf. But go with a thirst you could hang your hat on and be prepared for 12 hour debates and lots of singing.

There are numerous such tournaments each year all over Ireland, staged by the regional tourist boards in conjunction with the local golf associations. They cater for all combinations of teams, male and female, pairs and fours and they don't cut corners on the social side, either.

Or you could take the Royal Tour, playing the Royal courses of Belfast, Portrush, County Down and Dublin, where you could meet with Himself, Christy O'Connor Sr.. Now there's a blue-blooded itinerary for you.

And if none of that grabs you I'm afraid it's back to the dart throwing. Upon reflection, that's not bad promotional idea for Borde Failte. Should be worth a Guinness or three.....

Carnoustie Country: For the ultimate challenge in golf.

If the great links of Carnoustie didn't exist the county of Angus would still be a golfing mecca, such are the alternative attractions. On the other hand, if Carnoustie were the only course available the golfing world would still beat a path to its first tee. Many regard it as not merely the greatest links in Britain but one of the outstanding links in the whole of golf.

It's not a pretty sight. Carnoustie merits many adjectives but pretty isn't one of them. It has been described as "stark, evil, gigantic, brutal and monstrous." It is unrelenting in its challenge and sparse with its rewards. But you could play like your granny and still walk off the 18th green basking in the thrill of playing one of the world's great links. If you've played well your cup will runneth over.

Lying on sand dunes alongside the Firth of Tay, and thus exposed to the vagaries of wind and weather, it's a links with every golfing attribute and no glaring weakness. Length, accuracy and judgment are part of the armoury required: sound course management and a hot putter are imperatives, too.

No more than two consecutive holes run in the same direction, so the wind is an every-changing factor; the flat terrain underscores the required judgment, of distance and strategy, and a multitude of hazards – cavernous bunkers, out of bounds and the seemingly ubiquitous burns – demand the ultimate in concentration and imagination. Any golfer worth his salt should play Carnoustie and the card would be a reminder of one of his great days.

You'll want to play Carnoustie as soon as maybe but first, though, let's explore the surrounding golf attractions, links that will have your eyeballs spinning if you're a first time visitor.

Monifieth has two links managed by a trust, private courses over which five clubs play. Their clubhouses overlook the 18th green of the major course, known as the Medal, a rough-hewn links where great stands of pine trees form part of the tapestry, coloured by banks of golden gorse. This is the very essence of the game in Scotland. Golf has been played hereabouts for 450 years or more, at Monifieth probably since 1643. The sense of history is palpable.

Panmure, our next port of call, is a regular stop for true believers, where a pinewood path leads to a succession of links holes winding through undulating duneland to present a combination of beauty and challenge that defies description. A meandering burn, stands of trees and swathes of gorse will catch the eye, and more. Ben Hogan practised here for the 1953 Open Championship and was entranced. Quite simply, Panmure is a beauty and a barrel of fun... Go gently and enjoy.

Montrose is a resort town 30 minutes north of Carnoustie, a well-ordered place with two golf courses. The principal one is the Medal and history books have it that the course is the fifth oldest links in the world – and it looks it! This marvellous stretch of duneland could have no other use but golf. It would be sacrilegious! The present lay-out owes much to Tom Morris and Willie Park Jr. It's a rugged, venerable links that climbs to a cliff top above the beach where it undulates for nine holes before flattening out and turning inland at right angles. So the wind holds the key and it will get you one way or t'other.

Montrose has some spectacular holes, a few mild eccentricities but heaps of character. If you've a soft spot for things historic you must see the Medal course. They'll make you warmly welcome.

Location: Angus is on the east coast of Scotland about an hour to the north of St Andrews, beyond Dundee. So once you've had your fill of Fife's major attractions Carnoustie Country is no distance at all.

A bonus is the Carnoustie Golf Hotel. It's no secret that its construction brought the Open Championship back to Carnoustie in 1999 for the first time for 24 years. The return of the Open has encouraged other hoteliers and now there's no shortage of quality accommodation.

When to go: Except when there is snow, golf is playable year-round although winter weather can be unpleasant and the course conditions below par. In winter, too, mats for fairway shots are common and forward tees and shorter courses are standard. Summer and autumn, from July onwards, are best for golf: the weather can be surprisingly warm and the courses will be in top condition and at full stretch. Autumn is a delight.

Prestwick Old: back where it all began

The nervous tingling should begin as your flight prepares to land at Glasgow's Prestwick airport because below, stretching to the horizon, you'll see a moonscape of sand dunes dotted with a necklace of bunkers and emerald greens. Your flight will swoop so low that moments before touch down the sharp-eyed golfer could make a mental note of most of the flag positions of the day at Royal Troon and Prestwick Old and check the wind velocity from the fluttering flags.

For the impatient, the original home of the Open Championship is only a short ride from the airport. But don't rush things: this is one to savour; save it for the finale. It will be one of the many highlights of your stay.

Instead, begin your dream week at Barassie, then move to Irvine Bogside, building to a climax at glorious Western Gailes before girding your loins for what will be almost a spiritual experience at Prestwick Old. If that lot doesn't light your fire you should call the undertaker and book a plot: there's no hope for you....

At the other end of the scale are the great links listed in our preamble and we begin our magical tour at Kilmarnock Barassie.

It is a final qualifying venue for the Open Championship but the lovely aspect of this course is its combination of playability and challenge. At some 7,100 yards from the new championship tees it is among the longest courses hereabouts and a meandering burn, hidden depressions, fierce rough and gathering fairway bunkers at driving length all put a premium on precision and strategy. Patience is the watchword here, plus sound course management.

The Irvine course, too, has been used for final qualifying and although the card reads only a touch over 6,400 yards you'd be forgiven for thinking that it was measured at night using an elastic tape! It plays much longer than this, not least because the land is heavily undulating, there are several pulpit greens and long carries and generally it is trickier than a sackful of monkeys.

It is one of many such designs by James Braid who was producing strategic courses long before most people knew what he was talking about. He was the first architect to introduce variable flag positions and he devised some cunning spots here. It's all enhanced by a welcoming Edwardian clubhouse with stained glass in profusion and a locker room redolent of a by-gone era. Enchanting and not to be missed.

The Irish brogue was softer than usual but that was because of the reverence it carried. "When I die, and if I go to Heaven," he said, "I hope it's just like this."

We were standing on the 7th tee at Western Gailes. To our right lay the beach; beyond that, over the Firth of Clyde sparkling in the Spring sunshine, stood the Isle of Arran. A two club wind was warm to the skin. Sweaters had been discarded; sun visors were on duty. It's on days such as this that you know for certain that The Almighty is a golfer.

Like many of its contemporaries, the first links dating back more than a century, Western Gailes runs between the beach and the railway line that played such a part in the development of golf in Scotland. Here, the clubhouse is in a central position which brings the first seven holes to the north and the remainder to the south. Typically, they lie in line astern, the fruits of totally natural design before earth moving became the norm.

On many links the sea is largely hidden by towering sand dunes but here the player is constantly aware of its presence and its effect, visually and otherwise, and on a glorious stretch of holes from the 7th to the 13th it is in full view. This is vintage seaside golf: sand dunes in profusion, sea views at every turn, fast-running fairways and shining greens. Western Gailes is, quite simply, inspiring.

If Western Gailes is hauntingly beautiful Old Prestwick is simply haunting. For this is where the Open Championship began, back in 1860, and where it was staged 24 times. I recall a dramatic experience when I first played there, many years ago. It was July 1962 and I was there on the eve of the Open at Royal Troon, gathering colour and background for my preview.

It had been a lovely summer's day and as I teed up alone the late afternoon sunshine was was pouring shadows into the swales and fairway undulations, enhancing a picture of links golf at its most ethereal. After several holes my neck hairs began rising and I had the distinct feeling that I was not alone, that someone was at my side, an invisible presence..... It was nothing threatening; more inquisitive, perhaps.

The ghostly presence was a distraction for only a couple of holes; the ensuing bogeys were probably a disappointing deterrent, and when later I told the club secretary he gave a knowing smile and said I was not the first to have such an experience. Old Prestwick is like that, was the inference; haunting and ethereal.

The unknowing would perhaps imagine it as a small, quaint and old fashioned course, at odds with modern architecture, but not so. Venerable it may be, dating to 1851, but there's nothing backward about it.

Here's a links to test any of the modern giants of the game and their high tech equipment. From the club tees it's an exhilarating examination on a calm day; from the championship tees it can be a monster in anything more than a two club wind, which is about par for this area.

Designed by Old Tom Morris, it was initially a 12 hole course and the Open was decided over three rounds in a day, 36 holes being considered a fitting challenge for aspiring champion golfers.

The original 12 holes were extant when the 1881 championship was played there but by 1884 the course had been extended to 18 holes. Seven of the original holes are still in play, although new tees have lengthened them marginally.

Thankfully, many of the old features have been retained: the Cardinal bunker at the 3rd, with its vertiginous, sleepered ramparts is renowned as one of the golf world's famous hazards: the 4th, recognised as golf's original dog-leg, uses the Pow Burn as a deterrent to those brave and long enough to contemplate a carry over the bend; the 5th is redolent of Old Tom's blind par three at Lahinch, although Himalayas, as it is known, is longer and demands a stiffer climb up the hill that hides the green.

There's no shortage of eccentricity at Prestwick Old but there's excitement, romance and golfing adventure aplenty, too. It has everything you'd imagine of such a venerable links: vast expanses of heather and sand, cavernous bunkers, tightly guarded greens, sloping fairways, and the wind that oft times will make your eyes water.

Then there's the clubhouse, a golfing shrine and a place of great traditions but one of warm welcome, too. No golfer worthy of the name should pass through Ayrshire without spending a day here. He will leave spiritually up-lifted with his golfing education complete.....

Where to stay: No doubt about this, even in a region where good hotels abound. This is the players' choice when The Open comes to town. The Barcelo Troon Marine Hotel is 4* de luxe and overlooks the 18th fairway of Royal Troon and the shoreline towards the Isle of Arran. It recently underwent a £4 million refurbishment and offers everything a travelling golfer desires: ample parking, golf bag storage and drying, 24 hour room service, a renowned dining room with golf views and a welcoming bar. It has 89 spacious bedrooms and four suites, a health club with spa and sauna; a gym, squash courts and swimming pool. Glasgow is 35 minutes away, by rail or road; Prestwick Airport is 10 minutes and there are 20 golf courses nearby or a short drive away. Highly recommended on all counts.

Dining out:

Golfers love exploring the local night life and there's plenty of it around here, particularly fine dining in a region that's famous for its dairy produce, its meat and fish.

The latest in-place is Scotts of Troon, a visually stunning bar and restaurant alongside Troon's marina. It looks out towards the Isle of Arran and Ailsa Craig and is enchanting at sunset.

Scotts is large but with intimate corners, luxurious and elegant and offers the finest cuisine in the region with an expansive wine list. There are various menus, for breakfast lunch or dinner.

Somewhere quite different but of comparable quality is The Ship Inn, on the main street at Irvine. This is a quaint, old-style pub that's well worth a visit but it also has an outstanding dining room whose chef deserves greater recognition. Our meal here was the gastronomic highlight of the week, high praise indeed. We were a large group but our four course dinner went like clockwork and was so impressive we had a whip-round for the chef, as well as the staff. Highly recommended.

The Border Country:
a meander through a painted landscape

If your personal antenna is receptive the time warp will take effect as you leave the bustling town of Hawick behind, to the south. Stop your car for a moment on the near-deserted country road and you'll be enveloped in a hushed, all-pervading ambience of pure nostalgia. Those who can recall an Austin Seven and Woodbines in packets of five will get the picture.

This is the Scottish Borders, the place, they say, that time forgot. It's a picturesque amalgam of four small counties, miniature masterpieces of nature painted into the landscape between Northumberland and the Lothians. There may be nowhere comparable.

Stay glued to one of the three main roads that dissect the region and you'll pass through it in under the hour, probably none the wiser. Slip off the beaten track, though, and you could meander for hours, as the narrow roads rise and fall through countryside that will leave you wide eyed.

Comfortable old towns and ancient villages dot the map, many juxtaposed to the tumbling River Tweed which in places joins forces with the Cheviot Hills to mark the border with England. And, like the seemingly ubiquitous river, history awaits around every bend: great mansions and castles, ancient forts and four huge ruined abbeys stand as testimony to a violent, bloodstained past, when Border wars spanned centuries.

Now serenity reigns, evocative of a more gentle era when Sir Walter Scott, who was born and died nearby, would clip clop the country lanes in carriage and pair, pausing daily at his favourite outlook to view the Eildon Hills. The spot is known forever now as Scott's View. Legend has it that when the great author's cortège passed by, en route to his burial at Dryburgh Abbey, his horses stopped of their own accord, a last farewell. It hasn't changed. See it and you'll pray it never does.

George Ovens sums it up well. "The tranquillity is blissful," he says. "In the summer, when they're standing on each other's heads elsewhere, the roads are empty here."

Tall and lean and still an accomplished golfer after a life-long romance with the game, George is a Past President of the Scottish Golf Union. He's also the driving force of the bewitchingly beautiful St Boswells Golf Club, ingeniously laid out in only 27 acres of a verdant ribbon stretching along one bank of the Tweed. George took great pride in showing us around the teasing nine holer (5,250 yards, par 66) he helped re-establish in 1948 after a disastrous flood destroyed the course. The view from the elevated second tee proved his point.

The only constant sound was from the gurgling river. Across the water, deep in woodland at the foot of the Eildon Hills, stood the ruins of Dryburgh Abbey. On high ground in the middle distance, half hidden in the trees, a towered country house had all the appearances of a French château. The emerald course, fresh-mown, pristine, almost manicured, was deserted in the dappled early morning sunshine. It was difficult to resist whooping for joy.

That was a scenario oft-repeated during our visit. You won't have heard of most of the courses. Few have. They're overshadowed by the great Lothians links, an hour away to the north.

With a couple of exceptions, the Border courses nurse few ambitions towards championship status. A mixture of meadowland, parkland and moorland, their challenge is outweighed by their charm and peerless setting, although if you fancy yourself as a golfer you'll have a cracking time, for all that. You could anticipate par golf. Scoring it's another thing entirely.

As George Ovens says of St Boswells: "It's not a difficult course off the tees. It's the better golfers who hook into the river. It's a fatal attraction. If you've never hooked in your life you will here!"

He was right, but we managed to avoid the fleet of ducks. And a lost ball was a small price to pay for such a joyful golfing experience.

There are 17 courses in the region, most of them of nine holes but with several 18 holers. They're invariably in good order, all offering spectacular scenery, a warm welcome and astonishing value.

We shouldn't say this by rights, but if the green fees were doubled they'd still be a bargain. You could play 36 holes a day for five days and the green fees would stop just short of free golf.

The key is the Freedom of the Fairways programme devised by the Scottish Borders Tourist Board which, by staying at specific hotels, gives mid-week access to 14 courses. The major proviso is that you play a maximum of ten courses in five days and 36 holes on any one course during your stay. But it virtually equates to unlimited golf.

A budget-conscious golfing family or group eager to sample the unusual would be lavishly rewarded here. A bonus is that because the region is so compact everywhere is within easy reach. Several courses are in a cluster and all 14 of those in the Freedom package would be within a comfortable drive of a centrally located hotel. The passport brochure carries a map, details of all participating courses and lists a variety of accommodations from bed and breakfast farmhouses to the four star country house hotel at Dryburgh Abbey.

You won't need a tee reservation mid-week, but it's as well to phone the day before to establish availability. You'll find a contact number in the Freedom brochure because, at most of the nine hole courses anyway, the clubhouse will be unmanned during the day. This means, as a group of visitors had noted in the St Boswells' visitors' book: "Played nine, gone to the pub for lunch. Be back later." No one minded. It's par for the course.

You'll be on your honour to pay the green fees, too, although if you're a Freedom passport holder you'll simply stuff your daily voucher into the envelope provided and take a numbered ticket.

The St Boswells' honesty box is a wall-inlaid George VI mail box near the first tee. Or if you stop for a paper the village newsagent will sell you a green fee ticket. Such modern-day idiosyncrasies are part of the region's charm, redolent of other times and other values.

"Most visitors respect the system," said Willie MacRae, part-time secretary of the Melrose club. "The greens staff may feel disposed to challenge the few who don't."

Melrose, a neighbour to St Boswells, is another of those cracking nine holers that abound. Such is its quality it would be renowned if were 18 holes, although it wouldn't be more appealing.

It might be possible to squeeze in another nine, Willie reckoned, but that would detract from the quality of the existing lay-out, so they're content with the status quo.

Melrose, founded in 1880 and with an in-put from Old Tom Morris and Willie Park, is a big course as nine holers go. It covers 70 acres on the lower slopes of North Eildon, one of the chain of hills and a local landmark that towers over the course. It's not difficult walking, though. It opens with a gentle climb and then levels out to a plateau overlooking the town.

Thousands of trees have been planted over the years on what was a moorland site and, the sheer beauty of the setting aside, this means that most holes are hidden from their neighbours. The consequence is a sense of total isolation and infinite variety. The 18 hole card reads 5,579 yards, par 70, standard scratch 68, but a mark of its challenge is that the course record is a modest 66, even though only one hole is longer than 400 yards.

Play it and you'll discover why. Pay a visit from June onwards, when the course and its surrounding hills are ablaze with flowering gorse and heather and you'll be privy to one of the great sights of Scotland.

If your route is from the south, up the A7, Hawick will be the first town you'll bump in to. Stop awhile. Here's where Mr Pringle knits his sweaters. It's a pleasant place and if you're travelling with children there's an impressive new leisure centre, a model of its kind.

While the family enjoys the pool, you could steal away to nearby Hawick golf club for a round on one of the region's more memorable courses. Take your camera. This is one you'll want to record.

Set on a hill overlooking the town, it starts with a gentle climb for three or four holes. Then it levels out and the next ten holes are over an undulating plateau from where, it seems, most of Scotland is laid at your feet. Then there's a bit of a climb to the 14th green before the path turns downhill, from the 15th tee.

This is the high point of the course. You're 1,000 feet above sea level here. It's because of this altitude that Hawick is known as a "back end" course. Its growing season starts later than most and lasts longer than normal. It's a picture in late autumn.

It's a sound all-round test, very tight, particularly off the tee, although the tree-lined fairways are deceptively generous. The 6th and 7th, both long par fours, play as par fives for the average golfer, and there are several blind second shots. Be straight here, too.

The clue is in the paucity of sand. There are only seven bunkers which says much about the wind velocity usually encountered "up top". The card holds another clue: at 5,929 yards the par is 68, the standard scratch 69. Nick Faldo holds the professional course record with 64. He reckons the two opening holes — the first green is a double, shared with the 18th — are among the toughest he knows.

It's not a course for the less accomplished, but if you lived nearby you'd contemplate murder to become a member. A lovely old-fashioned clubhouse with an obliging resident steward frames a lovely picture.

From Hawick it's but a short saunter up the A7 to Galashiels, the geographical centre of the Borders, which brings St Boswells and Melrose within long iron distance. Even closer, though, is Ladhope, an 18 hole moorland lay-out that nibbles into the town's northern boundary.

Here's an opportunity you shouldn't pass up, but brace yourself! You'll need to be sound of wind and limb to play here, although the rewards, visual and sporting, are many.

The handbooks describe it as "hilly" but really there are only two holes guaranteed to leave you jelly-legged and gasping for mercy. The 10th and 11th holes fall just short of requiring the services of a sherpa but they give entrée to some of the most stunning scenery in Scottish golf. No pain, no gain, as they say in politics.

Those two holes aside, the averagely fit golfer will find the walk invigorating although anything more than a breeze will work wonders for the sinuses and the respiration generally! The breeze, indeed, is the principal hazard at Galashiels, a course like no other James Braid ever had a hand in. (He laid it out in 1920, but there's been a course on the site since 1884.)

There's only one bunker, for instance, at the new first hole. The fairways, winding around and over the undulating lowlands, are lush and expansive. What little rough there is will punish only the wildest of shots and the greens are quick and true. They're generally on the small side because several par fours are under 280 yards and would be drivable on good days but for the cross wind!

There's a trio of long par threes, a genuine three shotter — Braid's Delight is stroke index one and 524 yards of lush, rising fairway — and a three hole finish as tight as a miser's wallet!

Ladhope, then, is a sporty challenge (5,185 yards, par 67) that will bring one of golf's lasting memories. But a word of warning: if you're planning to play 36 holes choose a calm day! A most hospitable clubhouse, offering daily catering and a 12 hour bar service, completes an appealing prospect.

If you've followed our route so far you're two courses down with three to go. Add St Boswells and Melrose and you've one to go. Now you're in a pickle: it's decision time. Ten courses left and one choice to make. Life's tough, eh?

Let's state now that we were unable to see all 14 courses. We were there in April and the weather wasn't kind, nor the days long enough. And so with no disrespect to the rest, if we had one venue left we could narrow the choice down to two courses.

They're equidistant from Galashiels, both about 20 miles away, a long drive in this neck of the woods! They're also world's apart in style but so appealing that either could be top of our list.

Those familiar with it would agree that our penultimate stop could well be the Borders' finest. It is a gorgeous parkland course that when I visited had everything except a second loop — and that omission is being rectified as I write. If its specifications match the existing nine it will be a joy to behold.

Simply put, the Hirsel course at Coldstream is the Augusta of The Borders. Breathlessly beautiful and in immaculate condition, it also offers a stern challenge to the accomplished while being sympathetic to the lesser player.

Like Melrose, it is in a rolling woodland setting and with thick shrubbery, fierce rough, water and other hazards in abundance. Being lush — a tributary of the Tweed runs through it with a high water table the consequence — it plays every inch of its length. Founded in 1948, it is a course of strategic design with a fair margin for error.

The fairways are generous, as are the greens, but getting from one to the other calls more for precision than power. Two or three holes demand blind tee shots, and blind seconds as well if the drive is too short or wayward.

Few holes are longer than 350 yards but the terrain and holding fairways mean you'll be reaching for a short iron only when your second falls short.

Carry the brow of the hill from several tees, though, and you'll get an agreeable kick on. Shades of Augusta!

Added to this cornucopia of golf is a rare setting close to the village of Coldstream, birthplace of the famous guards regiment and part of the Hirsel estate of the Douglas Home family.

A cosy clubhouse offers seven day catering from March to September, so with lunch available you could happily play 36 holes here. Don't miss it.

From the east we move to the most westerly course in the region, a moorland course of great charm and quality.

The West Linton club is near the village of that name on the A702 a short distance south of Pencuik. The bare statistics say that it's a course set in 135 acres, measures 6,132 yards to a par of 69, equal to standard scratch. As usual, the figures hide a story.

It's a tale of two men, one ancient, one modern. The former was the founder whose dream began it all. Robert Millar, the club's first secretary, was the village schoolmaster, had attended St Andrews University and so, naturally enough, was a golfer.

Arriving at West Linton in the 1880s, he soon drummed up support for a golf course on land known as Slipperfield Moor. It was farmland then, but Millar's promptings helped establish a committee to lease about 40 acres for £5 a year.

Heavily influenced by the Old Course, Millar designed nine holes and, with one helper, laid out the course. It opened in 1890 with 42 members. It measured 2,100 yards.

Despite various unfulfilled plans for another nine, it stayed that way, with only minor expansion, for many years. Then, in 1974, Donald Fraser, still the club's treasured greenkeeper, designed and built a second loop on a further 135 acres the club had bought for £55,000. A new clubhouse had been opened in 1964 and, thanks to Donald's endeavours, a decade later West Linton was established in the forefront of Scottish Lowlands golf.

It is, says club pro Ron Tickle, a very difficult par 69, one requiring consummate accuracy, particularly to the acclaimed greens. There's some margin for error with the tee shot, unless a constant breeze develops ambitions, in which case a host of Donald's new bunkers make their presence felt.

Based on peat, it drains well and is invariably in good order, particularly later in the year. It's a classical moorland course that is fair but tough when the wind blows. The par threes are a feature: unusually, it has two of them to finish and a club legend tells of a member who came to the last tee needing par for an unprecedented nett 57. He found places no human foot had trodden before and took 15!

Don't be deterred, though. The drive from Galashiels will take 30 minutes and, the scenery aside, it will be time well invested.

While you're in the region you shouldn't miss a round at Peebles, a few miles from West Linton. Because of local demand, Peebles is not part of the Freedom package but £15 for a mid-week day ticket is a give-away price for what is considered the region's principal course.

Topographically, it's similar in style to Hawick: a climb to a wide plateau where most of the holes are laid out in open, rolling meadowland, then a gentle descent back to the handsome clubhouse.

It was as green as could be in April, so doubtless it plays long (6,137 yards, par 69) particularly when the wind gets up, which it does frequently. Hence the need for benevolent greens, which carry the signature of James Braid.

Opened in 1893, the course was for many years run by the municipality. It became a private club in 1991 and is going from strength to strength. If you're in the locality, telephone first (01721.20197) to ensure the first tee is free. They'll put the welcome mat out unless it's a competition day.

The latter is true of all the clubs involved in the Freedom package, including, we're told, those we were unable to visit. Like the ambience, the Borders hospitality will take you back in time. They're grand folk and the courses reflect the happy holiday aura that is a by-product of Scotland's little-known jewel in the south.

A brochure giving details of the Freedom of the Fairways programme is available from: The Scottish Borders Tourist Board, 70 High Street, Selkirk TD7 4DD. Freedom passports may be purchased upon arrival in the Borders, at local tourist board offices or the participating golf clubs.

Where to stay: Dryburgh Abbey Hotel, St Boswells, is an hotel that offers the ultimate in luxury, comfort and service. Hidden away in an expanse of gardens on the banks of the River Tweed and adjacent to the ruins of Dryburgh Abbey, this is an hotel deserving of the highest accolades. Up-market, needless to say, but good value, nonetheless. If the budget runs to it, a Borders golfing holiday with a base here would be unforgettable.

Contact: Dryburgh Abbey Hotel, St Boswells, Roxburghshire TD6 0RQ.

Kings Hotel, Galashiels. (3 Crowns): An up-market town centre hotel in Galashiels, this family-owned inn is ideally situated for courses in the Freedom package and offers excellent value. Refurbished in tasteful style, the Kings is a favourite rendezvous for locals dining out or celebrating. Only seven bedrooms, all en suite, offer all facilities and total comfort. Highly recommended for small groups. Mine host is golfer and will arrange tee times through the Freedom programme.

Contact: Kings Hotel, Market Street, Galashiels TD1 3AN.

Traquair Arms Hotel, Innerleithen. (3 Crowns):

A friendly country pub-hotel in the Tweed Valley town of Innerleithen, the Traquair has 10 en suite bedrooms, a cracking bar and an old fashioned dining room serving traditional cuisine by the chef/proprietor. Adjacent to town's nine hole course, it is convenient for Peebles (6 miles) Galashiels and West Linton (both 18 miles).

Tweed Valley Hotel, Walkerburn (RAC 3 Star, 4 Crowns Commended):

Overlooking the River Tweed and nestling at the foot of the Moorfoot Hills, this gracious former Edwardian mansion is a joy to behold. It has a Michelin-acclaimed restaurant and a cosy bar giving river views. There are 16 bedrooms, all large, all en suite and with every amenity. Hospitable service and a friendly local clientèle enhance one of Scotland's most appealing small hotels. Ideal for couples, groups or families. Golf arranged through Freedom package. Convenient for most courses. Merits a detour.

Taymouth Castle: beautiful, regal and serene

It's as well, perhaps, that the course at Taymouth Castle falls just short of the top echelon. That would detract from its naturally rustic charm. Better by far that it is simply a course of considerable challenge, played in a setting out of a travelogue.

A massive, forbidding castle dwarfs the wooden clubhouse behind the first tee. Just beyond the first green rise wooded hills, a natural wall that encircles most of the course, broken only to allow views of Loch Tay and its river, a silver fairway glimpsed through the trees. Taymouth Castle is not only one of the most beautiful courses you'll ever clap eyes on, it may be the most peaceful. The crack of club on ball is a reverberating rifle shot, a slightly raised voice an intrusion.

The course is rather more difficult than first signals indicate. Generous greens and wide fairways, winding between avenues of trees, invite you to open the shoulders. But you'll need to be straight off the tee; the deceptively shallow rough will snap your club face shut with the speed of a rat trap.

Avoid the burn that wriggles through the course, place the ball just so and on most holes the green makes promises that are not always kept. They are large, with some cunning pin positions, a problem compounded by what appear to be green side bunkers that are often some way short, hiding distance and foreshortening the shot.

Playing here is a battle of wits with the maestro himself: it's a Braid-designed course, as some distinctive features will testify. At 6,066 yards to a par of 69 it's a gentle stroll but its length in play is deceptive because it's generally flat and invariably lush. Most distance is gained through the air, even in summer.

You'll need to play it more than once to appreciate the nuances. By then you'll be hooked and have to stay for another day, which is excuse enough to sample the delights of the nearby Kenmore Hotel, where you'll pay your green fees. Dating to 1572 and the oldest inn in Scotland, it's part of a 400 acre family estate that includes the village, the course and the castle. You'll get no closer to heaven before you hand in your final card.

The Ayrshire Coast, part of the living history of Scottish golf

The oustanding aspect of golf in Scotland is the volume of superb, little-known courses, many of them a century old or more. They're part of the living history of the country and on the coastline of Ayrshire, home of Royal Troon and Old Prestwick, it's on daily display, like the Crown Jewels of Scotland.

Unlike those other royal baubles, though, these belong to an appreciative populace, to be enjoyed upon demand. Golfers bearing clubs on bikes and buses are a common sight although often they need travel only a short distance. Long established links were founded on common duneland close to many small towns. A century or more later they're even closer, often between the main street and the beach or the sea wall. Terraced houses nudging the fairways are a not uncommon sight.

Drive north from Girvan to Irvine via Ayr, Prestwick and Troon, a distance of no more than 30 miles, and you'll pass close to 19 coastal courses, 13 of them in the 12 mile stretch between Prestwick and Irvine. Among the lesser known are several council-run courses setting standards that would shame some English municipals we've seen. They prove what can be achieved by a local authority with the good sense to realise the value of golf as a public amenity.

The regional authority in Ayrshire manages eight courses and though disparate in degree of challenge they're comparable in quality. The little nine holer at Maybole is as flawless as Belleisle, the council's flagship, perhaps the best inland public course in Scotland and a venue for many major events.

Nor are they expensive. With an annual ticket costing £180 a local golfer could play at Belleisle virtually every day; that's about £2 per day! And he would also have access to Lochgreen and Darley, the council's two other Group One courses, at Troon.

Such largesse is extended to the thousands of visitors. A round at one of the three Group One courses will cost £12, the slightly less demanding Group Two quartet will cost £9. To egality add economy, in equally generous scoops.

A large dollop of history is an ingredient, too: Troon reeks of it but nowhere is it stronger than at Old Prestwick, founded in 1851, birthplace of The Open and venue for 12 of its first 24 championships, the last in 1925. Play the course on an autumn evening as dappled sunlight scatters shadows over the fairways and your neck hair will rise at the feeling that hidden eyes are watching... History here is tangible. At £45 a day ticket Old Prestwick some will find it irresistible. But there's good value to be enjoyed too at other private clubs, Prestwick St Nicholas for instance, and Kilmarnock Barassie. But they will be the finale to a glorious week. Let's begin our tour further south.

Girvan is an agreeable starting point: the scenery and the little golf course are worth a day of anyone's time and as a bonus a newly opened course nearby also merits a detour. We'll call there first.

Coming from the south you'll run across Brunston Castle golf club at Dailly, a tiny village on the B741 five miles east of Girvan. It was opened only in 1993 but already it's a glittering addition to the region's golf collection.

It was the brainchild of Bob Low, a Belgian diamond merchant who was bewitched by the region after a holiday at Turnberry and had an improbable dream of owning a Scottish golf course. He found the site, a 250 acre valley in a glorious pastoral landscape, and enlisted Donald Steel to design a course. A year later, with minimal excavation on a site tailor-made for golf, Donald had produced a work of rare beauty and challenge.

It measures 6,792 yards to a par and standard scratch of 72. Be advised every last inch is in play, partly because of the lush growth encouraged by the River Girvan which dissects the course and partly because of the sou' west wind. You'll be hitting lots of long irons.

The 9th and 18th fairways run parallel but every other hole plays in a different direction, usually through the wind, occasionally into it. Only four holes are remotely straight; the others bend at driving length from where fairway bunkers direct the accurate and snaffle the wayward.

The outward loop is generally level walking but the land rises from the 10th, where the second shot must fly the river, to the 11th green, the highest point from which Ailsa Craig is visible, beyond the valley at your feet. Someone should paint that picture.

Girvan is the southern-most coastal town in Ayrshire, convenient to the A76 and the M6, via Dumfries. It's a small, pleasant town and the King's Arms Hotel offers a convenient overnight stop for those wishing to play Brunston Castle and the town's municipal course.

A word of caution here: because of demand the starters at the local council courses cannot accept telephone bookings, although they will advise of availability. If you're intent upon playing them to a schedule you must either book your tee times in writing or use the services of the Ayrshire Golf Agency, which will provide a total package of accommodation and golf at public and private courses.

The district council offers two golf packages: a weekly ticket for £70 and a £50 pass which brings five mid-week rounds at any municipal course before 4.15pm. That proviso gives a clue: heavy local demand rises markedly after working hours and at weekends which means that the £70 pass, offering unlimited golf, has drawbacks for those wishing to play 36 holes a day.

This applies particularly in the peak golfing months of May and September when pre-booking is essential. Large groups playing a competition could find 36 holes impossible because tee times are allocated alternately to locals and visitors. Thus, a party of 24 could take up to two hours to tee off, putting a second round out of the question.

That said, the seven day pass offers good value for a small group visiting in July or August, the less busy months. Then, with maximum daylight hours and an early start, 36 holes a day is viable if you book your first tee time in advance. At that time of year a walk-up four ball will wait an average of perhaps 30 minutes before playing: just sufficient time for lunch after your morning round.

The Girvan course is no more than a minute from the Kings Arms Hotel so an early start doesn't mean crack of dawn! But whatever the hour the effort will be repaid: the scenery is breathtaking, the course impeccable.

It's in two sections: eight holes run down a spit of land alongside the sea; the remainder are inland, dissected by the river which, as at Brunston Castle, gives the course an emerald lushness that makes a mockery of the card. From the back tees it reads 5,095 yards over gently rolling ground to a par of 64. The rough is minimal, the fairways generous. There are four par threes on each loop and only two holes longer than 400 yards.

Sounds accommodating? Be warned that five of the par threes are in excess of 200 yards and the greens are far from large. It's a terrier of a course, but a playful terrier. You'll have great fun here. Take your camera.

From Girvan it's only a short drive north to Ayr, another attractive coastal town, where you'll find three more of those municipal courses. Two of them, Belleisle and Seafield, are neighbours in Belleisle Park just south of town. The other is Dalmilling, like Seafield a Group Two course, but on the northern outskirts.

Set in meadowland, it's a lovely walk and a pleasant, forgiving course for the less accomplished player. At 5,400 yards to a standard scratch of 66 it should hold no terrors for the competent. That's the theory, anyway!

Seafield has similar statistics but, tighter and more hazardous, it's made of sterner stuff, not least some evil bunkering. Many of the holes have a links flavour, although it's appreciably inland, in a partly wooded and frequently rolling landscape.

Like Girvan, Seafield has some long one shotters but they are nicely counter-balanced. Only three holes exceed 400 yards and several par fours will have you thinking of birdies. But many tee shots leave little margin for error and the greens are modest in size. It's a fun course, a perfect warm-up for the challenge to come. If you're intent on 36 holes you'll be advised to make this an aperitif for Belleisle where two rounds could be too much for most, particularly if the course is busy, when progress can be slow.

This is a sleeping giant, a fact disguised by the card which shows a relatively modest yardage of 6,477 to par and SSS of 71. Don't be misled: as a public course Ayr Belleisle is acclaimed as being only a whisker behind the Old Course and Carnoustie.

It's heathland-parkland in style with large stands of trees dictating the line of shot on several holes and a burn influencing others. Opened in 1927 to a design by James Braid, its original lay-out is still largely extant. A series of voracious fairway and cross bunkers, for instance, have been kept in play simply by extending the tees.

The greens are huge, with undulations ranging from subtle to severe, many with run-off banks around the edges. Most of them are heavily bunkered, several are on a plateau and surrounded by trouble, or elevated, with hummocks to catch or deflect anything short. You'll need your short game in good order.

This particularly applies to the par threes, perhaps the principal feature of the course. There are five, all of heroic proportions. All require accurate club selection and steely nerves, all have trouble lurking. Four of them will require long irons or better, depending upon the wind. The 3rd, for instance, is generally regarded as perhaps the toughest par three in Ayrshire. Belleisle will have you constantly on the defensive, but there are options aplenty. This is a strategic course par excellence, one to lift the spirits. Don't miss it.

It's said that more golf may be played in Troon than any other town in Britain with the exception of St Andrews. If that comes as a surprise then you're not aware that Troon has five courses, the two at Royal Troon and three outstanding municipals.

The three public courses in ascending order of challenge are Fullarton, Lochgreen and Darley, which adjoin each other and have a common clubhouse. Fullarton is similar to Dalmilling, a gentle golfing experience of 4,822 yards, par 64. The first hole at 442 yards is the longest by 70 yards and there are eight par threes. It's generally easy driving and the holes play short, particularly in summer. The greens, best described as miserly in size, can be hard and unreceptive. Whatever your handicap, play to it here and you're in form to tackle the next one up the ladder.

Although it was previously an Open qualifying course, Lochgreen is much more forgiving than its neighbour. Its fairways are more receptive; its greens, flat and generally quick, are bigger. There's minimal rough to bother the reasonably accurate driver and not too many bunkers and hazards.

It's not an ordeal, in a nutshell, but you'll need to get your head down to better your handicap. There's a demanding opening and the final four holes will wreck your card if you don't keep your wits about you. At 6,785 yards, par 74, its bark is worse than its bite. It's generally flat walking, and a lovely loop through the trees encompassing holes 11 to 14 bring a touch of woodland into the delightful equation. On a still day it's heavenly.

Darley is another kettle of fish entirely. A still day here is a prerequisite. The three opening holes give no hint of the waiting trouble. Then the heather, gorse and scrub become progressively thicker, the fairways progressively narrower. If that's not enough, a burn cuts across the line of play on six holes.

Darley follows the coastal perimeter of the site and becomes virtually links golf in which the wind exacerbates the problems posed by the narrow, scrub-lined fairways. Fortunately, bunkers are few so there's ample opportunity to play the half shot, the knock-down, predicated by the small, hard greens. At 6,501 yards, par 71, Darley is a lion of a course. It can be totally intimidating in a wind but links men who can drive it low and straight will relish the challenge. Others will be more at home next door, at Lochgreen.

As with Old Prestwick, it would be impossible to play Prestwick St Nicholas without being aware of its place in history. Of similar vintage to Old Prestwick, the club was founded in 1851 although the links moved location twice before settling on its present site in 1892. Deceptively difficult to play in any breeze at all, it's on a duneland site of modest proportions so there's not much spare land: everything is neat and tight. Hence the problems in a wind.

There are five blind tee shots but it's not a demanding driving course because the once feared heathery rough and gorse has largely disappeared. These days, at least you'll find your ball. But the fairways are tight and they're all bumpy. You'll wish for a third leg on occasion.

A number of fiercely bunkered plateau greens must be hit, or else! Often it's better to lay-up on the longer holes where there are cross bunkers in the approaches.

This is largely a second shot course whose demands are more technical than physical. Drive passably well and you'll frequently need no more than medium irons to many holes. That's when the fun starts.

It's a fair course, a good challenge at 5,952 yards, par 69, with only one par five and two other holes of any length at all. A number of short two shotters are models of their kind, bringing a lovely tempo to the round, and the homeward loop has three cracking par threes.

Then on to Barassie. A day here would be a memorable climax to any week of golf in Scotland. It may be the ultimate members' club and you'll leave green eyed at their good fortune. As befits a club of considerable substance and tradition, the facilities, on-course and off it, are unsurpassed, the fruits of a century of imaginative management from relatively modest beginnings. It's difficult to visualise improvements but we gather more plans are afoot...

They're uncommonly hospitable, too, as we discovered: a visitor carding an ace received a memento, a not unusual touch, it seems.

The lovely aspect of the course is its combination of playability and challenge. It's an Open qualifying course but Barassie won't intimidate the lesser player if he tempers his ambitions. It's a tricky links but not overly long or demanding.

Each hole poses different problems, because no two in succession are similar. A meandering burn, hidden depressions, fierce rough and fairways bunkers that gather a wayward ball at driving length, all put a premium on precision and strategy. The superb greens, without exception huge, undulating and slick, pose particular individual problems that are exacerbated if you miss them.

It's a links of benign beginnings, with only light rough on the early holes, but one that becomes progressively more testing, particularly off the tee. At 6,473 yards from the medal tees to a par of 71, there's only one par five on each loop and only three other holes are in excess of 400 yards.

Patience is the watchword here in more senses than one. Barassie is to be savoured for its condition, its technical challenge and its setting. It has few equals and no betters. Go gently and enjoy. It will crown a memorable week.

The Scottish Highlands: For night golf in broad daylight!

We were contemplating the cheese board and admiring a glorious Highland evening when a trio of golfers appeared on the green about 50 yards from the hotel's picture window that framed our view. It was just after nine pm. Recognising them as hotel guests, I voiced the thought that if they didn't look snappy they'd miss dinner.

Not so, replied our waiter. "They've already had dinner. It's quite normal here to golf afterwards. It will be light for hours yet at this time of year."

We were about 75 miles north of Inverness, the capital of the Highlands: it was June and in that month thereabouts they enjoy the longest summer days in Britain. They stretch from 2am until midnight and the golf is endless. For golfers this is the Promised Land. Buy a day ticket (all good value) anywhere in the Highlands and you could play until you drop from exhaustion or fall victim to terminal boredom.

Any journey to Scotland is a voyage of discovery but none is more richly rewarding than that which takes the golfing visitor to the nation's spiritual heartland. Knowing golfers whisper the names and drool: Royal Dornoch, Nairn, Boat of Garten, Tain, Golspie, Strathpeffer and Brora, to list a few. This is the stuff of golfing dreams in settings that defy description. It explains why many make it an annual pilgrimage, by-passing the golfing delights en route

Take the view from that dining room window, for instance: in any direction it will stop the breath. The Brora links, laid out by James Braid, occupies a voluptuously undulating site between the great Sutherland Hills and a dazzling white beach that stretches for miles in either direction. To the north stands the gaunt edifice of Ben Dhorian; to the south, across the Moray Firth, is the headland of Tarbat Ness. The serenity is so tangible it would support a coat hook.

Brora is as old-fashioned and welcoming as a log fire in your granny's kitchen. It's not a tough course to play or to walk, but it's no pushover: a wriggling burn, the hummocks and Braid's bunkers see to that. But the fairways are magnanimous: hook or slice and you'll always have a shot of sorts, but it will need a few seconds thought and some dexterity. While you're ruminating you can admire the views!

Nor is it long, not much more than 6,000 yards from the back so there's lots of mid-iron shots to be played. But there's only one par five and a trio of testing two shotters that can be the very devil in a breeze, which also spices the short holes.

This general description applies to a legion of the smaller clubs in the Highlands. Unlike Royal Dornoch and Nairn, they may not be of international repute but see them and you too will want to make this an annual golfing pilgrimage.

Five miles south of Brora and just short of Dornoch is Golspie, a links with lush fairways and a section of heathland. It runs along the shore of the Moray Firth, which in the past century has reeled in a ribbon of about 100 yards of the links section. They've built a sea wall now, so all's well.

The course is roughly the shape of a shepherd's crook. The links bit runs down the shaft, along the beach, and four heathland holes form the hook, around a pond. They're new by Highland standards. James Braid laid them out in 1926 when he up-graded the course. Those four apart, all the greens are originals, dating to 1910, although there was a nine holer here in 1899.

A mark of Golspie's standing is that it was a qualifying course for the 1985 British Amateur Championship played at Royal Dornoch. It's a shade shorter than Brora, with five par threes and no par fives, which makes it a touch more demanding, particularly as they say that if you have to look for a ball at Golspie you may as well re-load and forget it.

The first point to make about Tain is that it may well be the best-kept course in the Highlands and some way beyond. That's why Ian MacLeod has been adjudged green keeper of the year in Scotland and among in the top five in Britain.

Unappealing courses are rare as hen's teeth in the Highlands but this one will have your eye balls spinning. It's quite a test, too, although very fair, a strategic course of tight fairways laid out like strips of crumpled carpet edged by broom and gorse.

Tain is a links with a major difference. Through it runs a river, which must be crossed three times, and some parts have the appearance of sandy parkland. Members don't lay too many bets when the prevailing wind's on duty. It's a westerly and a cross wind on many holes. It brings all sorts of complications in the summer when the fairways are full of fire and bounce.

Few will demur that the center piece of Highland golf is Royal Dornoch. A round here is almost a spiritual experience. Ancient before Old Tom Morris was a pup but as modern as the internet, the Dornoch links are a model for any aspiring golf architect and a dream to play for the Tour pro or high handicapper alike. Tom Watson once popped in for a round and stayed for three days. He said he'd never had so much fun on a golf course. Play it on a fine summer's day, when the gorse is in full fig and the dunes are mounds of gold, and you may experience nothing like it.

It's a totally natural links, as are all the great ones, although Dornoch undulates more than most. As at Royal County Down, a jewel of equally incandescent brilliance, the fairways are all hummocks, swales and knolls, snaking between the dunes and linking greens of incomparable placement and form. Most if the latter are plateau or pulpit, and range in size from very large to vast, so huge that simply to move the flag stick is to change the character of the course in a breeze.

All of them are crowned, inverted saucers, so any miscued shot will trickle off and down, frequently with punishing results. This became the mark of Donald Ross, once the green keeper and professional here, who learned his trade under Old Tom at St Andrews. He transposed the style when he left Dornoch for Pinehurst in 1898, later to become the doyen of American golf course architecture.

At 6,700 yards Royal Dornoch is not long on the card; it simply plays long, oddly enough most markedly on a still day, according to the club's veteran professional Willie Skinner.

"The east wind is best," he'll tell you. "It helps a little on some holes, although it's across on several others."

Dornoch is a fair course, a strategic test *par excellence*. Blind shots are not anathema here, and although the rough is fierce the fairways are as generous as the greens, albeit crooked and with many judiciously placed bunkers.

Memorable sport aside Royal Dornoch, set on the shores of Embo Bay, has a serene ambience that's common to the Highlands, borne of geographical isolation and a hallowed place in golfing history. It's an imperative experience for those who care deeply about the game, one worth whatever detour is necessary.

In fact not much of a detour is required, although to drive from London would take two days. The trick is to fly into Inverness, the capital of the Highlands. This is an hour to the south of Dornoch but only a few minutes away from the well-scrubbed town of Nairn where an equally venerable links is part of the Highland pilgrimage.

Well over a century old, Nairn is frequently the venue for major events, the most recent being the 1994 British Amateur and the 1998 Walker Cup match between amateur teams from Britain and America. It is a magnificent links, comparable to Dornoch in stature although quite different in character.

Large, well-guarded greens of impeccable quality are a principal feature of a design that carries the marks of Old Tom Morris and James Braid. Edged by the beach, which forms a lateral hazard on the opening holes, it is exposed to every sea breeze as it runs out and back, with a minor diversion inland from the 13th tee. Hookers will relish Nairn but they should beware of over-cooking it: the gorse and whins are impenetrable, the rough knee-high.

In anything more than a breeze, a head wind on the opening loop, this is a giant of a links, one of the many jewels in the crown of Highland golf.

Where to stay:

The Links Hotel, Brora (AA & RAC 3*). A first class hotel in an idyllic setting, with views over the course to the sea. The nearby sister hotel, the Royal Marine, has a leisure centre and swimming pool. Both offer golf packages.

The Golf View Hotel, (AA 4*). Seabank Road, Nairn.

A sumptuous hotel with a renowned dining room and, close to the links, a favourite with golfers. Facilities include large gardens, tennis, pool, sauna and putting green. It has common ownership with the Royal Golf Hotel overlooking the links at Dornoch. Both highly recommended.

A journey along Scotland's Golfing Highway

Scotland's golfing jewels are on display all over this enchanting country but you won't find a finer collection than that hiding away in the region known as East Lothian, across the bay from St Andrews.

The access road is the A198 but it's known as the Golfing Highway. It wriggles along the coast from a point near the ancient Musselburgh links, a few miles east of Edinburgh, almost to venerable Dunbar, calling at a succession of comfortable old villages en route. The stretch in question runs for little more than 20 miles but packed into it are 15 links of the top echelon, with several parkland courses a little further inland.

Savour these names and let your imagination run wild: Muirfield, Musselburgh, Longniddry, Kilspindie, Luffness, Craigielaw, North Berwick, Dunbar and Gullane, which has three links. Craigielaw aside, all are more than a century old and part of the nation's golfing history.

Your only problem in the face of such riches is where to play? This would depend largely upon the duration of your visit and also on your budget. Presumably, most would like to include Muirfield in their schedule but it's not inexpensive. and a round at one the other principal links would be roughly one quarter of the cost.

For a stay of two or three days you could perhaps play Gullane, Craigielaw and Dunbar. Gullane has three courses, numbered in seniority: #1 is a final qualifying course for the Open; #2 is comparable in quality and has staged various major events; and #3 is somewhat shorter but no less challenging and enjoyable.

Dunbar, more than 150 years old and oozing history and tradition, is also a final qualifying venue and while Craigielaw is a new links it is one of masterful design and presentation. So much so that it has already staged several national events, amateur and professional.

Best value: For those groups planning a longer stay an advantage is that, seasons and daylight permitting, most clubs offer greatly reduced rates for twilight tee times, usually from about 3.30pm. Day tickets for 36 holes, too, are good value and all clubs offer sound catering to complete your day out.

When best to go: Go in autumn, when the weather is usually agreeable and the tourist crowds are thinning, and you'll find the countryside at its best and life being conducted at an amiable pace. The courses will be uncrowded, as will hotels and restaurants, and good value will be part of the package.

Getting there: The region is well under the hour from Edinburgh airport where a pre-arranged taxi will whisk you to your hotel. Better still, if you're coming from England you could travel by rail.

The train journey from London Kings Cross to Edinburgh Waverley station takes about four hours 40 minutes, with halts at Peterborough, Newcastle, Carlisle, Durham and Darlington, and this is far superior, in time and comfort, to flying. Once in Edinburgh, it's forty minutes to North Berwick, just beyond the half-way point along the coast.

Getting about: From this central point, or from the villages of Gullane or Aberlady, several golf courses will be no more than a few minutes away. For a small group it's a blissful situation and economical, too. A local taxi company has a fleet of people carriers manned by golf-knowledgeable drivers so you can let your hair down after golf or over dinner without a worry.

The accommodations: There's no shortage of good quality accommodation but we know two from personal experience. Those who prefer smaller establishments would delight in the charming Duck's, a pub-style hotel with a renowned restaurant that is part of Kilspindie House, in the village of Aberlady.

On a grander scale, the imposing 5* Macdonald Marine Hotel overlooking the North Berwick links is the favoured stop for players in the Open Championship. Both offer every facility, including all-inclusive golf packages, and are warmly recommended.

When to go:

Except when there is snow, golf is playable year-round although winter weather can be unpleasant and the course conditions below par. In winter, too, mats for fairway shots are common and forward tees and shorter courses are standard. Summer and autumn, from July onwards, are best for golf: the weather can be surprisingly warm and the courses will be in top condition and at full stretch

A memorable hole: The 14th at Lundin Links, Fife

Its name is Perfection and it is well named. It has every attribute of an outstanding par three and if Lundin Links were anywhere else in Britain its 14th hole would be as renowned as Troon's Postage Stamp or Calamity Corner at Portrush.

Instead, the course is over-shadowed by the golfing conurbation of nearby St Andrews and thus one of Scotland's finest links remains a true hidden gem. Any one of several holes at Lundin would fall into the category of memorable but the 14th is a masterpiece.

Take its length, for a start: at 175 yards it won't intimidate the average club golfer. Sure enough, the prevailing breeze comes in over the beach off Largo Bay at two o'clock, which can add more than a few yards at times. But obligingly it also pushes the ball away from the OOB wall, thirty yards or so from the back right corner of the green, which separates Lundin from neighbouring Leven Links.

That apart, the tee sits atop a steep hill, eighty feet or so above the green, and unless the flag is on the front edge the bottom of it is clearly visible. A slightly fat or under-clubbed shot will be severely punished, of which more anon, but if you've judged the distance correctly you can be a touch askew without meeting disaster.

There's room for error on three sides of the green although, if you're going to miss it, left is preferable: there's a sizeable bail-out area, just short of hummocky rough. All you'll have is a pitch from a tight lie over sand....

The gently concaved green is symmetrically circular, 25 yards by 26, with a slightly lower tier occupying the front quarter. It has a ring of five evenly-spaced bunkers, with a 30 yard entrance between those front left and front right. But they're all saucer bunkers: a gentle splash shot will leave a putt, albeit a long one that bears close scrutiny. So it's a generous target area. All plain sailing so far.

The problems? Discounting the wind, they're largely psychological. Just to the right of the tee is a jungle of trees and rough, deep enough to hide an elephant, that runs down the slope before thinning out into a belt of gorse running across the fairway at the bottom of the hill. Beyond that, twenty yards from the front edge and lurking in sand dunes which hide the green approaches, is a steep-faced pot bunker.

Now here's the piquant situation: a rank bad tee shot, even a top, will trickle down the close-mown hill leaving a pitch over the trouble. An over-clubbed shot, straight, pushed or pulled, will still leave the chance of a par if you've a short game worth the name.

It's that in-between shot, one hit a touch fat or under-clubbed, that will end in the consommé — and if it finds the gorse don't even bother looking. It is possible to just fly the cross bunker and get a kick forward off the down slope but that's akin to winning the national lottery. Don't bank on it.

The problem is compounded by that high tee, of course. From that elevation it's easy to under-club, and even a slight breeze can add fifteen yards.

I was there on a still autumn day and with the flag in centre-green saw a low handicap club member hit a five iron to fifteen feet, the ball rolling no more than four feet after pitching. But it's frequently a long iron, he said, and in extreme conditions he has hit the driver.

Take three here, any way possible, and as Lee Trevino would say, "get outta town;" walk away smiling from a truly memorable and picturesque hole.

SOME OF THE HIDDEN JEWELS OF GOLF HERE AND THERE....

Wales, where a red carpet awaits golfing purists

They keep a welcome in the hillsides, to be sure, but there's a red carpet covering the coastline of Wales, too. It over-lays a succession of glorious links, some world famous but most little-known jewels hiding in quiet corners of this lovely land.

Roll the names around the tongue and savour the prospects: Royal Porthcawl, the venerable figurehead of Welsh golf; Tenby, the principality's oldest club; Royal St David's, its jewel in the crown; Aberdovey, Pyle & Kenfig, Southerndown, all a match for any one, and the miniature masterpieces of Cardigan Bay and Borth, that purist's delight.

And this is only a brief selection: there are as many to the north, plus an array of parkland courses, ranging in quality from the rustic to the regal, that dot the timeless mountains in the interior.

For many years the number of Welsh courses was static at 111. But they've had a rush of blood to the head of late: the last tally was 170, and climbing. In consequence, the game has become an important plank in the nation's tourist market.

Access is convenient and a bonus is the association of 40 or so superior hotels collectively known as Welsh Rarebits. These run the gamut from an ancient former abbey at Tenby to elegant country houses, olde worlde village pubs and secluded farm houses. Although independently owned, they have a common bond: superior accommodations and cuisine. It's the perfect scenario for discerning golfers who can leap-frog from one stop to the next between golf and dinner.

Those traditionalists to whom links golf is the ultimate could have their fill by working their way westwards on the M4 from just beyond the Severn bridge. Tarry overnight at The Great House Hotel at Laleston, for instance, and Royal Porthcawl is only minutes away, with Southerndown and Pyle & Kenfig on opposite flanks.

There's a trio to summon up the blood! Southerndown is really elevated downland but it's in sight of the sea, exposed to its winds and in many respects plays like a links. It's a thoroughbred, too, with a pedigree that lists Willie Fernie, James Braid, Herbert Fowler and Harry Colt among the architects to have shaped its destiny since 1905.

They used to stage the Piccadilly Masters and the Martini International there but these days it would be too short for tour events at 6,417 yards. Par-70 but SS 72 says much, and at that elevation — it has a bird's eye view of Porthcawl — the finish would turn the knuckles white in anything more than a breeze.

Similarly Pyle & Kenfig, a creation of Harry Colt that has nine of the toughest links holes in the UK and a snaking loop of downland. Here standard scratch is two strokes higher than the par of 71 and any score close to par will win most bets.

Pyle, too, is somewhat overshadowed by Royal Porthcawl although its quality confirms its place in the great triumvirate of golf in the southern reaches of the country.

But then, most British courses would play second fiddle to Wales' premier links which over the years has staged virtually every amateur event worth talking about, not least the 1995 Walker Cup.

The essence of Porthcawl, the marvellous design aside, is the terrain which slopes sharply down to the sea. Consequently many greens tilt awkwardly, a factor compounded by severe undulations and, in several instances, a lack of width that predicates an approach up the length of a narrow green that often as not is slick and wind-swept.

So the tee shot must find the correct line, avoiding bunkers large enough to hide a Panzer tank, and even on the larger greens — some are vast — precision of both shots is paramount.

It's fair to say that even with relatively flat greens Royal Porthcawl would be a major test of technique: the greens that grace this jewel place it in the highest echelons of the game. And we haven't even mentioned the wind and the gorse....

If you're within striking distance of the M4 this trio of clubs promises a matchless golfing weekend; if time allows, more delights await further along the coast.

It's imperative that you detour to the Gower Peninsular, an oasis of serenity that's a magnet for holidaymakers and now a mecca for golfers. Stay a night or two at the luxurious Fairyhill Hotel and you'll be no more than 15 minutes away from a clutch of courses in settings that defy description.

Perhaps the best known is Penard, a cliff-top course that's half links, half moorland and all red-blooded challenge with a series of pulpit greens that demand an imaginative short game. It's only a whisker over 6,000 yards but par-71 and when you learn that it was designed by James Braid you'll simply have to play it.

Then there's Clyne, almost as venerable, equally as imposing, slightly shorter but just as demanding of precision. They say Clyne's greens set the standards hereabouts but the good folk at Langland's Bay might have a comment on that score.

Set on a headland between Carswell Bay and Langland's Bay, this course lies in two valleys overlooked by several holes on higher ground. The views may be without peer in British golf and the short 16th is special, even by local standards.

They say it's parkland but the course is a bit linksy, a bit moorland, a bit breezy and a bit hard! The card says 5,857 yards, par-70, SS 69, but it doesn't say that many shots are "up" to add length and confound anything lacking authority to greens on the small side. It's a joy but such is the welcome the most difficult bit is actually escaping the clubhouse long enough to play!

Another course that mustn't be missed is the newest, known as The Gower. It opened in June 1997 to a design by Donald Steel and is on two levels with several small lakes and lots of wildlife.

Ever the minimalist, Steel has utilised a lovely site to its ultimate without upsetting the rhythm of nature. His signature is large greens but they don't intrude on a tranquil setting that in every other respect appears unchanged.

If you're not fussed about playing links golf a stay on The Gower would be just the ticket with four such courses on your doorstep. And the Fairyhill people will make your arrangements, some at reduced green fees, and provide detailed directions.

It would be a shame, though, to come this far and eschew the extra leg to Tenby in neighbouring Pembrokeshire. So to hell with the expense; sell the pig and head west. It's not far.

Even non-golfers will give a vote of thanks when they sight the once-fortified town clinging to the cliffs above Carmarthen Bay. History permeates the higgledy-piggledy cobbled streets, spanned by archways and lined by ancient buildings, one of them the oldest church in Wales.

The town is visible from Penally Abbey, now a sumptuous hotel that's worth any detour. From its breakfast room you can also see the venerable links where it runs onto the beach across the bay. If there's a finer sight on a summer's morn then someone's keeping it secret.

Founded in 1880, this is the birthplace of Welsh golf, now a majestic links that was redesigned by James Braid in his hey day. His marks are legion and all have stood the test of time on a succession of superb holes that still attract national events.

Like most well-tramped links of such vintage a certain renewal eventually becomes imperative and that is now under way. The greens have long been the club's pride and joy and now the tees and bunkers are under-going piece meal reconstruction and irrigation is being introduced at the rate of two holes each year.

It all adds up to a pretty penny but, like renovating any national treasure, it's an investment that will pay rich dividends for another century or more. Not to be missed.

Just for variety there's a new course hereabouts, too, a pretty parkland on the outskirts of town that has all the makings of something special.

It's called Trefloyne Golf Club, it is owned by a local quarry company who didn't skimp in the construction — it's to USGA specifications — and whose efforts are now being rewarded with a growing membership and a steady flow of visitors.

The course measures 6,635 yards from the back to par of 71, equal to SS, and has a nice tempo, with some testing one shotters and a couple of formidable par fives: the 18th is 580 yards. It opened in May 1996, is maturing well and they were putting the finishing touches when I popped in.

On the subject of new courses, two other South Wales clubs are worth noting not least because both will soon have resort-style hotels and all the usual facilities.

You'll know about Celtic Manor, no doubt; what you may not know is that a third course, now bedding down, will open next spring and that the gracious old hotel, which began with 17 rooms, will by January have 400!

With 1,000 acres, a huge golf academy and the largest clubhouse in Britain, Celtic Manor has already made its mark on the national game. It has two courses by Trent Jones Sr, the major being the Roman Road course that's a real man-eater from the back pegs, and the shorter Coldra Woods course.

But the Roman Road course, now being re-routed and amended, will play second fiddle when the Wentwood Hill course, designed by Trent Jones Jr., comes on-stream. They're talking Tour events and then some and there's serious money involved...

Big things are happening, too, at the Vale of Glamorgan Golf Club, just off the M4 only 10 minutes from both Bridgend and Cardiff. It began as a nine holer in October 1993 but obviously struck a chord with local golfers: there were 500 members within seven weeks!

So it became 18 holes in May 1995 and is now 27, spread over 225 acres of sublime parkland. Soon there'll be a 125 roomed hotel and a major leisure centre and all the bits and pieces one associates with a resort.

The newer 18 holes are the major course. It's known as The Lakes, a 6,500 yarder with five one shotters and five par fives and with water in play on 10 holes. As an indication of the quality, the Welsh Professional Championship will be staged there for the third time this year and, like Celtic Manor, the owners are looking beyond that, to even bigger things.

That's the story of golf in Wales in the 1990s. There's no stopping it....

Where to stay: The Great House, Laleston, Bridgend. The main house, with a celebrated restaurant, dates to 1550; several bedrooms are in cottages overlooking the courtyard. All is 5* standard. Convenient for Royal Porthcawl. Highly recommended.

Fairyhill Hotel, Reynoldston, Gower. A country house dating to 1720 and set in 24 acres of gardens, Fairyhill was the AA Hotel of the Year for 1997. Exquisite sums it up. Renowned dining room, luxurious bedrooms, impeccable service.

Penally Abbey, Tenby. Worth any detour for award-winning cuisine or accommodation. Historic, romantic, memorable, intimate, a rare example of an elegant country house overlooking the sea and golf. Set in five wooded acres on the site of a 6th century abbey. Only 12 rooms, all de luxe.

How to book: For a guide to all 43 Welsh Rarebit hotels contact Welsh Rarebits, Tyglyn Aeron, Lampeter,Ceredigion. SA48 8DD.

Bewitching golf in legendary Somerset

Somerset is a beguiling county, a Pandora's Box of beauty, history and legend. Devon and Cornwall play a siren song just beyond the far horizon but only the iron-willed could by-pass Somerset and golfers shouldn't think of it.

From the limestone Mendips to the russett-red Quantocks and the brooding Blackdowns, the cider apple county nestles in a bed of hills that serrate the horizon from virtually any viewpoint. A ragged, picturesque coastline completes a bewitching plethora of natural distractions.

There are legends aplenty, too, of castles and battlefields and King Arthur's knights, and here the Reverend Toplady was inspired to scribble Rock of Ages while sheltering from a Mendip storm not far from what is now the alluring golf club of that name.

Walk the Mendip course and you'll be overcome by a similar reverence; your well-bred instinct will have you repairing any divots or pitch marks. The fairways are of an astonishing quality that extends through every facet of this delightful and elegant downland course.

Set in deeply undulating, heavily wooded countryside, it gives entrée to spectacular views from the peak, some 1,000 feet above sea level. On a summer's day there's no more glorious sight in golf, although, as the good reverend discovered, altitude brings mixed climatic blessings!

There's a gentle climb to open, holes four to ten are played over a rolling plateau, followed by a descent. Nothing too strenuous, although the wind at that altitude will oft-times summon up the blood and exacerbate that slice!

At 6,330 yards, par-71, here is a course whose pedigree matches its charm. The club was founded in 1897 but moved to the present site in 1913 when Harry Vardon laid out the first nine holes. It became an 18 holer only in 1965. The architects were Ken Cotton and the redoubtable Frank Pennink and the quality shows through.

Not least is a lovely tempo and variety. After a gentle up-hill start every hole counterpoints its neighbours, with five short two shotters and five long ones. There are three genuine three shotters for the average player, a trio of delightful par threes and the finishing hole, like the first, is a short par four.

The architectural delights, like the vista, are equalled by the presentation, and there's an interesting tale about the architect of that.

His name is Richard Flower, he's been the club's greenkeeper for more than 20 years and the club champion for 10 of those! He still plays off three. As a greenkeeper he is plus three. His endeavours compliment one of the true hidden gems of English golf. Well worth a detour.

Stockley Park: A silk purse from a sow's ear....

Entrepreneurs seeking a role model for golf developments should drop in at Stockley Park, near Heathrow. Local authorities running golf courses would benefit by having a look, too. Here's how a pay-and-play facility should be designed, built and operated.

It's a project that has transformed the London Borough of Hillingdon, eradicating a hazardous eyesore and replacing it with an attractive green belt vista that, golf aside, offers a variety of indoor and outdoor leisure pursuits to an appreciative populace. Just hearing the story lifts the spirits.

For two centuries, until 1985, the 360 acres had been a sprawling landfill site, a tip for the capital's waste that offended eyes and nostrils. Hillingdon's residents must have wondered what they'd done to deserve it.

Now it's a wooded rolling country park with nature trails, ten soccer pitches, an equestrian centre and a golf course, complete with lakes, already recognised by the organisers of the Senior and Challenge Tours. The locals can't believe their luck.

The statistics behind the transformation boggle the mind: 3,000,000 cubic yards of refuse were moved to create hills and raise the land levels by 200 feet, all layered with top soil over the sewage cake used for the grass seed root zone. They tell me that 1.6 million worms (wonder who counted 'em?) were introduced to break up the sub soil clay. Then it was all contoured, irrigated, and planted with 4,000 semi mature trees and 140,000 saplings.

Now there's a two storey futuristic golf clubhouse with every facility and a leisure club that offers squash, swimming and horse riding. All pay and play. It's public facility sport, 21st Century-style.

See it and you'll know that the course is by Robert Trent Jones Sr. Lots of water, acres of jig saw bunkers, huge greens of disparate contours: it couldn't have been designed by anyone else.

There are a few flat bits here and there but the vista from the clubhouse terrace is one of voluptuously rolling fairways winding through the trees, twisting and turning as they go. Don't stray too far because in places they're barely 25 yards wide. Be straight, though, and clear the rise that marks many fairways and the down-slope will stretch your drive. But beware the cunningly-placed bunkers and, on three holes, the water. The further you hit it the greater the risk.

Tees and greens are to USGA specifications and the equal of any you'll find. The undulating greens are slick in summer, but they hold the ball well so be accurate with your approach or you'll find yourself in three putt territory..

And because the land is now elevated, up to 200 feet in places, there's always a breeze up top. It's a big, demanding course from the back pegs, a good test from further forward and it's improving as those trees mature.

A joint venture between a local business consortium and the PGA European Tour, with a 75 year lease from the local council, the Stockley Park complex opened in June 1993 with a no-nonsense, value for money policy.

The daily green fees are modest for a Home Counties course and there are discounts for five and seven day ticket holders who pay an annual fee of £84 and £120 respectively.

There's an annual season ticket, which virtually equates to club membership with handicaps and weekly competitions, for £840. That was limited to 350 applicants: it was sold out in five weeks. Such was the demand, such is the quality. Merits a detour.

Prestbury rewards a misguided detour

Prestbury Golf Club is a hidden gem in both senses of the term. Tucked away in a lovely corner of Cheshire, it takes some finding but, unless you're running late for your tee time, searching the patchwork of picturesque country lanes will enhance a delightful day.

Another bonus is that the course was designed by Harry Colt, with assistance from John Morrison. That's sufficient justification for any misguided detour: in this case the attractions are ten fold. It is a beauty in every respect.

Prestbury is laid out in 120 acres, all sumptuously rolling and wooded, with a further 40 devoted to a practice area. A stream runs through it, too. In some spots there are views of the distant Pennines in Derbyshire. Tranquillity and beauty contribute in tandem.

Originally, one suspects, it would have been moorland with scant flora. Over the years, though, several thousand trees have been planted, mostly in strategic clumps, others as a backdrop to tees and greens, and the image now is one of cultured parkland.

With two differences: the site is on the crest of a huge sand belt that runs through the centre of Cheshire. The course also stands at an altitude of about 300 feet, so the combination of sand and wind brings fast draining qualities rare in the parkland genre. Here bents and fescues dominate.

The altitude also means a later growing season than is found in more sheltered areas. It doesn't peak until late June but it holds its quality until early winter. A golden autumn evening would be one to savour. You'll view the members with green eyes, and not only for the course. The clubhouse is a gem, too.

The original, a whitewashed cottage some 250 years old, is now a staff residence adjacent to a large, two storey building that 200 years ago was a farm stores, stables and a hayloft. It has mullioned windows, beamed ceilings, arched doorways and an ambience impossible to imitate. These days the hay loft is a charming dining room, the stables part of the members' lounge. I've seen no more appealing clubhouse.

Prestbury is a club of considerable substance and tradition, qualities attributable to the founder members whose foresight has been passed on down the generations. Change is not anathema here but it has always been the subject of deep reflection. The clubhouse has, by necessity over the years, been extended here and there but always in sympathy with the original and never without taste. The seams defy detection.

Similarly with the course: the constitution denies any architectural change without the acquiescence of the architect and the express permission of the members. Harry Colt has passed on, of course, but these days Martin Hawtree has followed his father as the club's consultant architect, with similar intent, an impenetrable barrier to council members seeking posterity.

Its benefits are obvious: subtle up-grading and the trees excepted, the course is virtually as Colt and Morrison last saw it, except that these days it is vastly superior in presentation and outlook. Suffice to say that Anthony Davies, formerly of Wentworth, is one of only five master greenkeepers in Britain and a former greenkeeper of the year. It shows at every turn.

It's a site of marked undulation but such is the design that only one hole, the 9th, requires an uphill shot of any severity, although there are several pitches to elevated greens. Most tee shots, indeed, are downhill, albeit blind, and some are teasing dog-legs.

But that's unavoidable on such a natural course and in any event there's virtually no rough to speak of, the fairways are as wide as can be. A strategic fairway bunker is usually visible: just miss it and you'll be in the correct spot, particularly if you've carried the rise. If that's beyond you, hit it somewhere near the marker posts and you'll find your ball, although if you're too wide getting the thing onto the green won't be quite so easy, despite their generous size. Fanciers of Colt's bunkering will appreciate this point.

There's a hint of Mackenzie in some greens. The par four 9th has a narrow, three tiered green and others have folds that suggest that Mackenzie, who did some work with Colt about the time Prestbury was laid out in 1920, had an influence on the design, even if he wasn't present. Variety abounds, there's not a weak hole and the four par threes are superb.

It's not a championship course — those blind shots wouldn't best please some professionals — but it's a sound test demanding versatility and imagination. Strong drivers will drool. For many years the pro record was 68, three under, by Max Faulkner. These days it's 67 although professionals seldom play there. It looks an awesome challenge from the back pegs.

County fixtures are not infrequent, and visitors are made most welcome during the week, even societies, though these are restricted in size and may play only on Thursdays.

Prestbury is one to savour. Give yourself an extra half hour for the detour around the local countryside and you'll arrive uplifted and raring to go.

Location:
Near Prestbury village, two miles NW of Macclesfield on the A538.

Nailcote Hall: a short course in tournament history

Nine hole courses don't usually fall into my ambit simply because there are so many 18 holers to be discovered and to write about as venues for golfing breaks. So the odds of my reviewing a nine hole, par-three course were about equal to Tiger Woods being named Man of The Year by the Feminist Tendency.

Until, that is, I popped into the four star Nailcote Hall, down there in Shakespeare country, to discover that they're successfully re-writing golfing history in the form of the British Short Course Championship.

Those who can remember Craven A's and Morris Eights will recall the annual event staged between 1933 and 1973 over the little course at the Palace Hotel, Torquay, in the days before the European Tour was a glint in John Jacob's eye.

The prize money wasn't much but it was better than nothing, which was the alternative that week, and all the big names in British pro golf would trot down there once a year for the annual knees-up and 36 holes of fresh air and fun.

Henry Cotton and Ted Ray were among the winners and so was dear old Charlie Ward, another former Ryder Cupper, who at 87 years of age teed it up at Nailcote in the revived event last June. The winner was Peter Baker who pocketed £3,000 for being three under par after 36 holes.

That's right: three under after 36. This on a course just light of 1,000 yards, where the longest hole is 145 yards and the shortest is 87. A push-over it is not, with first class bent greens, slippery in the summer, that are crowned or elevated and guarded by bunkers or water. The condition was flawless; the pro's loved it.

There's a smashing hotel, of which more anon, and there's only 15 acres all told, of which eight are dedicated to the golf course. A bonus: it's great practice on the most important part of the game and you'll never have more fun in broad daylight. You could whiz around in under the hour but you'll want to do it again, and again. It's quite addictive.

What's more it's free. There's no green fee. Of course, you'll have to stay in the hotel but that's no hardship. For a romantic break with golf thrown in I can think of few places more appealing.

The hall, set in established gardens, dates to 1640: they say Oliver Cromwell, old Lemon Lips himself, once stayed there but I'll wager it's more fun these days!

There are 38 en suite rooms, acres of polished timber, lots of stained glass windows, low beams and log fires. There's a cosy piano bar, a library and lounges, and the Oak Room restaurant is about as good as it gets in the gourmet stakes.

To ring the changes, there's a modern wing with a conference centre that's home to a Mediterranean-style restaurant and Rick's Bar, named for the owner, Rick Cressman, but redolent of the original that featured in the movie *Casablanca* This is where it all happens each weekend, with live entertainment and dancing for those who like to shimmy.

But if you're there with a golfing sweetheart the Oak Room is the place to be. Have a slap-up dinner, a bottle of something memorable by candlelight and an early night ready for the golf in the morning. Old Cromwell will never know what he missed!

MISCELLANEOUS MUSINGS UPON THINGS GOLF

Finally, after 500 years, the wait is over!

The golfers of St Andrews spent 500 years without a public clubhouse but, prevarication over, they built one in 15 months. At £3 million it looks a snip and well worth the wait.

Until now visiting golfers have been forced to change their shoes in the nearest car park and hump their clubs down to the first tee, their spikes scraping sparks on the town pavements. Showers? Forget it. Maybe a pint? There's the pub. A sandwich? Ditto. Back to the hotel? You said it.

It wasn't a barrel of fun after playing through a rain storm and although the situation had a certain rustic charm it wasn't really in keeping with image of the Home of Golf. Non-complaining Brits were pretty stoic about it; the Japanese simply bowed, smiled and said "ah so", but Americans, accustomed to country club luxury, were aghast at such an uncouth paucity of basic facilities.

Not now, though. Returning visitors won't know what's hit 'em. The objective, said Peter Mason, of the St Andrews Links Trust Management, was a clubhouse equal to international standards. And that's just what they've produced.

It's elegant, opulent even, with every amenity, plus the greatest views in golf. It overlooks the the 1st, 17th and 18th holes of the Old Course: they're right there, through the windows if you're inside, down below if you're on the upper balcony or the landscaped roof garden. A roof garden at St Andrews? Told you it was opulent.

Externally it's a handsome edifice, designed in keeping with its historic setting, with external walls and pillars of honeyed stone, the roof of Westmoreland green slate. It has, in effect, four fronts, each side with an attractive entrance leading onto landscaped gardens guarded by dry stone walling.

The building is of three storeys, not counting the turret, but only 33 feet of it is visible: the foundations and basement level, which houses the service facilities, have been dug into a sand hill, to maintain the necessary low profile.

(They had to shift 3,000 tons of sand and pump out 250,000 gallons of rising sea water per day before the foundations were made waterproof.)

All in, it has 20,000 square feet of floor space on the two floors which will open to the public in May: there's a reception area, starter's office, changing rooms for men and women with 370 handsome lockers and, yes, even showers! There are bars, a large lounge with all-round picture windows giving the aforementioned views, a dining room and space for a pro shop. All with wall to wall carpet , décor and furnishings to match.

It's where all golfers will check in and for those due to play the Old Course there's even a chauffeured golf cart shuttle up to the first tee and back.

It will be a grand spot to watch the climax of the 1995 Open but you'll need to be a member of the Royal & Ancient to have access. They've booked it for the duration of the championship.

After 500 years they probably felt like a change of view!

Golfing esoterica: Did you know that....?

There was no such thing as "a teeing ground" until about 1875. Before then our golfing forebears teed up on the putting green, using a pinch of sand.

The first Rules of Golf, devised in 1744 by the Gentlemen Golfers of Leith (later to become The Honourable Company of Muirfield) stipulated that after holing out the ball should be teed up "within one club length of the hole."

By 1828 this had become "no less than two club lengths and no more then four." An appreciation of putting surfaces was evidently emerging because this was later extended to "no less than four club lengths or more than six" and by about 1870 the distance stipulated was "no less than eight and no more than 12 club lengths."

The formal teeing ground was first mentioned in 1875 and in 1882 the amended Rules of Golf referred to "the tee" rather than the distance from the hole. In 1893 the teeing ground was accurately defined for the first time as "two marks in line at right angles to the course (the fairway) and two club lengths in depth."

There was no mention of the proximity to the hole: the tee was placed a short distance from it and conveniently positioned for the next hole. Thus were taken the first steps towards golf course architecture, where the tee and its hole became an entity. It was a development that was to change the very nature of the game and have lasting implications.

In the early years of the game course maintenance was at best rudimentary and the results rustic. Scythes and sickles had replaced rabbits and sheep for grass-cropping purposes but the length of grass on the fairways still served to shorten shots and stretch courses, and even the best greens were uneven in both surface and response.

When the teeing ground was accurately defined, the game's architecture took a giant leap forward. The modern golf course began to emerge.

By this stage, too, hand-pushed grass cutters had become more readily available: putting surfaces assumed a consistency previously undreamed of, thanks to Edwin Budding. He was a Gloucestershire man who produced what was the world's first lawn mower. Aside from committing future generations of men to an unending weekend chore, he changed the concept of golf course maintenance. The gang mower was not far behind.

It is not known precisely when Budding unveiled his first lawn mower but the patent was taken up by Ransomes, then manufacturing ploughshares, who in 1832 obtained a licence to build the first commercial model. Within two decades, their promotional literature proudly announced they were turning out around 70 to 80 such machines annually, complete with rollers–a vital component — and catch-boxes. By the time the teeing ground was introduced, it's fair to assume, most golf clubs would have availed themselves of this revolutionary invention which would transform their courses beyond anything previously imagined. The two developments merged into common usage to initiate another upsurge in course construction.

The original rules of golf were devised in 1744 when the world's first golf society was formed by a group of Edinburgh businessmen who played over the five hole links near the Port of Leith.

Until that time matches had been individual affairs, privately arranged for wagers, invariably followed by dinner at a nearby hostelry and the consumption of copious quantities of claret, invariably the subject of the wagers..

Then it was decided to stage a formal competition, the winner to be declared Captain of The Golf, and they requested the Burghers of the City of Edinburgh to donate a silver club as a trophy for what was intended to be an annual event.

The City Elders agreed to this with two provisos: that to protect the Burghers' investment, as it were, the group form a recognised society; and that the competition for which the silver club was to be donated on loan should be open to all.

Thus was formed the Company of Gentlemen Golfers of Leith, later to be the Honourable Company of Edinburgh Golfers of Muirfield. They still have the silver club and the original of the "Articles and Laws in Playing at Golf".

Until 1744 the rules governing play were as informal as the groups who played. They were local rules, devised to suit the conditions and the course over which they were used. But visitors to the open competition, it was realised, would not be conversant with such rules, only their own. Hence the need for universal laws.

In 1754 the 22 Noblemen and Gentlemen of Fife, later the Royal & Ancient, adopted the Articles for their first open competition. They formed the basis of the Rules of Golf we know today. There were thirteen of them and they defined the requirements and penalties, many of which are still in effect ("He whose ball lyes farthest from the hole is obliged to play first") and they all relate to what we know as match play.

The Articles were simple because that was the nature of the game. The ball was played where it was found and if by chance it could not be played "Allow your adversary a stroke for so getting out your ball." Complications ensued, though, with regard to the manner of deciding the winner in what was a non-knockout match play competition.

So in 1759 it was decided by the Gentlemen of St Andrews that "whoever puts in the ball at the fewest strokes over the round shall be the winner." Thus did the Rules bring about the invention of stroke play.

How an invalid carriage changed the face of Florida

Like the charming story of the founding of Pinehurst as the world's first golf resort, the history of how Florida became Golf State USA also has remarkable beginnings. It all started because of an invalid... The setting: the Boca Raton resort in Palm Beach, a winter hide-away for film stars and other wealthy celebrities in the years between the wars. In those days it was known as the Cloister Inn and it had one of the few golf courses in the region, one built simply as a hotel facility.

It seems that a couple of vacationing New Yorkers decided to try the strange game they saw being played but, being on the wrong side of 50 and unaccustomed to walking further than a waiting limo, they couldn't finish the course.

"Pity," they agreed. "It's a crazy game but fun." Then the sight of a friend tootling around the resort in a motor-driven three wheeled invalid carriage gave them a bright idea... If they could get one of those things converted to carry some golf sticks, they said, their problem would be solved. Another chum came up with a suitable conversion... and the age of the golf cart was born. Before you could shout "fore" their rudimentary cart had spawned an industry. Soon there were hundreds of carts zooming around and, to meet the demand, golf courses began springing up like mushrooms in a farmyard, many built on land reclaimed from swamps that covered almost half of the State..

Then along came another bright idea when it was realised that golf courses had lots of unused land just perfect for building second homes for the seriously wealthy seeking winter sunshine. Soon there were 100 golf courses, then 500, then 1,000: today there are more than 1,500 courses across the State, each with hundreds of second homes on the fairways. "Gated communities" they call them, part of the country club set that is synonymous with the State.

And that was the start of the multi-billion dollar Florida real estate boom that continues to this day. It all began with an invalid carriage that is now a treasured exhibit in the Pinehurst museum: the world's first golf cart at home in the world's first golf resort...

Not a lot of people know that, even in Florida... And how many golf carts are there in America? We doubt that anybody knows that...

Prayer mats prove a blessing

The committees of clubs with courses having winter drainage problems will be interested in a development that has paid rich dividends in Scotland. It's a simple way of protecting the course during climatic excesses and making winter golf more enjoyable.

Players carry small mats of artificial grass — eight inch squares are perfect — from which to hit the ball. It's permissible to anchor the mat with a tee peg, which may also be used for teeing up, a boon on big holes stretched by winter conditions. The benefits are two-fold: no divots and consistent lies for every shot.

The movement seems to have started at Monifieth GC, near Carnoustie, a couple of years ago and when the benefits became obvious the Carnoustie management followed suit.

The result: the fairways of the Open Championship course have never been in finer condition and now the Links Management body at St Andrews have introduced the scheme to save an estimated 150,000 divots each winter.

The Scots call them prayer mats. They've proved a blessing.

Old tyres make the Algarve a greener place

It is quite a stretch of the imagination to link a mountain of old car tyres with the development of de luxe golf resorts but such an obtuse connection exists. It is part of an ingenious invention that promises to transform the golf course construction industry.

The masterminds behind Castro Marim, a 500 acre estate in the eastern end of the Portuguese Algarve and close to the Spanish border, have changed the whole concept of resort development. They have devised a subterranean irrigation system that makes sprinklers obsolete, obviates hollow tining and verti-cutting and reduces water wastage and the use of pesticides (that's where those old tyres get into the act...) as well as unsightly debris and delays to play.

There's also a computerised drainage network that gathers surplus water, directs it into a reserve lake, one of 15, all inter-linked, from where a solar powered pump returns it into the system.

Then there's a fleet of solar powered golf carts, with satellite controlled computer screens giving on-course directions..... One could accurately describe Castro Marim as revolutionary.

That's all good copy, as we say, but the big story has been a secret until recently, largely because it's out of sight, underground. Its product name is Leaky Pipe, it is created from old tyres converted by granulation into porous rubber piping about the thickness of a slim cigar and formed into mesh in eight inch squares. Like a mammoth rubberised chicken wire, if you can imagine that. This is laid onto a carpet of two inch thick desiccated sponge just below what will become the root zone of the embryonic golf course and connected to a network of pumps running down the edge of each fairway.

Once the root zone and top soil have been spread, shaped and seeded over tees, fairways, rough and greens, as required, the pumps are primed and fired and computer-controlled irrigation gets under way. The water leaks from the pipes into the sponge which acts as a reservoir and feeds the grass roots. It is a concept so simple and yet so radical....

No, there's not a sprinkler to be seen. The first 18 holes of what will be Castro Marim's Atlantic course — there'll eventually be 36 holes — are complete. They look a picture, a vista of striped emerald fairways and checker board greens. And, a couple of spring showers aside, not a drop of water has fallen on them.

The advantages are multiple and varied: the system saves up to 50 per cent on water costs because there is no evaporation or run-off; it reduces maintenance, is labour saving and assists greens staff and golfers alike because it doesn't hinder progress as do sprinklers. More, it reduces the use and wastage of pesticides and nullifies the threat of disease caused by surface moisture.

Nor does it end there: twice a year the pipes are allowed to empty and compressed air is pumped into the system to aerate the roots, thus negating the need for hollow tining and verti-cutting! Again, no delays to work or play and no unsightly mess associated with the old-fashioned method or getting air into the root zones.

"The objective is a totally eco-conscious resort ," said Marc van Gelder, the marketing manager. "Here we recycle everything and reduce pollution to the absolute minimum."

It's a philosophy that has already won an International Green Globe award for ecological initiative. Eventually, when the concept is in common usage, it will make a small but significant contribution to one of the world's major environmental headaches, what to do with all those old tyres.....

Pyjamas are de rigeur for golf's dawn patrol !

Here's an idea for those clubs with a large playing membership who experience problems apropos the weekend starting sheet.

It comes from Mill Green GC, Herts, where one weekend tee time each hour is blocked out in yellow, signifying it has been reserved for booking on the day for those members unable to get to the club during the week.

Groups without a time draw straws, the loser being despatched to the club at first light to reserve a slot. It's known as the dawn patrol and, no, it's not abused, no matter how exalted the members involved.

A former president of the EGU, who lives about a mile from the club, was recently spotted in pyjamas and dressing gown waiting for the doors to open.

Drawing the short straw is tough but the loser takes it stoically. And of course he wastes no time in conveying the news to his bed-bound partners. I gather 6.05 is the current Sunday record....

HUMOUR

The new cutting edge of golf technology

Beware the sick golfer is a time-honoured adage we've all heard at some point in our golfing lives. Like me, you've probably discovered it's a truism based on absolute fact, endorsed when you've drawn the short straw in a four ball and found a crock in opposition.

Given a minor injury of a nature which is no barrier to playing — a fractured fibia, perhaps, or a severed cartilage — any golfer worth his corn will invariably produce close to the best form of his life. Anything less — double pneumonia or acute dengue fever spring to mind from personal experience — will have him beating his handicap by a handsome margin, leaving the rest trailing in his wake of soggy tissues.

A devout toper will tell you that a simple brink-of-the-grave hangover is worth three holes start any Sunday morning, providing your partner is drilled to pick the ball out of the hole, thus nullifying the danger of your head falling off as you bend to retrieve the happy outcome of your third successive sixty foot putt.

There are drawbacks, though, to this form of self-inflicted debilitation. It seldom persists for the full 18 holes, particularly on a bitingly brisk, hoary February morning when the combined effects of a force five wind and a walking rate only marginally slower than that displayed by the winner of the Olympic 400 metre final works wonder for the old brain box, surging the blood around the body in the fast lane and sweeping away the debris from last night's debauch.

Before you know it you've regained consciousness and, contemplating your card in the cold light of a winter's morn, realise with a jolt that you're four under par after eight holes, at which point the wheels fall off and you play the remaining 10 in 27 over!

After many years of research, not least in the field of self-inflicted injury, I have reached a conclusion on the odd state of affairs whereby a sick golfer will leave a healthy one feeling worse than when he started.

It is this: I think a sick man, or one recovering from a recent illness, is simply glad to be out on the course, grateful for small mercies and not expecting much in the way of reward. Relieved of the ritual, self-imposed pressures of attempting yet again to better the course record, he plays well within himself and swings the club easily. This serves to keep everything in its prescribed place and the ball flies down successive fairways as straight as frozen rope.

The end result is usually in the order of two bogeys, ten pars and six birdies, including a pair of twos, for a net 58 and a bulging wallet.

Consider the reverse: how often have you arrived at the club feeling full of the joys of Spring and eager to consummate your well-being with a good score, only to play at your worst?

Why? Because you expected too much; you tried too hard. You began badly, tried harder and became progressively worse. Your day was doomed from the outset.

Meanwhile, your opponent, hung over to the point of being terminal, couldn't give a continental. He doesn't expect to live much beyond lunch, anyway, and the end can't come soon enough. He swings slowly, simply because of the pain he's enduring, and his tempo, positively funereal, becomes established from the start.

He misses a couple of four footers due to the fact that he can see two balls and his hands are shaking something awful, but that apart he can't put a foot wrong and wins in a canter. He heads for the bar contemplating a hair of the dog as you ponder opening your veins in a warm bath....

Now, a hangover is more pleasurable pain than a fractured fibia, though it may not seem so at the time, but I'm sure that not all of you would care to get tanked up every night before golf simply an as aid to form. That would incur too many penalty strokes at home and adversely affect the old connubial bliss, if you're fortunate to enjoy that happy state.

By chance I stumbled across an alternative recently, one that has similar effects but is marginally less painful than a hangover or a broken whatsit and is appreciably easier on the liquidity: ie; it's less expensive.

It came about, indeed, because of a certain paucity of funds — a quite temporary state of affairs, you understand — at a most unpropitious moment. It was during the Cheltenham Festival race meeting, to be precise, and my Irish connections had advised of a good thing going in the 2.40.

"Don't make it favourite," I was told, "but if you have a few spare bobs this is money in the bank, each way."

Well, I had just returned from Hawaii and the spare bobs I had at that moment wouldn't have bought a cup of cold water but I happened to know that Miss Fitch, who runs our office, had refilled the petty cash box the day before.. It now being Saturday she was away, engaged in arm wrestling or playing hockey with the boys, and it took but two minutes to locate her cunningly contrived hideaway.

The smile on my face dissipated when I also discovered that, being of a suspicious nature, she'd taken the key with her and probably had it stuffed down her shin guards even now!

There being only 40 minutes to post time I went at it with a hammer and chisel but such was my haste that I gashed my right hand on a jagged edge and was forced to seek succour at the local out-patients departments where a particularly sadistic Scot cracked bad jokes as he engaged in a little embroidery with a blunt needle.

I missed post time, which was just as well because the nag was still running the next day, but a bonus ensued quite unexpectedly and I managed to replace the damaged petty cash box before Miss Fitch twigged, substituting the new one from my golf winnings.

How could I win at golf with my hand stitched? I hear you ask.

That's the bonus. Plagued by a life-long hook I discovered that my wound negated the strong right hand grip that causes it. I simply let the left hand do the work, taking its mate along for the ride.

The consequence was that, not expecting a score worth a crumpet, I played well within myself, hitting the ball like an arrow for 18 holes. I cleaned up, I can tell you, showing a handsome profit even after buying drinks for the vanquished and a replacement cash box.

That was some weeks ago. My first wound has healed nicely and the stitches from the second will come out soon, fortunately not before the final of the club foursomes championship in which I am involved, thanks to my new-found system.

For those similarly afflicted who don't cavil at the sight of a drop or two of blood and a modicum of pain, an old fashioned razor blade does the job nicely. You should start the incision on that bit of loose skin between the right thumb and base of the forefinger and gently work around ....

Bloopers I have made in pursuit of scoops I have missed....

Bloopers? Tell me about 'em. During a life time in the golf writing business I've experienced more bloopers that scoops. Well, quite a few anyway.... and a couple involve bathrooms.

I was one of a group of golf writers gathered for the opening of Montecastillo, a golf resort near Jerez, in Spain. We'd played the resort's new Nicklaus course and repaired to the hotel for a lunch that lasted into the early evening.

"Right ho, chaps," said our host, finally. "Dinner in an hour. I suggest we meet in the bar in 30 minutes. Suits and ties required."

"OK," said clever dick me, knowing that a certain colleague possessed of notoriously short arms and deep pockets would probably turn up late for his own funeral. "Last man in buys the drinks."

Already suitably lubricated, off we all raced to clean up and change. I'd stripped off and turned on the shower when the fun began.

The shower was one of those with a six foot hose suspended above the bath. Except that this hose was lying in the bath. And was about to rear out of control.

Obviously, I turned the tap too far because the hose leapt out of the bath like a demented snake and began writhing around the bathroom, spraying water everywhere. I made a grab for it but, being barefoot, slipped on the wet, tiled floor and ended base over apex. Well, attempting to subdue a snake by wrestling with it while simultaneously trying to turn off the tap meant that I achieved neither.

By now the bathroom floor was a lake so I left the snake to its own devises and, laughing my silly head off, staggered upright and cut off its water supply.

The flood by now threatened to seep onto the bedroom carpet so I had to spend several minutes mopping it up. Then, using a hand towel, the only one not soaked, I dried off and hurriedly dressed.

I reached the bar to loud cheers. Yup, I was last man in, of 24. My explanation provoked considerable hilarity, as did my expense claim. But I dined out on the yarn for several months. It makes me chuckle even now.

On another occasion I'd retired for a soak after a long day driving in Colorado and achieved similar results in hotel bathroom desecration.

It was a big bath, designed for two people, and had a control panel for several water jets to create a massage effect. Being tired and without thinking too much, I turned on the taps and popped in a generous dollop of bath oil in preparation for a langorous soak.

Minutes later, now stripped, I returned to find bubble foam already cascading out of the bath. By the time I'd deciphered the control panel to turn the thing off the foam was a foot deep on the bathroom floor, already creeping into the bedroom and make a bee-line for the door and the corridor outside....

Near panic. What to do with an unquantifiable load of foam? Couldn't put it in the bath: that was already full. The toilet bowl? I tried, but too small.... Ditto the hand basin. There was only one avenue of disposal.

I opened the bathroom window and began scooping the stuff out using the waste bin.... Fortunately I was on an upper floor of multi-storey hotel and the stuff simply floated away on the breeze blowing over the golf course. I gather that the the greens staff were suitably bemused....

An hour later order had been restored. Most of the foam had gone where ever foam hides in retirement, the bathroom was pristine again, although the bedroom carpet was on the moist side of damp, and I was more exhausted than ever. Didn't have the energy to get dressed for dinner. So I dried off and went to bed.

This travel writing business is not all it's cracked up to be. Memo to self: don't put bath oil in a jacuzzi......

EPILOGUE

My Life and Career in Golf: How it all began

Most people exposed to it have been deeply affected by literature but in my case it changed my life, bringing rewards beyond measure and value. It made me what I am today and I can't imagine where or what I would otherwise have been.

More than 65 years later I still recall the incident that instilled in me the love of books that was to have such a lasting effect and shape my life and consequently the lives of my family to come, possibly for generations....

The year was 1946, I was 14 years old and a pupil at the Huntingdon Secondary Modern School in Nottingham. We were in class awaiting the results of our annual examinations and school life was at a hiatus on one of the final days of what would be our final term. In relaxed mood, our form teacher entertained his 44 pupils with reminiscences of his early days, at university and in teaching.

Mr Baines was a man of middle age, an imposing figure much admired by his pupils for his patience, his fairness, his pleasing personality and a wicked sense of humour. He was a gifted teacher who won results without recourse to strict discipline, a gentle and often humorous admonition ("Do that again, Ward, and I'll have you beheaded at dawn") bringing the occasional miscreant to heel, seldom using the leather strap across the palm that was the accepted method of punishment in that era.

For among other things he taught us about self-discipline and self-respect. Good behaviour was endemic. Most of us actually enjoyed lessons, particularly those he supervised.

In those days, before education became a political football for social engineers and headline-hunting politicians, pupils stayed put in their own classrooms, except for specialist subjects such as science and woodwork. The teachers came to us, not the reverse as happens today, but Mr Baines was largely ever-present. Known as our form teacher, he took lessons in several subjects and would accompany us for the weekly afternoon on the sports field. For two years he was a father figure to many of us.

Like most youngsters in that immediate post-war era I would leave school at 14 after what had been a truncated but balanced education that some might kindly describe as "adequate." Certainly the results from Huntingdon would be not merely highly regarded today but envied by most local authorities in Britain.

Pupils were adept at mental arithmetic, spelling and punctuation; could write essays in well-formed English, and knew the significance of all or most of the important dates in history. We had instruction in science and art and a command of general knowledge that in those days was a curriculum subject. The end result was a considerable distance removed from a classical education but most of us would grow into productive, socially adept and responsible citizens.

So that informal afternoon with Mr Baines was something of a watershed: half of me was anticipating a new phase of life; the other half was reluctant to leave the security of school. Not for the first time, Mr Baines would fire my imagination, in my view one of the keys to all forms of endeavour.

I can't recall how the subject arose but suddenly he was telling, virtually confiding, about how his love of books had become a power, almost the engine, in his life. He was recounting his reading list and giving examples of some of the plots and characters of the books he had known.

Then he said something that 65 years later still resonates in my memory. He was talking about Daphne du Maurier's novel *Rebecca*, the much-loved minor classic that has seen various versions on film and is still popular in printed form.

Imagine, he said with theatrical overtones, opening a novel in which the first sentence reads: "Last night I dreamt I went to Manderley again." The class was silent; the inference was heavy with expectation and a hint of foreboding. To a boy we knew precisely what Mr Baines meant. That first sentence had us collectively entranced. We were as hooked as he had been with his discovery years before. We had been introduced to the power of words.

I couldn't wait to read the book. The following day I went to the city's municipal library, became a member and searched it out. Two days later I went back for more, then more. I lost count of the number of titles I withdrew over the four years until I left Nottingham. I devoured books with an insatiable hunger, from Dickens to Dostoyevsky, Jack London to D.H.Lawrence, Caldwell to Henry James, Scott Fitzgerald to Hemingway. They all became friends; the latter indeed became my mentor, in a metaphorical sense at least. How this happened might defy credulity for most people.

Finding employment was a simple matter in those days and my first job was as an office boy for a firm in the lace industry, called upon for minor clerical work and mail collection. A year later I was promoted to shipping clerk, completing in-coming orders for transportation. One morning each week I attended technical college to learn the mechanical aspects of making lace and thought that eventually I might become a designer. I shudder now at the thought but fortunately, a couple of years later, in 1950, an escape route appeared. My new life was about to get a kick-start.

At 18 I was conscripted for National Service and found myself in Germany with the RAF Regiment. Two years later I was demobbed and, after exploring the limited options available, I joined the Nottingham City Police. It was rewarding work but my spell in Europe had given me a taste for travel and I searched for further pastures. So after two years I transferred to the Colonial Police and, from a choice of possible postings, selected Bermuda.

While in Germany I had boxed all over Europe for the RAF, hence my itch for travel, and as the sport was popular in Bermuda I began appearing in local tournaments.

Among these was a monthly event at the US Air Force base known as Kindley Field, now Bermuda's airport. I became known to the staff there and was intrigued to learn that the University of Maryland ran what was known as extension courses for service personnel wishing to better themselves. Delighted to hear that these were open to the Bermuda public, I applied and was accepted for a two year course in American Literature and English. Thanks to Mr Baines, another building block in my life had fallen into place.

The course called for attendance twice weekly under a full time tutor of the university seconded to Bermuda for the project. He was a replica of Mr Baines, albeit with an American accent. We got on famously and a small class brought virtually one to one tuition. I was inspired.

We studied a good deal of American literature but the necessary dissertation was on Hemingway, whose books were already familiar to me. I'd read much of his work and the examination subject was his classic, *For Whom The Bell Tolls*.

This wasn't a degree course but I received high marks for the dissertation, the study filled a void in my educational *curriculum vitae* and was to prove an invaluable lever in my progress in life.

As a sportsman I had become well known to the local newspaper writers and was friendly with the sports editor of the *Bermuda Royal Gazette*.

Chatting after one of my fights, I told him about my experience on the university course and my subsequent writing ambitions, until then simply a hobby. He suggested I write a sports column as a trial and it proved good enough to become a regular feature in the newspaper. When the editor offered a full-time post I could barely believe it and accepted on the spot. It was to prove the launch pad for a career I could never have dreamed of.

It didn't end there: I joined the paper just as the island's tourist board launched the Bermuda Goodwill Golf Tournament, an international pro-am that attracted teams from around the globe. I was a recent convert to golf but when the sports editor needed a golfer to cover the tournament he discovered I was the only reporter who played the game. So I was appointed official golf writer for the *Royal Gazette*. I never looked back.

After three further years in Bermuda, and hoping to better myself in journalism, I returned to Nottingham and joined the *Evening Post*. This lasted for a year until, through an Australian newspaper executive I had assisted on his visit to Bermuda, I was offered the position of European Sports Editor in the London office of the Australian Consolidated Press, the holding company for the *Sydney Daily Telegraph* group. Incredulous at my stroke of luck, I must have floated down Fleet Street, then the news-gathering capital of the world, on a daily basis.

My job took me all over Britain and Europe, covering sporting events involving Australians or likely to be of interest down under. Soon I was a regular at Wimbledon, the Open Championship, rugby internationals, grand prix racing, Test cricket matches, athletics, world title fights and virtually every major event on the European sports calendar. I was in heaven.

This happy state lasted for three more years until the cruel winter of 1962/3 reminded me why I'd left England in the first place. My Bermudian wife was desperate for some sunshine: so we packed our bags and headed for Australia. It was November 1963.

The rest, as they say, is history. I joined the *Sydney Daily Telegraph*, was head hunted by the *Sunday Mirror*, where in time I became News Editor, then found myself out of work because of a protracted city-wide journalists' strike. I went freelance as editor of *Golf Australia* magazine and, in consequence of my production duties, met the female publisher of a local newspaper at the printers our respective companies used. A few weeks later she was murdered for what she was about to publish on organised crime and corruption. I felt constrained to investigate her killing but in consequence, after death threats, was forced to leave Australia in 1978 and return to London.

In time I became editor of *Golf News,* then Travel Editor for *Golf Monthly* magazine, which meant that I spent the next few years circling the globe reviewing golf resorts and generally acting, once again, like the luckiest man alive. Following a management buy-out in 1999 I left *Golf Monthly* to launch my on-line magazine which has kept me gainfully occupied ever since.

I've written several books, chiefly on golf and travel but also an expose, disguised as a novel for legal reasons, on the murder that drove me away from Sydney. Now 80 years old, I'm still working as a golf writer, reading at least one book each week and have plans to write two more. That Baines fellow really started something, didn't he?

Other books by Barry Ward

The Good Value Golf Guide to Scotland (1995)

Golf in Morocco, Land of Wonders (1996)

A State of Terror (2001)

The Nelson Conspiracy (2008)

Printed in Great Britain
by Amazon.co.uk, Ltd.,
Marston Gate.